Eclipse Cookbook™

Other Java™ resources from O'Reilly

Related titles

Eclipse
Java™ in a Nutshell
Head First Java™
Head First EJB™
Programming Jakarta Struts
Tomcat: The Definitive Guide

Learning Java™
Java™ Extreme Programming
   Cookbook
Java™ Servlet and JSP™
   Cookbook™
Hardcore Java™
JavaServer™ Pages

Java Books Resource Center

java.oreilly.com is a complete catalog of O'Reilly's books on Java and related technologies, including sample chapters and code examples.

OnJava.com is a one-stop resource for enterprise Java developers, featuring news, code recipes, interviews, weblogs, and more.

Conferences

O'Reilly brings diverse innovators together to nurture the ideas that spark revolutionary industries. We specialize in documenting the latest tools and systems, translating the innovator's knowledge into useful skills for those in the trenches. Visit *conferences.oreilly.com* for our upcoming events.

Safari Bookshelf (*safari.oreilly.com*) is the premier online reference library for programmers and IT professionals. Conduct searches across more than 1,000 books. Subscribers can zero in on answers to time-critical questions in a matter of seconds. Read the books on your Bookshelf from cover to cover or simply flip to the page you need. Try it today with a free trial.

Eclipse Cookbook™

Steve Holzner

O'REILLY®

Beijing · Cambridge · Farnham · Köln · Paris · Sebastopol · Taipei · Tokyo

Eclipse Cookbook™
by Steve Holzner

Published by O'Reilly Media, Inc., 1005 Gravenstein Highway North, Sebastopol, CA 95472.

O'Reilly books may be purchased for educational, business, or sales promotional use. Online editions are also available for most titles (*safari.oreilly.com*). For more information, contact our corporate/institutional sales department: (800) 998-9938 or *corporate@oreilly.com*.

Editor:	Brett McLaughlin
Production Editor:	Mary Anne Weeks Mayo
Cover Designer:	Emma Colby
Interior Designer:	Melanie Wang

Printing History:

June 2004:	First Edition.

 This book uses RepKover™, a durable and flexible lay-flat binding.

ISBN: 0-596-00710-8

[M]

Table of Contents

Preface

This book will help you find the answers about Eclipse, today's premier Java Integrated Development Environment (IDE). Eclipse is a great tool, but it's also a complicated one, and not everyone has the time to spend days trying to unravel it. That's where this book comes in; it unravels Eclipse for you.

Eclipse has long been needed in the Java world. There have been Java IDEs before, but not like this one. And if you've just been using the Java command-line compiler, javac, there's no comparison at all; Eclipse will revolutionize your programming. Eclipse is terrific because it's built to handle the details for you—syntax checking, error handling, adding imports as needed, targeting builds, commenting out blocks of code with a click, putting *.jar* files on the build path, refactoring, even reformatting your code. Eclipse makes it all happen for you. However, actually making it happen in Eclipse is up to you, and there's a steep learning curve.

This book reduces that learning curve. Got a problem? Just look up the appropriate recipe to find out how to solve it. Want to go back to the previously edited location? See Chapter 2. Want to extract an interface from your code with a few clicks? See Chapter 4. Want to create getter and setter methods with a few more mouse clicks? Check out Chapter 3. How about connecting Eclipse to a CVS repository? Take a look at Chapter 6.

This book lays out Eclipse, from the basics through the advanced. It's designed specifically to bring you up to speed on nearly any Eclipse question without wasting time. Eclipse is where the action is in Java today, and this book is all about mastering Eclipse.

What's Inside

This book is Eclipse from cover to cover. We will solve hundreds of Eclipse problems, and discuss dozens of issues, from installing all the way to reinstalling if some catastrophe occurs. And we're going to take a look at what Eclipse 3.0, now in beta form, has to offer as well. Here's an overview of what's inside the book:

Chapter 1, *Basic Skills*
> This chapter covers the basics—all you need to use Eclipse and handle routine tasks, including getting and installing Eclipse.

Chapter 2, *Using Eclipse*
> This chapter is all about the Eclipse workbench and what it offers. Covered are items such as editors, views, perspectives, and how to work with them in depth.

Chapter 3, *Java Development*
> Eclipse excels at Java development, and this chapter starts our Java development. Here we'll use the Java Development Tools (JDT) to create and work with Java projects, classes, methods, code, and so on.

Chapter 4, *Refactoring, Building, and Launching*
> Refactoring handles the task when you need to rename or move elements in your code and update every occurrence throughout that code. This chapter covers refactoring and many advanced Java tasks. It also covers building projects and launching them, including setting launch configurations.

Chapter 5, *Testing and Debugging*
> Where would an IDE be without debugging? The Eclipse debugger is first rate, and you'll get the story in this chapter, including breakpoints, breakpoint hit counters, watchpoints, changing your code on the fly, and a great deal more.

Chapter 6, *Using Eclipse in Teams*
> Eclipse also is built to be used in teams, and this chapter covers how to use Eclipse with a Concurrent Versions System (CVS) server so that code can be shared. You'll see how to connect Eclipse to a CVS server, how to store Eclipse projects in a CVS repository, how to check your files and projects, and more.

Chapter 7, *Eclipse and Ant*
> Ant is the best build tool for Java, and Eclipse comes with Ant support already built in. This chapter covers how to create Ant build files, how to execute them, and what you can do with Ant in Eclipse.

Chapter 8, *SWT: Text, Buttons, Lists, and Nonrectangular Windows*
> The Standard Widget Toolkit (SWT) comes built into Eclipse and is an extensive GUI API designed to replace Java's AWT and Swing. This first chapter of SWT coverage includes the basics on SWT as well as getting started with basic widgets such as buttons, lists, and composites, and how to create nonrectangular windows.

Chapter 9, *SWT: Dialogs, Toolbars, Menus, and More*
> This chapter on SWT covers more SWT widgets, including advanced widgets such as dialogs, toolbars, menus, and tables. You'll also learn how to embed AWT/Swing windows in SWT applications.

Chapter 10, *SWT: Coolbars, Tab Folders, Trees, and Browsers*
> This final chapter on SWT covers more SWT widgets: coolbars, tab folders, trees, and browsers.

Chapter 11, *JSP, Servlets, and Eclipse*
> Eclipse and web development are natural partners, and this chapter covers developing web applications with Eclipse, including JSP, JavaBeans, and servlets. You'll also learn how to create deployment packages for web applications.

Chapter 12, *Creating Plug-ins: Extension Points, Actions, and Menus*
> This and the next chapter illustrate how to create your own Eclipse plug-ins. In this chapter, you'll get the details on extension points, actions, and creating plug-in menus.

Chapter 13, *Creating Plug-ins: Wizards, Editors, and Views*
> This chapter concludes our focus on plug-ins; here, we'll create plug-ins that display wizards, views, and editors in Eclipse.

Conventions Used in This Book

The following typographical conventions are used in this book:

Plain text
> Indicates menu titles, menu options, menu buttons, and keyboard accelerators

Italic
> Indicates new terms, URLs, email addresses, filenames, file extensions, pathnames, directories, and Unix utilities

Constant width
> Indicates commands, options, switches, variables, types, classes, namespaces, methods, modules, properties, parameters, values, objects, events, event handlers, or XML tags

Constant width italic
> Shows text that should be replaced with user-supplied values

 This icon signifies a tip, suggestion, or general note.

 This icon indicates a warning or caution.

Also in this book I use a number of conventions. For example, menu items are separated with an → like so: File → New → Project. To make them stand out, new lines of code are highlighted when they're added, and I indicate more code yet to come with three dots. Here's an example:

```
for (int loopIndex = 0; loopIndex < 10; loopIndex++)
{
    TabItem tabItem = new TabItem(tabFolder, SWT.NULL);
    tabItem.setText("Tab " + loopIndex);

    Text text = new Text(tabFolder, SWT.BORDER);
    text.setText("This is page " + loopIndex);
    tabItem.setControl(text);
        .
        .
        .

}
```

What You'll Need

Any software you need in this book can be found online for free, including Eclipse. This book was written using Eclipse 2.1.2, as well as an early version of Eclipse 3.0. Chapter 1 discusses where to get Eclipse, as well as how to install and configure it.

I'll also discuss where to get other software, from the Tomcat web server to CVS servers. For that matter, you'll also be developing your own software to use with Eclipse when you create plug-ins in Chapters 12 and 13.

Everything you need is available for free; just download it. I'll show you where to get it all. No problem.

Using Code Examples

The code developed in this book is available for download for free from the O'Reilly web site for this book *http://www.oreilly.com/catalog/eclipseckbk*. (Before installing, take a look at *readme.txt* in the download).

This book is here to help you get your job done. In general, you can use the code in this book in your programs and documentation. You don't need to contact us for permission unless you're reproducing a significant portion of the code. For example, writing a program that uses several chunks of code from this book doesn't require permission. Selling or distributing a CD-ROM of examples from O'Reilly books *does* require permission. Answering a question by citing this book and quoting example code doesn't require permission. Incorporating a significant amount of example code from this book into your product's documentation *does* require permission.

We appreciate, but don't require, attribution. An attribution usually includes the title, author, publisher, and ISBN. For example: "*Eclipse Cookbook*, by Steve Holzner. Copyright 2004 O'Reilly, 0-596-00710-8."

If you feel your use of code examples falls outside fair use or the permission given here, feel free to contact us at *permissions@oreilly.com*.

We'd Like to Hear from You

Please address comments and questions concerning this book to the publisher:

O'Reilly Media, Inc.
1005 Gravenstein Highway North
Sebastopol, CA 95472
(800) 998-9938 (in the United States or Canada)
(707) 829-0515 (international or local)
(707) 829-0104 (fax)

There's a web page for this book that lists errata, examples, and any additional information. You can access this page at:

http://www.oreilly.com/catalog/eclipseckbk

To comment or ask technical questions about this book, send email to:

bookquestions@oreilly.com

For more information about books, conferences, Resource Centers, and the O'Reilly Network, see the O'Reilly web site at:

http://www.oreilly.com

Basic Skills

1.0   Introduction

If you're a Java™ programmer, Eclipse is the best thing since sliced bread. Eclipse not only takes the rough edges off Java development better than any other product, but also it's a free download!

Even if you develop with just the Java compiler, javac, Eclipse can make life easier for you. In fact, Eclipse's Integrated Development Environment (IDE) makes the development process as close to fun as it can get: the first time that Java programmers fire up Eclipse and start to use it, they often find themselves thinking, *This is great!*

As with any extensive programming tool, however, Eclipse has a learning curve. In this chapter, we will brush up on fundamental Eclipse skills, from installing Eclipse to creating a simple Java application. Some of these skills are covered for the sake of reference, and you already might be adept at them, while others might be new to you. The goal with this book is to push the Eclipse envelope; to do that, you must have the solid foundation this chapter provides.

1.1   Getting Eclipse

Problem

You want to try out Eclipse.

Solution

Eclipse is a free download, and you can pick it up at *www.eclipse.org*. Just click the *Downloads* link located on the left side of that page.

Discussion

The current download URL is *www.eclipse.org/downloads/index.php*. The download page appears in Figure 1-1.

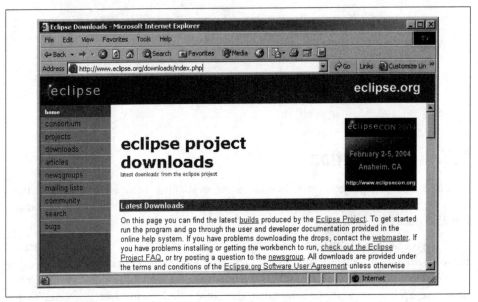

Figure 1-1. The Eclipse download page

Click a mirror site close to you, choose the version of Eclipse you want, and then select your operating system (Eclipse works with everything from Linux to AIX to Windows). The download starts automatically.

You can download four different versions of Eclipse:

Release builds
> These releases are for general use. In most cases, when you download Eclipse you'll use one of the release versions. These builds have been tested, and the chance of coming across serious bugs is minimal. If Eclipse were for sale, this is the version that would be selling.

Stable builds
> Stable builds are much like beta versions. The Eclipse team treats this build as relatively stable, but you might run across problems, as in any beta version. If you're interested, this is where you'll find forthcoming Eclipse features.

Integration builds
> These are a step below stable builds; their components have been fairly well tested, but the way they operate together still might be problematic. If things work out OK for an integration build, it might be made into a stable version.

Nightly builds

The most experimental and risky of all publically available Eclipse builds, these are created every night by the Eclipse team, and they come with virtually no guarantee. My experience with these builds suggests that you can run into substantial problems, so beware here.

Usually, you'll pick the most recent release version of Eclipse. Allow some time for the download; depending on your operating system, most current release versions are more than 60 MB.

See Also

Chapter 1 of *Eclipse* (O'Reilly); the Eclipse site, *www.eclipse.org*; the technical articles at *www.eclipse.org/articles/index.html*; the newsgroups at *www.eclipse.org/newsgroups/index.html*; the current and upcoming versions page at *www.eclipse.org/eclipse/development/main.html*.

1.2   Installing and Running Eclipse

Problem

You want to install Eclipse and get it running on your machine.

Solution

After you've downloaded it, installing Eclipse is not hard: unzip or untar the Eclipse download, and you're ready to go. Because you've downloaded the version of Eclipse targeted to your operating system, you'll find the executable file as soon as you uncompress Eclipse. To run Eclipse, just run that executable file.

Discussion

One of the great things about Eclipse is the ease with which you can install it. Wherever you unzip or untar it is its home. You also can have parallel installations of Eclipse; just decompress it in the various directories you want and run the executable file, such as *eclipse.exe*.

Users of big, invasive IDEs will appreciate the fact that Eclipse installs quickly, does not require multiple reboots, and does not include hidden spyware. Windows developers will be relieved to learn that Eclipse does not install itself in the Windows registry, with all the attendant problems that can cause. So, (re)installation is painless.

When you first run Eclipse, you'll see the *Resource perspective* by default, as shown in Figure 1-2. As discussed in the Recipe 1.6 later in this chapter, a *perspective* presents an arrangement of windows to the user. If you open a particular perspective over and over, you'll always get the same set of windows. The Resource perspective is a general perspective that is good for resource management, particularly file handling. But we're not going to work with it here because everything we need, including virtually all functionality that the Resource perspective offers, is in the Java-oriented perspectives, particularly the Java perspective, discussed later in this chapter.

 The Resource perspective doesn't have to be your default perspective. Select Window → Preferences → Workbench → Perspectives to choose a default perspective. Java programmers often select the Java perspective here, which is the main perspective for Java development.

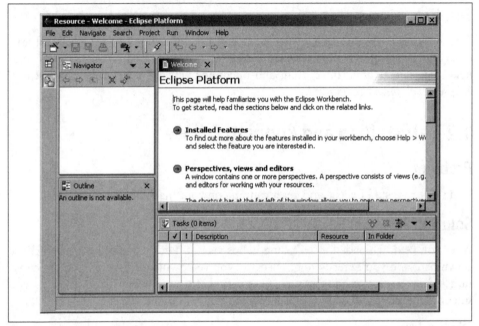

Figure 1-2. The Resource perspective

 You must have Java installed on your machine to start Eclipse. If you start Eclipse for the first time and see a dialog box with a message beginning with the sentence "A Java Runtime Environment (JRE) or Java Development Kit (JDK) must be available in order to run Eclipse," download and install Java first. You can get Java for free at *http://java.sun.com/j2se/*.

After installing Eclipse, you can make it easier to run by connecting a shortcut to it. In Linux or Unix, add the Eclipse directory to your path, or use `ln -s` to create a symbolic link to the Eclipse executable. In Windows, right-click the executable file in Windows Explorer and select Create Shortcut from the context menu that opens, then drag the new shortcut where you want it.

> ## Speeding Up Startup
>
> In general, Eclipse starts fairly slowly, but you can improve startup performance (if you're an Eclipse novice, you might want to wait on this until you have more experience). Startup is often slow because of the number of things Eclipse has to do. To speed up the startup process, reduce the number of plug-ins you have, close views and editors before quitting Eclipse, and remove unessential projects from the workspace. You can even fine-tune the Java virtual machine (JVM) that Eclipse uses. For example, you can give it more memory with a startup argument such as `-vmargs -Xmx512m`, which gives the JVM 512 MB of memory to work with, eliminating a lot of swapping to disk.

See Also

Recipe 1.6 on perspectives, views, and editors; Recipe 1.3 on understanding the Eclipse workspace; Chapter 1 of *Eclipse* (O'Reilly).

1.3   Understanding Your Workspace

Problem

What's meant by the term *workspace*? And what's a *plug-in*?

Solution

Although you might think of Eclipse as a Java IDE, it comprises a number of components that act together behind the scenes in Eclipse's workspace. A plug-in is a software tool that accomplishes a specific task in Eclipse, such as allowing you to edit an Ant file, compile a Java file, or drag and drop GUI elements. The workspace, along with the Eclipse workbench, the team component, and the help component, are all parts of the overall Eclipse platform, and serve as the foundation for plug-ins to interact with the Eclipse core software.

Discussion

The Java IDE you work with is the *Java Development Toolkit*, or JDT. The JDT is not an integral part of Eclipse; it's a plug-in. Eclipse is really composed of the Eclipse Platform, which provides support for other tools. These tools are implemented as plug-ins, allowing the platform itself to be a relatively small software package.

Eclipse comes with a number of plug-ins, including the JDT. Another important plug-in is the *Plug-in Development Environment* (PDE), which enables you to develop your own plug-ins. If you want to develop in a language other than Java, you get the corresponding plug-in for that language, and many are available.

Besides using different programming languages, you can change the human language that Eclipse uses as well. Different languages often are supported with what are called *plug-in fragments*. Plug-in fragments are available for numerous languages, including Japanese, Korean, German, French, Italian, Portuguese, Spanish, and even traditional and simplified Chinese.

Knowing the parts of Eclipse is essential to working with it for anything but the most casual use. If you don't have at least an idea of what parts do what, you'll end up confused when you encounter the barriers between these components, which can make Eclipse's behavior seem inconsistent. For example, when you know that the JDT is different from other plug-ins, you won't be surprised when options available in the JDT aren't available in other plug-ins.

The Eclipse Platform consists of several components: the platform kernel, the workspace, the workbench, the team component, and the help component. You can see an overview of these components in Figure 1-3. Plug-ins are loaded when Eclipse starts; the plug-ins also appear in Figure 1-3.

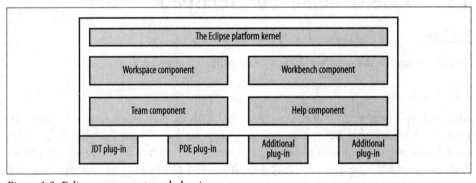

Figure 1-3. Eclipse components and plug-ins

The Eclipse platform kernel

Everything starts with the platform kernel. The platform kernel is written in native code, and its job is to load the rest of Eclipse; the kernel warns you if it can't find a workable Java installation to run the rest of the application. The kernel also loads the Eclipse plug-ins.

The workbench component

The workbench is Eclipse at its most basic. The workbench window displays the menus and toolbars you saw in Figure 1-2 (the menu and toolbar items that are displayed are put there by the perspective you're currently viewing).

Although you load different plug-ins, each with different windows and menu systems, the workbench is what displays them. The workbench is designed to look like a native application, targeted to your operating system. In Linux, it looks like a Linux application, in Windows, a Windows application, and so on.

> Targeting Eclipse's graphical user interface to the operating system is a somewhat controversial issue. The workbench is built using Eclipse's own Standard Widget Toolkit (SWT) and JFace packages (built on top of SWT), which use operating-system native components in their displays. Doing that in a Java application is still a contentious point, as you'll see when we discuss SWT and JFace later in Chapters 8, 9, and 10.

The workspace component

The workspace component in Eclipse manages your resources, including what you store on disk. Eclipse manages your resources in *projects*, and by default each project is managed by the workspace component in the Eclipse *workspace* directory. You'll learn more about projects later in this chapter in Recipe 1.5.

> Your project doesn't need to be in the workspace directory; you can use other directories, even networked directories. To select a different location, uncheck the "Use default" checkbox when you give the name of the project to create, and fill in the directory you want to use instead.

The workspace component manages all the resources in a project, including your code. It also manages changes to your code and to other files, giving you access to a stored history of the changes and even enabling you to compare those changes graphically. The workspace also communicates with plug-ins such as the JDT, making history and file information accessible.

The team component

The team component gives you version control for your code, and it supports file sharing. If you've developed software in a corporate environment, you might already have worked with source code control and repositories. Code is stored in a repository and checked in or out as needed, which means the changes to the software can be tracked.

Coordinating changes that teams make to the code means you can avoid the kind of random overlapping changes that will cause utter chaos otherwise. Eclipse integrates well with the Concurrent Versions System (CVS), the de facto standard for version control (except perhaps in Microsoft shops, where Visual SourceSafe still reigns supreme). In fact, the team component can act as a CVS client, which interacts with a CVS server that maintains the code repository from which team members can retrieve code. We're going to take a look at how this works in Chapter 6.

The help component

The help component is Eclipse's documentation system for providing help. It's an extensible help system; plug-ins can provide their own help, in XML-formatted form, to tell the help system how to navigate their documentation.

Plug-ins

Eclipse is extendible via plug-ins. Plug-ins can set up their own perspectives, editors, views, wizards, and more. For example, the JDT is a plug-in that adds its functionality to what the workbench already provides. Besides using some of the more than 450 plug-ins available for Eclipse, we're also going to build our own starting in Chapter 12.

1.4   Running Multiple Eclipse Windows

Problem

You want to run multiple Eclipse windows at the same time, possibly including different versions of Eclipse.

Solution

Launch Eclipse more than once, and you'll get multiple Eclipse windows.

Discussion

Running multiple Eclipse windows is not a problem, as shown in Figure 1-4.

You have choices here, as explained in the following sections.

Multiple Eclipse windows, same workspace

To open multiple Eclipse windows using the same workspace, select Window → New Window. It's a good idea to use this technique if you want to work in two different perspectives (such as the Java and Debug perspectives) at the same time in different windows.

Multiple Eclipse windows, multiple workspaces

You can launch Eclipse so that it uses the workspace of your choice instead of the default one. To do that, enter `eclipse -data newWorkSpacePath -showLocation` on the command line. This starts Eclipse with the workspace given by *newWorkSpacePath* (the `-showLocation` option makes windows show their location, making it easy to

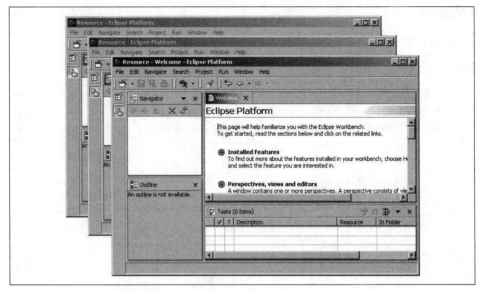

Figure 1-4. Running multiple Eclipse windows

remember where you are if you launch multiple windows). You would use this technique if you want to partition projects into different workspaces to keep them separate.

Multiple Eclipse installations

You can have multiple Eclipse installations on the same machine, including different versions. Just unzip or untar them in different directories; they won't conflict. This can be useful if you want to try out some of the new features in nonrelease builds, or if you don't want to start Eclipse from the command line to work with different workspaces.

Runtime workbench

You can launch a runtime workbench by selecting Run → Run As → Run-time Workbench. This can be useful to test plug-ins, as we'll do in Chapter 12. The plug-in you're developing will appear in the new workbench, ready to be tested.

1.5   Creating a Java Project

Problem

You want to start programming some Java. Where do you start?

Solution

Select File → New → Project.

Discussion

In Eclipse, all code—Java or otherwise—has to go into a *project*, and creating Eclipse projects is a basic skill. Projects organize your files, classes, libraries, and exports. Over the next few recipes, we're going to create a Java project that will use the code you see in Example 1-1 to display some simple text, "Stay cool."

 Creating a Java project is a basic skill, and this chapter is all about basic skills. However, there's much more that we don't have space for here. For additional details on creating Java projects, see Chapters 3 and 4.

Example 1-1. The FirstApp.java example

```java
public class FirstApp
{
  public static void main(String[] args)
  {
    System.out.println("Stay cool.");
  }
}
```

To get started, create a new Java project by selecting File → New → Project in Eclipse, and then open the New Project dialog, shown in Figure 1-5.

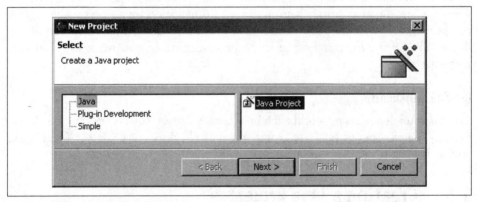

Figure 1-5. The New Project dialog

We want to create a Java project, so select Java in the left pane and Java Project in the right pane. Click Next, and in the next dialog name the project FirstApp, as shown in Figure 1-6.

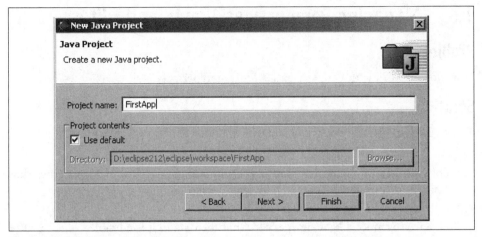

Figure 1-6. Naming a project

Click Finish to finish creating the project. (If you click Next, additional options for creating projects appear in the dialog that opens, but this chapter deals with basic Eclipse skills; you can learn more about project creation options in Chapter 3.)

If you've opened Eclipse for the first time and/or the Resource perspective is the only perspective open, Eclipse will ask you if you want to switch to the Java perspective, as shown in Figure 1-7. Click Yes.

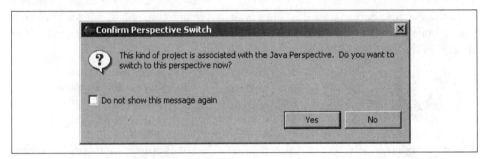

Figure 1-7. Switching perspectives

After this new project, *FirstApp*, is created, it's opened in the Java perspective. We've already discussed perspectives informally, but now that we're about to work with them directly we'll take a more in-depth look in the next two recipes. We'll continue developing the code for this example in the recipes that follow.

See Also

Recipe 1.8 on creating a Java class; Chapter 1 of *Eclipse* (O'Reilly).

1.6   Managing Perspectives, Views, and Editors

Problem

How do you work with Eclipse *views*, *editors*, and *perspectives*?

Solution

To use Eclipse, you need to know what view, editor, and perspective mean:

View
> This is a window that gives you a graphical display of your data, whether that data is text, bulleted lists, a GUI, images, and so on.

Editor
> An editor is much like a view, except that the data in it is editable. When you're working on your code, you edit it in an editor, which is usually the central window displayed in the workbench.

Perspective
> A perspective is a well-defined collection of views and editors. When you open a perspective, its views and/or editors appear in the workbench.

Discussion

Views display data but don't let you edit it; editors both display data and make it editable. Because screen space is always at a premium in GUIs, views are often stacked one on top of another. You select the one you want to see using tabs that appear on the edge of the stacked views.

 If you want to reopen a view you've closed by mistake, select Window → Show View, and choose the view you want from the menu that appears.

When you open code or other resources, their data will appear in an editor so that you can work on it. Eclipse automatically selects the right editor for the resource you're opening, based on the resource's file extension: the JDT's Java code editor for Java code (*.java* files), an XML editor if you have one installed for XML files (*.xml* files), and so on. You even can open Microsoft Word documents (*.doc* files) in an editor; Eclipse displays a Microsoft Word window in the editor space using Windows Object Linking and Embedding (OLE).

You can set which Eclipse editor or external program to use to open a specific type of file based on its file extension. Just select Window → Preferences → Workbench → File Associations, select the file type, and associate an editor or program with it (if nothing else, you can use Eclipse's default text editor). You also can run programs outside Eclipse as external tools, invoked by selecting Run → External Tools. To add and configure external tools, select Run → External Tools → External Tools.

Editors are where you do most of your work, developing code and working with other resources. For instance, you can develop a GUI in an editor by dragging and dropping controls when using a plug-in that provides that functionality (for more information on using a plug-in that enables you to design GUIs in this way, see Chapter 9).

You can have a number of editors open at the same time, and they'll appear stacked in the center of the workbench. You select the editor you want to work with by clicking the corresponding tab at the top of the stacked editors (or by selecting Window → Switch to Editor, which displays a list of editors you can switch to). You close an editor simply by clicking the X in its associated tab (or by selecting Window → Hide Editors, which toggles to Window → Show Editors after hiding an editor).

As noted earlier, a perspective is a collection of views and editors that open and close as a group. For example, the Java perspective displays a set of views and editors appropriate to Java development. These include the Package Explorer view, which displays a clickable hierarchical class structure of the Java files in the project, and the JDT editor, which supports Java syntax checking, quick fixes for syntax errors, and so on. The Debug perspective, on the other hand, displays views and editors appropriate to debugging, including watch windows, the output console, a watch window for variables, and so on.

Perspectives usually appear by themselves, following your lead (the Java perspective opens automatically when you create a Java project, for example), but you also can open Eclipse perspectives explicitly by selecting Window → Open Perspective, and then choosing a perspective from the submenu that appears. To close a perspective, select Window → Close Perspective.

When you open a perspective, icons appear in its *shortcut bar*. (The shortcut bar is located on the far left in the Eclipse window. Refer back to Figure 1-2, in which the icon for the Resource view—showing a file and a folder—appears.) Once you open a perspective, Eclipse remembers that you used that perspective at least once and an icon for that perspective appears in the shortcut bar. To switch to that perspective, just click the corresponding icon. To remove icons from the shortcut bar, right-click the icons, and click Close. The icon at the top of the shortcut bar (showing a perspective with a + sign) enables you to open new perspectives.

Perspectives have a predefined set of views and editors built in. When you select a perspective, that set of views and editors appears automatically. By defining a set of perspectives, Eclipse makes your job easier because you don't have to open the specific views you want every time you want to write or debug code. You also can create (as well as delete) your own perspectives.

To get a handle on these concepts by way of an example, take a look at the next recipe, in which we dissect the Java perspective.

See Also

Recipe 1.3 on understanding the Eclipse workspace.

1.7   Mastering the Java Perspective

Problem

What is the Java perspective, and what can I use it for?

Solution

You can see the parts of the Java perspective, as presented by the Eclipse JDT, in Figure 1-8. The Java perspective is showing *FirstApp*, the project we've been developing over the previous few recipes (you can see this project in the Package Explorer on the left side of the figure).

Discussion

This is the main perspective you use for Java development; if you're going to be using Eclipse on a daily basis, this is the perspective you'll be staring at a lot. In other words, this is your development environment.

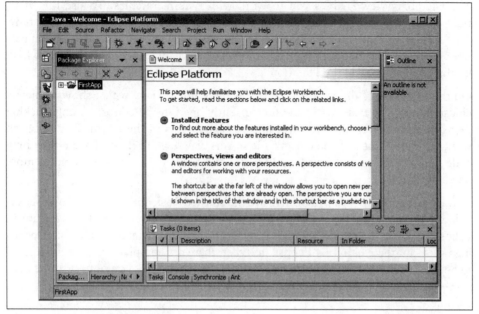

Figure 1-8. The Java perspective

You also can open the Java perspective at any time by selecting Window → Open Perspective → Java.

Take a look at the Java perspective in Figure 1-8. At the top of this perspective are the standard workbench menu bars and toolbars, now populated with the items for the Java perspective. You're going to get familiar with those items in this and in coming chapters.

You move the toolbars in Eclipse by dragging them. If you don't want to move the toolbars inadvertently, select Window → Lock the Toolbars.

On the left side of Figure 1-8, you see the Package Explorer and Hierarchy views stacked on top of each other. You can use the tabs at the bottom to flip between these two views.

The Package Explorer view is especially important for Java programming and is the view you use most frequently in Java development. It gives you an overview of your projects in Java terms, enabling you to navigate through files and classes. Double-clicking an item in the Package Explorer opens that item in the central editor window in the Java perspective.

The Hierarchy view enables you to work with type hierarchies. To use this view, right-click an item in the perspective's editor, and choose Open Type Hierarchy. This makes the item's type hierarchy appear in this view as a clickable inheritance tree. Working with an item's type hierarchy like this can be great if you want to look up the syntax of an inherited method.

On the right side of the Java perspective is the Outline view, which shows a hierarchical view of the elements in the file currently open in the editor. Double-clicking items in this view enables you to jump to those items in the editor. Being able to work with an outline of the current file in this way is good if you have a very long code file and are tired of scrolling 20 pages at a time. This view is covered in more detail in Chapter 2.

At the bottom of the Java perspective are the stacked Task and Console views, selectable via the tabs you see in Figure 1-8 (as in most GUIs, space is at a premium in Eclipse, and you'll often see views stacked). The Tasks view gives you a list of pending tasks, put there either by Eclipse (as when there are compilation errors that need to be fixed) or by you as reminders. The Console view shows you output to the console—for example, our first sample application will write the text "Stay cool." to the console.

In the central window of the Java perspective is a Welcome message that explains such concepts as perspectives, views, and editors. This central space is where editors are stacked, and you select between them with the tabs that appear at the top (the Welcome message's tab is shown in Figure 1-8). Unlike views, you enter text and data in editors, and the JDT editors are specially designed to work with Java. In addition to being the place where you enter Java code, JDT editors also feature an abundance of hidden power, such as syntax highlighting, syntax checking, automatic code completion, and more.

 When you open the Java perspective, the icon for that perspective, signified by a small J, appears in the shortcut bar shown on the left in Figure 1-8.

See Also

Chapters 1 and 2 of *Eclipse* (O'Reilly).

1.8   Creating a Java Class

Problem

You want to create a new Java class in an existing Java project.

Solution

When you have the Java perspective open and have a Java project selected in the Package Explorer, you can create new classes in Eclipse in several ways. You can use the toolbar item with the circled C icon, you can select File → New → Class, or you can right-click a project in the Package Explorer and select New → Class in the context menu. All these methods open the New Java Class dialog.

Discussion

The New Java Class dialog is shown in Figure 1-9.

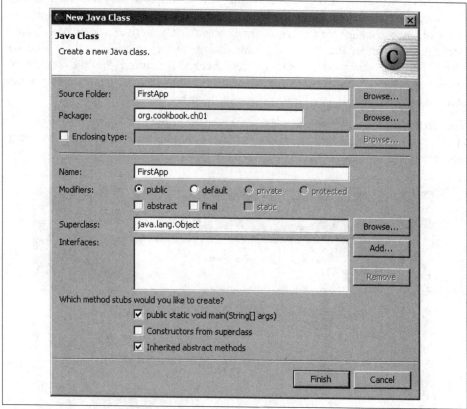

Figure 1-9. Creating a new Java class

Over the previous few recipes, we've been developing a short Java project, *FirstApp*. Now we're going to use the following code to display a message in that project:

```
public class FirstApp
{
  public static void main(String[] args)
  {
```

```
    System.out.println("Stay cool.");
  }
}
```

Creating Java classes is a fundamental skill for most Eclipse developers, so I'm going to cover the basics here. Note the options in this dialog: you can set a class's access specifier as public, private, or protected; you can make the class abstract or final; you can specify the new class's superclass (java.lang.Object is the default); and you can specify which, if any, interfaces it implements. Class creation is covered in more detail in Chapter 3.

In this book, you'll put examples into Java packages to avoid any conflict with other code; here, we use packages named after the example's chapter, such as org.cookbook.ch01. Enter the name of this new class, FirstApp, in the Name box and the name of a new package for this class, org.cookbook.ch01, in the Package box. Note in particular that under the question in this dialog "Which method stubs would you like to create?" that we're leaving the checkbox marked "public static void main(String[] args)" checked. Doing so means that Eclipse will create an empty main method automatically. Click Finish to accept the other defaults.

This creates and opens the new class, FirstApp, as shown in Figure 1-10. Open the *FirstApp* project in the Package Explorer, and double-click the FirstApp.java entry under the org.cookbook.ch01 entry to open the new code.

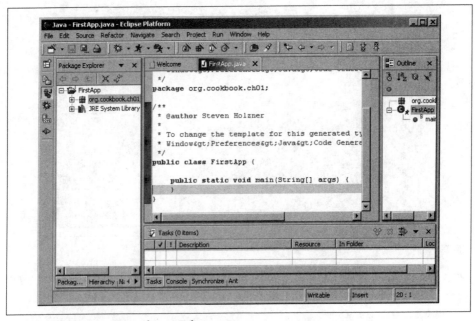

Figure 1-10. Opening a Java class in Eclipse

You can see the code the JDT has already written in this figure—note the package statement that creates the `org.cookbook.ch01` package. You also can see the `main` method Eclipse has added to our class. This new class will be stored in its own file, *FirstApp.java*, in the Eclipse folder *workspace\FirstApp*.

At this point, simply enter the code for this class directly in the editor and you're set. You also can use Eclipse's code assist to make things easier, as covered in the next recipe.

1.9 Completing Code Automatically

Problem

While entering code, you forgot the name of either a method you wanted to call or some of a method's parameters.

Solution

Use Eclipse's *code assist* (also called *content assist*) to help out. When you enter the name of an object or class in the JDT code editor followed by a period (.) and then pause, code assist displays the members of that object or class, and you can select the one you want. You also can bring up code assist at any time (e.g., when you've positioned the cursor inside a method's parentheses, and you want to see what arguments that method takes) by pressing Ctrl-Space or by selecting Edit → Content Assist.

Discussion

Code (or content) assist is one of the good things about using a full Java IDE. It's an invaluable tool that accelerates development, and it's a handy resource that you'll probably find yourself relying on in time. In the code example we've been developing over the previous few recipes, enter the following code to display some text:

```
public class FirstApp
{
  public static void main(String[] args)
  {
    System.out.println("Stay cool.");
  }
}
```

To work with code assist, enter `System.` in the `main` method of the *FirstApp* project, then pause. Code assist displays the classes and methods in the `System` namespace, as shown in Figure 1-11.

Double-click out in the code assist list so that code assist inserts that member into your code, insert a period so that the phrase now reads `System.out.`, and pause again. Code assist now displays the methods of the `out` class. Double-click the code

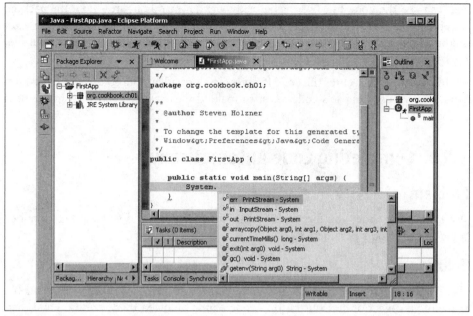

Figure 1-11. Using code assist

assist suggestion println(String argo), and code assist inserts the following code into the main method:

```
public class FirstApp
{
  public static void main(String[] args)
  {
    System.out.println( )
  }
}
```

Edit this to add the text Stay cool.. Note that code assist adds the closing quotation mark automatically as you type:

```
public class FirstApp
{
  public static void main(String[] args)
  {
    System.out.println("Stay cool.")
  }
}
```

As soon as you enter this code, Eclipse displays it with a wavy red underline, shown in Figure 1-12, to indicate that a syntax problem exists. Rest the mouse cursor over the new code, and a tool tip appears, also shown in Figure 1-12, indicating that a semicolon is missing. Note also that a red box (displayed in stunning black and white in the figure) appears in the *overview bar* to the right of the code. Clicking that box jumps to the error, which is handy if you've got a lot of errors and a long code file.

Deprecated methods also are underlined automatically in the JDT editor, but in yellow, not red. Syntax warnings in general are displayed with yellow boxes in the overview bar.

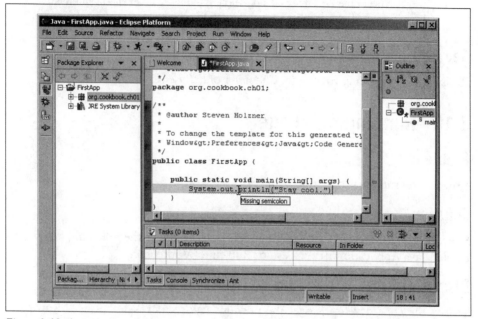

Figure 1-12. A syntax error message

Add that semicolon now to the end of the line to give you the complete code and to make the wavy red line disappear.

Eclipse can format your code automatically, adding indents and cleaning up the source code nicely, which is great if you're pasting code from somewhere else. Just select Source → Format, and Eclipse will handle the details. In time, you'll probably find yourself using this feature more often than you expected.

Finally, save the file by clicking the disk icon in the toolbar or by selecting File → Save. An unsaved file appears with an asterisk before its name in its editor tab (as shown in Figure 1-12), but the asterisk disappears when the file is saved. If you don't save a code file before trying to compile and run that code, Eclipse will prompt you to do so. We'll run this code in the next recipe.

To sum up, code assist is a great tool for code completion, and it will start automatically when you insert a period (.) in the JDT editor after the name of an object or class. You also can make code assist appear at any time while you're typing code; just press Ctrl-Space or select Edit → Content Assist.

 You can configure code assist to fit your own coding style. In the left pane of the Preferences dialog select Window → Preferences, and then Editor. Then click the Code Assist tab to configure it as you like.

See Also

Recipe 1.10 on running your code; Chapter 1 of *Eclipse* (O'Reilly).

1.10   Running Your Code

Problem

How do you run Java code from Eclipse?

Solution

Select Run → Run As. In the list that appears, select one of the following items: Java Applet, Java Application, JUnit Test, or Run-time Workbench.

Discussion

To run the code developed over the previous few recipes, select Run → Run As → Java Application (Eclipse will prompt you to save the file if you haven't already done so). Figure 1-13 shows the results, with the output of our code, Stay cool., appearing in the Console view at the bottom.

 Before running a Java program for the first time, it's a good idea to check if Eclipse is using the JRE or JDK you want it to use. By default, Eclipse locates an installed JRE or JDK, but it might not be the one you want to use (for example, Eclipse might have located the JRE installed for a browser you're using). To check which JRE or JDK Eclipse is using, select Window → Preferences to open the workbench preferences. Select Java → Installed JREs in the tree pane on the left to display the Installed Java Runtime Environments preference page. The JRE or JDK Eclipse is using is checked; you can check other JREs or JDKs to make Eclipse use them instead. We'll discuss adding other JREs and JDKs in the next chapter.

And that's it—you've developed and run your first Java example.

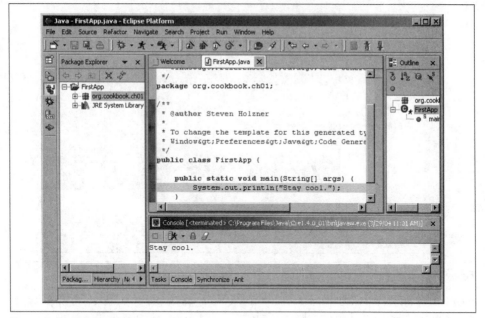

Figure 1-13. Running Java code

1.11 Running Code Snippets

Problem

You want to test just a section of code, without having to get a whole program to run.

Solution

There's another convenient way to run Java code in Eclipse: you can use a *scrapbook page*. Scrapbook pages enable you to execute code, even partial programs, on the fly. Using scrapbook pages isn't an essential skill in Eclipse, but it's a useful thing to know.

Discussion

After you've created a scrapbook page, you can copy and paste code to that page and run it. Create a scrapbook page by selecting File → New → Scrapbook Page. Enter a name for the page, such as ScrapPage, in the File box, and click Finish. The new scrapbook page is stored in the Package Explorer as *ScrapPage.jpage*, as shown in Figure 1-14.

Enter the code you want to run in this new page. For instance, to run the example code in the *FirstApp* project we just ran, enter the following code in the scrapbook

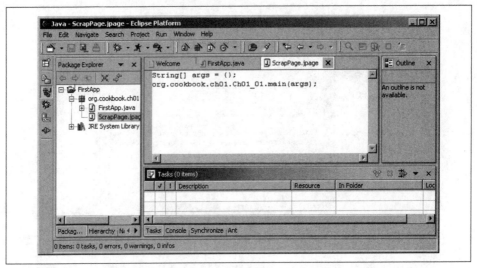

Figure 1-14. Using a scrapbook page

page; note that to reach the main method of our example, you have to qualify its name with the name of the package it's in:

```
String[] args = {};
org.cookbook.ch01.FirstApp.main(args);
```

You select the code you want to run in the scrapbook page by highlighting it. In this case, select all the code in the scrapbook page, right-click it, and click Execute, or select Run → Execute. (If you need imports for the code in the scrapbook page, right-click the scrapbook's code, and select Set Imports in the context menu.)

 Execute runs the code in a scrapbook page, but another option also exists. If you select Display instead, the net return value of the code you've selected appears in the scrapbook. This technique is useful if you don't want to stud your code with println statements.

1.12   Fixing Syntax Errors Automatically

Problem

Eclipse indicates that you've got syntax errors in your code, but you don't want to have to loop up the correct syntax in the Java documentation.

Solution

Let Eclipse's Quick Fix suggest solutions. When you see an error/light bulb icon in the marker bar to the left of the JDT editor, click it for solutions to the error, and select the solution you want.

Discussion

Quick Fix is a great tool; as far as I am concerned, if Eclipse did nothing else, it still would be a worthwhile program to use just because of its Quick Fix feature. Of all the built-in components of the JDT, Quick Fix is a real favorite among programmers because it enables you to fix syntax errors almost instantaneously.

For instance, say you want the example code we've developed in the previous few recipes to also display the date and time. You might use code such as this:

```java
public class FirstApp {
    public static void main(String[] args) {
        Date date = new Date( );
        stayCoolText = "Stay cool.";
        System.out.println(stayCoolText + " Date now is " + date.toString( ));
    }
}
```

You might spot a few errors here; Eclipse certainly does, as indicated by the X icons in the marker bar to the left of the editor in Figure 1-15.

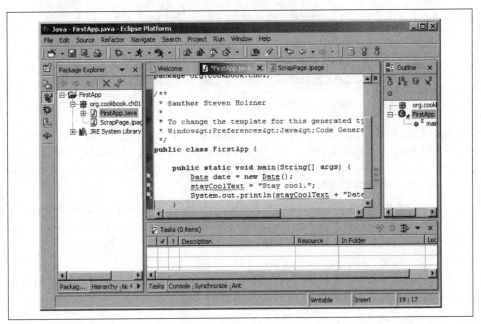

Figure 1-15. Using Quick Fix

Although Eclipse indicates that errors exist, it doesn't leave you in the cold. If Eclipse has a Quick Fix solution to offer, a light bulb will appear next to the X icon, also shown in Figure 1-15.

Tackle the first error by letting the mouse rest over the icon in the marker bar, which brings up a tool tip indicating that the Date class can't be resolved, as shown in Figure 1-16.

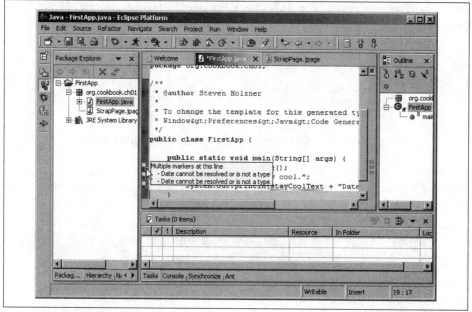

Figure 1-16. Getting the description of an error

To start Quick Fix and see what the JDT suggests, click the light bulb icon. You can see those suggestions in Figure 1-17; note that Quick Fix also indicates the code it's proposing to add. Double-click the import 'java.util.Date' suggestion to import the Date class so that it can be resolved.

That resolves the first problem in the code. The next problem is that the variable stayCoolText hasn't been defined before being used. You can see the Quick Fix suggestions in Figure 1-18; double-click the Create local variable 'stayCoolText' option.

The third error also was there because stayCoolText hadn't been declared, so that one is fixed now as well. Here's the final, fixed code:

```
import java.util.Date;
    .
    .
    .
public class FirstApp {

    public static void main(String[] args) {
        Date date = new Date();
        String stayCoolText = "Stay cool.";
```

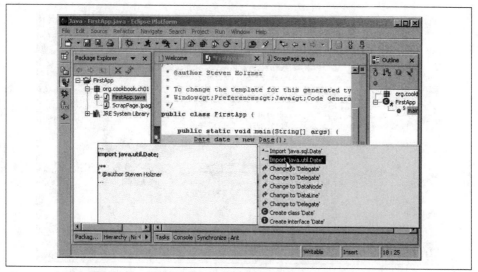

Figure 1-17. Quick Fix suggestions

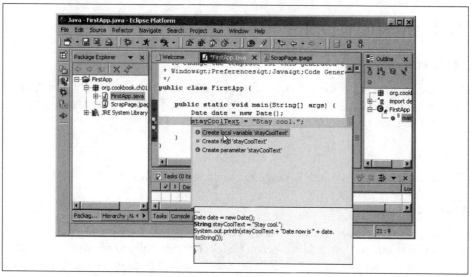

Figure 1-18. Fixing the error

```
        System.out.println(stayCoolText + " Date now is " + date.toString( ));
    }
}
```

After fixing these problems with Quick Fix, you can run the code, as shown in Figure 1-19, with no problems.

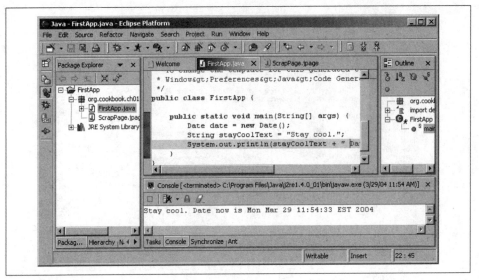

Figure 1-19. Running the fixed code

1.13   Keeping Your Workspace Clear

Problem

As you create more projects, your workspace gets cluttered. Eventually, the Package Explorer contains dozens of projects, old and new, and you've got to scroll to get to the ones you want.

Solution

To remove a project from the Package Explorer, simply delete it.

Discussion

Deleting a project *does not* necessarily delete the actual files used for the project. When you want, you can add the project back. For example, to remove the *FirstApp* project, just right-click it, and click Delete. Eclipse will display the Confirm Project Delete dialog box, as shown in Figure 1-20.

Make sure the "Do not delete contents" radio button is selected, and then click Yes to remove the project from Eclipse. The project will disappear from the Package Explorer.

Clicking the other radio button in this dialog will make Eclipse delete all the files and their contents in the project, so don't do that if you want to use the project again later.

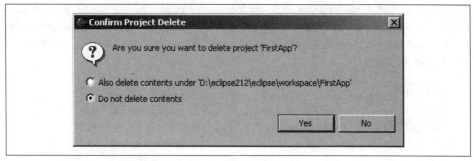

Figure 1-20. Removing a project

If you want to work with the project again, just import it back into the workspace. Right-click the Package Explorer and open the Import dialog by selecting Import from the context menu, or by selecting File → Import. Select Existing Project into Workspace and click Next. In the next pane, click the Browse button, select the *FirstApp* folder, and click OK.

Click Finish to import the *FirstApp* project again. The project reappears in the workspace. Removing projects from the workspace like this and importing them again as needed is the easiest way to reduce workspace clutter. We'll take a longer look at this issue in Chapter 3, when we start handling working sets.

See Also

Recipe 3.17 on creating working sets.

1.14   Recovering from Total Disaster

Problem

Your installation of Eclipse has become hopelessly fouled up.

Solution

Just save any of the projects from the *workspace* directory that you want to retain, delete the decompressed files and directories, and unzip or untar the Eclipse download again. After replacing the saved projects in the *workspace* directory (omitting any suspect projects that might have caused the problem in the first place), you're set.

Discussion

One reason people like Eclipse is because they have control over the (re)installation process. This is in stark contrast to other IDEs, some of which are massive and do so many things behind the scenes that you can never trust them.

Note that you also can migrate projects from one version of Eclipse to another simply by copying project folders into the new version's *workspace* directory. This doesn't always work with major revisions of Eclipse, but with minor revisions, it works like a charm.

 Eclipse doesn't install itself using the Windows installer, so there's no need to use the Windows control panel's Add/Remove Programs entry to manage Eclipse installation.

CHAPTER 2

Using Eclipse

2.0   Introduction

This chapter is about mastering Eclipse in everyday use. Chapter 1 gave you the basics; this chapter is designed to give you a working knowledge.

As with any complex tool, you might want to change things about Eclipse as you work with it more and more. So, in addition to teaching you how to work with Eclipse, this chapter also teaches you the many ways in which you can customize Eclipse, from moving views to creating your own perspectives.

When it comes to customizing Eclipse, one dialog stands out over the rest: the Preferences dialog, which you open by selecting Window → Preferences. This dialog is shown in Figure 2-1.

I encourage you to become familiar with this dialog. The Preferences dialog is the home of Eclipse customization, especially workbench customization. Want to automatically close all editors when you exit Eclipse (which enables Eclipse to start more quickly next time)? Select Window → Preferences → Workbench → Editors and then check the "Close all editors on exit" checkbox. Want to make editor tabs appear on the bottom of editor windows? Select Window → Preferences → Workbench → Appearance, and click Bottom in the Editor tab position box. Want to specify what editor or program Eclipse should use to open files with a certain file extension? Select Window → Preferences → Workbench → File Associations, choose a file extension, and click the Add button. Problem solved.

But as powerful as the Preferences dialog is, it's just the beginning of the customization story. Eclipse can be customized in thousands of ways. Read on to get a grip on tailoring Eclipse to match your requirements.

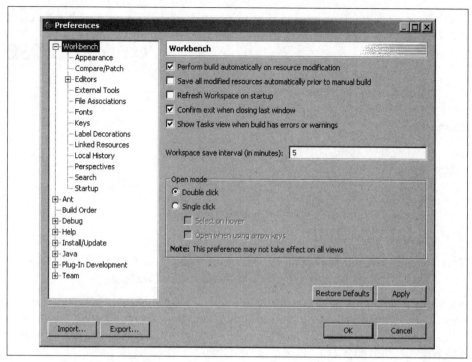

Figure 2-1. The Preferences dialog

2.1 Showing/Hiding Views

Problem

Where did the Console view go? It was here a minute ago.

Solution

To show a view, select Window → Show View, and choose the view you want to show. If the view you want isn't visible, select Window → Show View → Other, and choose a view from the dialog box that Eclipse presents of all views it knows about. To close a view, click the X button in its tab.

Discussion

It's easy to close a view accidentally or to work in a perspective that doesn't display a favorite view, such as the Console view that displays text sent to the output console. Just open the view by selecting Window → Show View.

For example, to add the Navigator view to the Debug perspective, open the Debug view (covered in Chapter 5) by selecting Window → Open Perspective → Debug.

Then add the Navigator view by selecting Window → Show View → Other → Basic → Navigator.

 If you want to save the newly configured perspective, select Window → Save Perspective As. For more information, see the Recipe 2.21 later in this chapter.

Some perspectives try to stack too many views on top of each other, which can make scrolling to the right tab annoying. Now that you know you can open views again as needed, you should have no qualms about closing extra views to remove clutter.

See Also

Recipe 5.3 on starting a debugging session; Chapter 1 of *Eclipse* (O'Reilly).

2.2 Moving a View or Toolbar

Problem

The Package Explorer should be on the right, shouldn't it?

Solution

You can drag toolbars and views in Eclipse, and they'll dock on the various edges of the Eclipse window. Figure 2-2 shows the Package Explorer being dragged to a new location.

The Package Explorer now appears on the right, as shown in Figure 2-3.

Besides being dragged, toolbars also can be broken into segments. Each toolbar features a graspable handle (the upright 3D bar at the left edge of the toolbar). By dragging this handle, you can resize the segments in the toolbar, as well as show or hide additional controls.

 You might not like working in an environment in which you can accidentally move toolbars, so select Window → Lock the Toolbars to hold things in place. If a perspective becomes scrambled as a result of accidental mouse movements, select Window → Reset Perspective to reset the perspective.

Discussion

You also can drag editors, but you can't mix items in the editor and view areas. The editor area is the center of the Eclipse window, and Eclipse won't allow you to drop any views there, or drop an editor on top of a view.

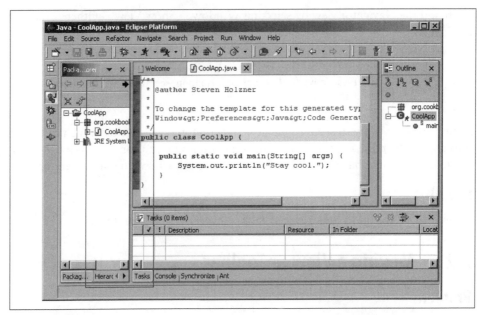

Figure 2-2. Dragging a view

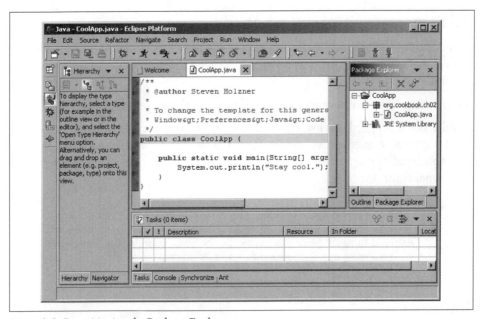

Figure 2-3. Repositioning the Package Explorer

See Also

Chapter 1 of *Eclipse* (O'Reilly).

2.3 Accessing Any Project File

Problem

Many perspectives will hide files; you want to get access to a specific file (or files) in your project.

Solution

The Navigator view in the Resource perspective gives you access to all the files in a project, without exception.

Discussion

Some perspectives hide files. For example, Eclipse stores project information in an XML file named *.project*, but many views, such as the Java perspective's Package Explorer, will hide that file. The *.project* file for a sample project open in the Resource perspective is shown in Figure 2-4.

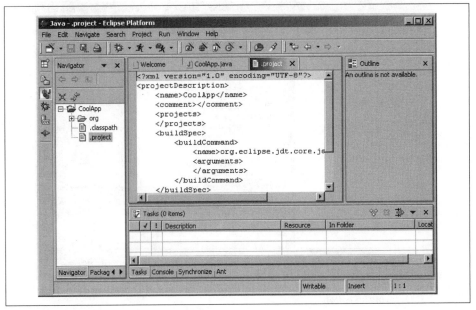

Figure 2-4. Using the Resource perspective

Some Java-oriented perspectives also support the Navigator view. Many Java programmers ignore the Resource perspective completely, but some Java-oriented views will hide various files from you. To get access to them all, don't forget about the Navigator view; it's always available in the Resource perspective as well as in some of the Java perspectives.

2.4 Tiling Editors

Problem

Although you can switch editors by clicking their tabs in the editor area, sometimes it's more desirable to have two editors open at once, e.g., when you're comparing two files visually.

Solution

You can drag editors and can tile the editor area with them.

Discussion

When you drag an editor and position it near an edge of the editor area, you'll see an arrow, as shown in Figure 2-5, which indicates that dropping the editor will dock it on that edge.

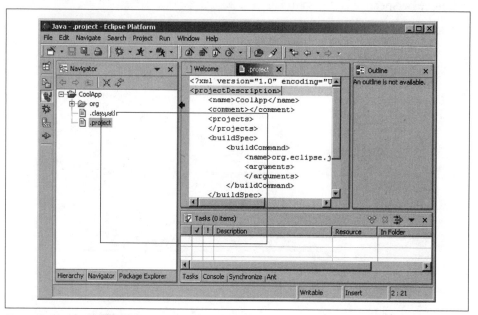

Figure 2-5. Dragging an editor

The new, tiled editor presentation is shown in Figure 2-6.

To restore an editor to its original position, just drag it back to where it was.

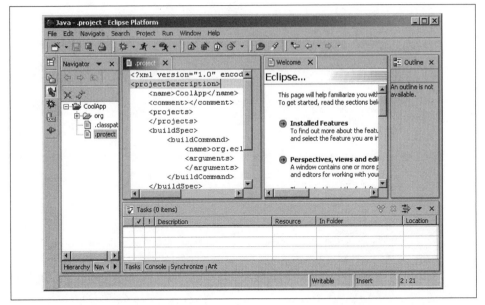

Figure 2-6. Tiling editors

You can open an item in an editor by dragging the item from a view such as the Package Explorer and dropping it on the editor area.

2.5   Maximizing Views and Editors

Problem

The Eclipse window is crammed with menu bars, toolbars, views, and editors. Sometimes, editing your code seems too cramped an experience.

Solution

You can maximize views or editors simply by double-clicking the view's titlebar or the editor's tab, something few people know.

Discussion

Figure 2-7 shows a maximized view of the JDT editor.

Double-click the view's titlebar or the editor's tab to restore it to its original size.

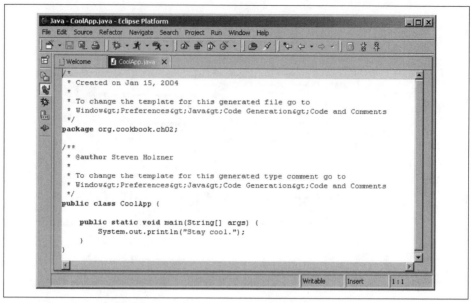

Figure 2-7. Maximizing an editor

As with many IDEs, Eclipse can feel crammed at times, especially when you're working on large documents. You might end up feeling like you're peering through a nest of distractions at the code you need to edit. To solve this problem, just double-click the editor's tab to maximize the editor.

2.6   Going Back to the Previous Editor

Problem

You've got 20 editors open, and scrolling through all those editor tabs to navigate between them is taking a long time.

Solution

Use the workbench editor's navigation history, which works much like a web browser's history. Just click the back arrow in the workbench toolbar as you would in a web browser to go back to the previous editor. (Or use Navigate menu items such as Navigate → Backward, or keyboard shortcuts such as Alt-Left Arrow.)

Discussion

When you work with Eclipse on extended projects, you'll find the editor area filling up with editors. And as the editors get more cramped, Eclipse makes their tabs smaller and the text in them more abbreviated. The more editors you have open, the more difficult it becomes to move between them. One way to ameliorate this problem is to bear in mind that you can use navigation controls to move between recently used editors.

2.7 Going Back to the Previous Edit Location

Problem

While editing, you switched to another editor to make sure that you had the name of a variable right. But you have 15 editors open. How do you get back to the exact line of code you were editing?

Solution

Select Navigate → Go to Last Edit Location (Ctrl-Q), which moves you back to the location where you last made a change in an editor. You'll also see a button for this function in the toolbar when working with editors.

Discussion

Eclipse lets you easily move between edit locations, a valuable addition to any programmer's toolset. If you can't see these buttons in your current perspective, you might need to add them by selecting Window → Customize Perspective → Other → Editor Navigation).

2.8 Linking Views to Editors

Problem

The items selected in a view are not tied closely to whichever editor is open. Switching editors, or even closing an editor, does not change the selection in a view by default.

Solution

Click the Link with Editor button.

Discussion

Many views, such as the Resource perspective's Navigator view and the Java perspective's Package Explorer, enable you to synchronize with editors. To synchronize, click the Link with Editor button shown in Figure 2-8.

By linking a view with an editor, you tie that view to the editor so that the view will always show the file currently being edited.

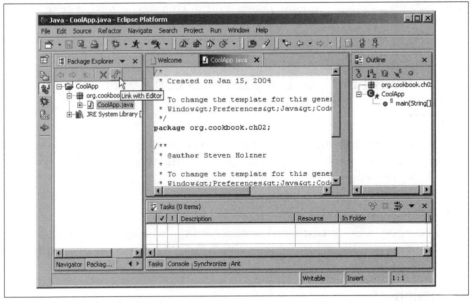

Figure 2-8. The Link with Editor button

See Also

Chapter 1 of *Eclipse* (O'Reilly).

2.9 Reordering View and Editor Tabs

Problem

You've got more than a dozen editors open, and the two you're working with are at opposite ends of the stack. As a result, you must scroll back and forth over all the editor tabs to work with the two editors you need. Isn't there a better way?

Solution

You can rearrange the order of the view and editor tabs as you prefer in Eclipse. Just drag the tab(s) to the order you want.

Discussion

This is a useful skill that few Eclipse developers know about, even those who use Eclipse everyday. When you open a large number of editors, as when you're working with multiple projects, you might find yourself surfing the editor tabs to find the ones you want. To avoid that, you can drag and drop those tabs in the order you want, grouping the editors you're currently working with.

2.10   Navigating from an Editor to a View

Problem

It's easy to navigate from a file in a view to an editor showing the file. Just double-click the file in the view. However, what if you want to go backward; from the editor showing a file to the view showing that file?

Solution

Select Navigate → Show In, and select the view you want from those that appear in the submenu.

Discussion

For example, if you're editing a Java file, select Navigate → Show In, and the Package Explorer will open. The file you're currently editing will be selected.

2.11   Creating a Key Binding

Problem

You find yourself performing a specific task, such as adding a bookmark or adding tasks to the task list, over and over. You want to assign a simple key combination to such tasks.

Solution

You can customize Eclipse by adding key combinations to dozens of Eclipse tasks.

Discussion

To see which tasks are available, select Window → Preferences → Workbench → Keys, and choose the task you want to automate, such as adding a bookmark. Then choose a key sequence you want to associate with the task, as shown in Figure 2-9.

2.12   Displaying More Resource Information with Icons

Problem

You want to turn on label decorators to get additional information about icons and buttons.

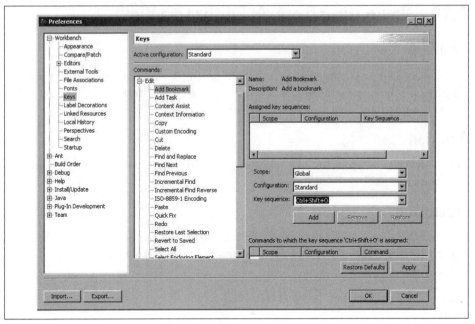

Figure 2-9. Assigning a key combination to a task

Solution

Select Window → Preferences → Workbench → Label Decorations.

Discussion

Label decorations augment the standard Eclipse icons displayed in various views. For example, if you archive a code file in a CVS repository and have label decorations turned on, the file's icon displays a small gold cylinder that isn't there otherwise.

To turn on label decorations, select Window → Preferences → Workbench → Label Decorations, and select which decoration you want to use, as shown in Figure 2-10.

We're going to use label decorations with Eclipse and CVS in Chapter 6. Once you've turned on label decorations, you can see at a glance which files have been stored in the CVS repository.

See Also

Recipe 6.6 on labeling files using version control.

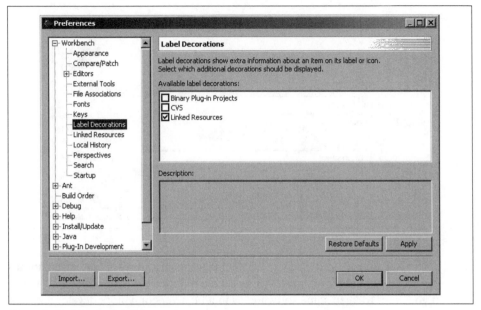

Figure 2-10. Selecting label decorations

2.13 Using a Different Workspace

Problem

You want to use a nondefault workspace for an Eclipse project.

Solution

Uncheck the "Use default" checkbox when you name the project in the first pane of the New Project dialog, and fill in the directory you want to use instead.

Discussion

When you create a new Eclipse project, Eclipse stores it in its *workspace* directory by default. You can, however, make it use another directory, regardless of the type of Eclipse project you're creating. To select a different location, uncheck the "Use default" checkbox when you name the new project in the first pane of the New Project dialog. Then fill in the directory you want to use instead.

You can see how this works in Figure 2-11, in which a new Java project is created and stored in the directory *c:\myworkspace*.

Using a nondefault workspace is a good idea in many cases. For example, you might be working with code on a network. In this case, you should store the code where other software can use it (in Chapter 8, we're going to store and develop code where

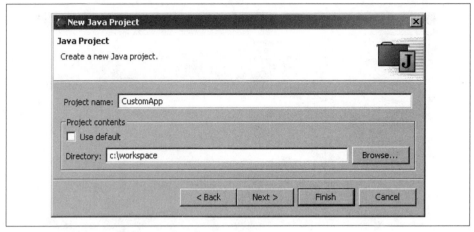

Figure 2-11. Creating a custom workspace

the Tomcat web server can find it, which means using the Tomcat installation's *webapps* directory as the workspace). It's also a good idea to use a nondefault workspace if you want to keep some software, as in a beta version you're developing, separate from the current version of the software.

2.14 Creating a Task

Problem

Eclipse tasks in the Tasks view serve as reminders of things you need to do. For example, compilation errors appear in the Tasks view; you can click them to jump to the lines containing the errors. So, how can you add and manage your own tasks to the Tasks view?

Solution

You can create a task in the Tasks view by right-clicking the view and selecting New Task. This opens the New Task dialog, in which you can create the task.

Discussion

The New Task dialog is shown in Figure 2-12. Enter the name of the new task, select a priority level, and click OK.

 You also can create a new task by right-clicking the marker bar in an editor and selecting Add Task. You can also click the button with three + signs in the Tasks view's toolbar.

The new task will appear in the Tasks view, as shown in Figure 2-13.

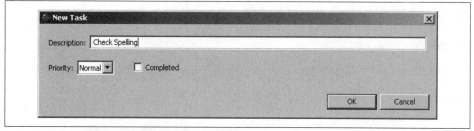

Figure 2-12. Creating a new task

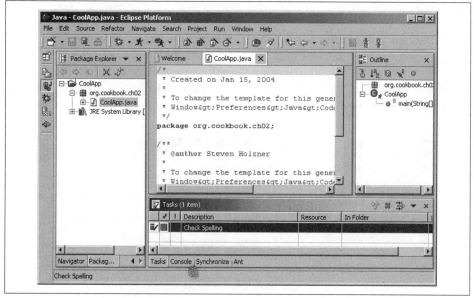

Figure 2-13. The new task

You can delete tasks you add to the Tasks view by right-clicking them and clicking the Delete button or by selecting the tasks and pressing the Delete key.

Tasks also have a completion status, which you can set by right-clicking the tasks and clicking Mark Completed. When you want to delete all completed tasks, right-click the Tasks view, and click Delete Completed Tasks.

See Also

Chapter 1 of *Eclipse* (O'Reilly).

2.15   Creating a Bookmark

Problem

You want to come back to a location in a file at a later time.

Solution

Create a bookmark by right-clicking the marker bar in an editor and specifying a name for the bookmark in the New Bookmark dialog.

Discussion

You're editing code, and suddenly it's quitting time. How can you save your place? Create a bookmark, and come back to it later by double-clicking that bookmark in the Bookmarks view. You create the bookmark by right-clicking the marker bar and naming the bookmark in the New Bookmark dialog. The bookmark will appear in the marker bar, as shown in Figure 2-14.

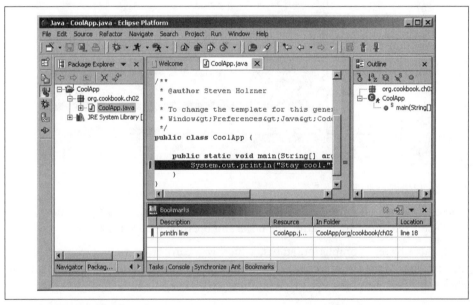

Figure 2-14. Using a bookmark

When you want to come back to the bookmarked location later, just open the Bookmarks view by selecting Window → Show View → Other → Basics → Bookmarks. You can see the bookmark we created in the Bookmarks view at the bottom of Figure 2-14; double-clicking it opens the bookmarked line in an editor.

As you'd expect, bookmarks work even if the file with the bookmark is closed; when you double-click the bookmark, that file opens automatically.

2.16   Creating a Fast View

Problem

Territory is always at a premium in IDEs; views can be stacked, but when you've got too many of them, it's frustrating to have to search for the right tab.

Solution

Use fast views to free some space in the Eclipse window.

Discussion

Transforming a view into a fast view adds it as an icon in the shortcut bar (that's the bar at extreme left in Eclipse, where the perspective icons appear). Clicking a fast view's icon makes it slide open until you're done with it. When you click outside it, it will slide closed automatically. For example, you can see the Bookmarks view made into a fast view in Figure 2-15.

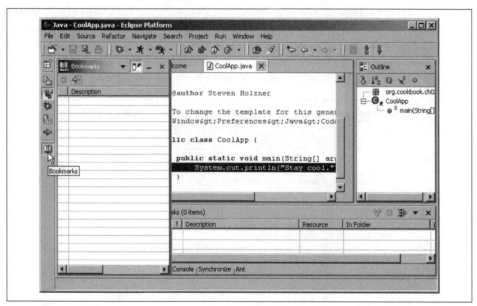

Figure 2-15. Creating a fast view

You turn a view into a fast view by selecting Fast View in its system menu, and you reach a view's system menu by right-clicking its name in its titlebar. When you turn a normal view into a fast view, an icon for the fast view appears on the shortcut bar. Right-clicking a fast view icon in the shortcut bar and deselecting Fast View restores it.

2.17 Customizing Help

Problem

You're browsing the Eclipse help system, and some of the help pages are very long. You want to search the text in those pages, but you notice that the Eclipse help browser doesn't let you search the current page.

Solution

Use your own browser instead.

Discussion

Eclipse uses a custom version of the Tomcat web server to display help documentation. While the help system is open, you can find the direct URL of the help topic you're looking at. After launching your own browser, you can navigate to that URL.

To get the URL of a help topic, right-click the topic, and select Create Shortcut, which creates a shortcut to the help topic. For example, my URL for help on bookmarks is *http://127.0.0.1:1203/help/index.jsp?topic=/org.eclipse.platform.doc.user/concepts/cbookmrk.htm*. You can double-click the shortcut or enter the URL in a browser to view the help page in your browser, as shown in Figure 2-16. You're free to search individual Eclipse help pages with your browser's Edit menu.

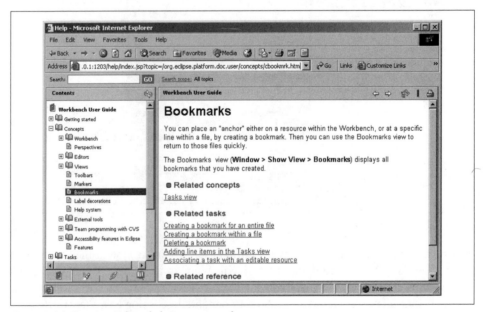

Figure 2-16. Opening Eclipse help in your own browser

A recent addition to Eclipse enables you to bookmark help topics in the Eclipse help system. To create a bookmark, click the Bookmark Document button on the toolbar, and the bookmark will appear in the Bookmarks tab. Just double-click a bookmark to go back to the help topic indicated.

You can even customize the Eclipse help system to use your favorite browser by default. Just select the browser option you want in the Window → Preferences → Help page, as shown in Figure 2-17.

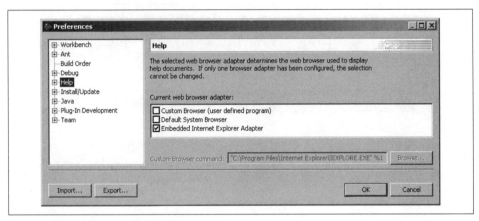

Figure 2-17. Configuring the help browser

You say you don't want to wait for the help system to open? What you're actually waiting for is the Tomcat web server to start so that it can serve help documents to the Eclipse Help browser. If you just want to check whether some topics match what you're looking for, click the Search button in the Eclipse toolbar and the Help Search button in the Search dialog. Enter the text you want help on, and click Search. The Search view then appears with matches in the help system. Here, you can see if your search returned any interesting matches to your query, all without having to launch Tomcat. However, if you see a match you're interested in, the help browser has to start up for you to view the topic's contents.

2.18   Restoring Deleted Resources

Problem

A needed file was deleted by mistake, and you want to restore it.

Solution

No problem. Restore the file using the container project's Restore from Local History context menu item.

Discussion

To restore a deleted file, right-click the file's project, and select Restore from Local History, opening the dialog shown in Figure 2-18. In the figure, a *.class* file that was deleted is restored.

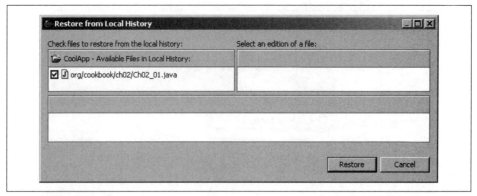

Figure 2-18. Restoring a deleted file

 Because the Java perspective's Package Explorer doesn't display all files, including *.class* files, you'll need to switch to the Navigator view in the Java perspective or use the Resource perspective if you want to restore *.class* files.

2.19   Customizing a Perspective

Problem

You want to change the menu choices and toolbar items in a perspective.

Solution

Use the Customize Perspective dialog, which you can open by selecting Window → Customize Perspective. The dialog is shown in Figure 2-19.

 After you've set Eclipse preferences, you can export those preferences so that others can use them as well. To do this, click the Import and Export buttons in the Preferences dialog.

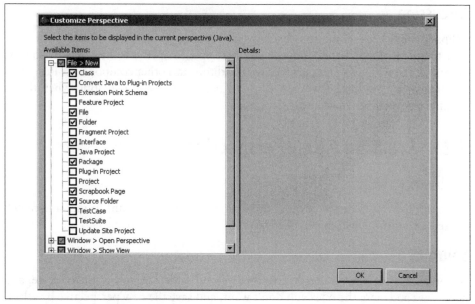

Figure 2-19. Customizing a perspective

The Preferences dialog enables you to customize menu choices and toolbar items, but it doesn't really enable you to "customize" perspectives (and in fact, the items you can add to menus usually are available under the Other menu choice anyway). To learn how to customize a perspective, see Recipe 2.21.

See Also

Recipe 2.20 on restoring a perspective; Recipe 2.21 on creating a new perspective.

2.20   Restoring a Perspective

Problem

One of Eclipse's perspectives was rearranged, and too many views were closed. How do you restore the perspective to its original condition?

Solution

If a perspective becomes scrambled to the point of being unrecognizable, you can restore it to its original state by selecting Window → Reset Perspective.

Discussion

Eclipse always keeps numerous backups and restore points in its memory. In addition to those platform- and file-specific backups, Eclipse also has default starting points for the windows and perspectives of editors and other components. Reset Perspective gives you that behavior with just a mouse-click and is helpful when things become cluttered and confused.

2.21 Creating a New Perspective

Problem

None of the built-in perspectives is quite right for you. You want to mix and match to create your own custom perspective.

Solution

No problem. Just open a perspective that's close to the one you want to create, add new views and close the ones you don't want, and save the new perspective by selecting Window → Save Perspective As.

Discussion

The Save Perspective As dialog is shown in Figure 2-20. This new perspective, named Debug2, adds the Navigator view to the Debug perspective.

Now you're free to open your new perspective whenever you want, as shown in Figure 2-21. Very cool.

 To delete a custom perspective, select Window → Preferences → Workbench → Perspectives, choose the perspective you want to get rid of, and click Delete.

Being able to create your own perspectives is very cool, and is something virtually no other IDE offers. You've got the opportunity here to mix and match views and create something totally new. Get creative!

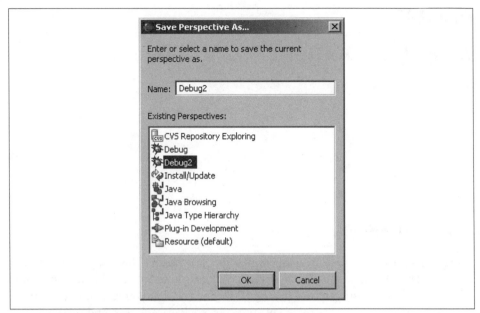

Figure 2-20. Creating a new perspective

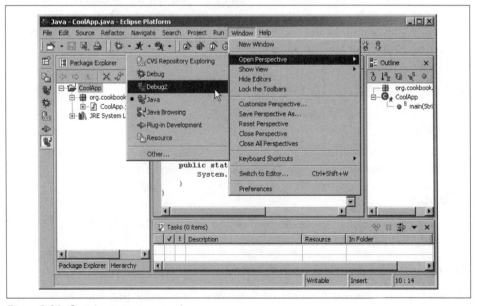

Figure 2-21. Opening a new perspective

CHAPTER 3

Java Development

3.0   Introduction

A great majority of Eclipse developers develop Java code. This chapter begins our focus on Java development. We'll cover a lot of ground in this chapter, including everything from speeding up the Eclipse JDT editor so that you can enter code more quickly, to using the JDT to create Java projects, packages, classes, and methods.

The Eclipse team is always thinking of techniques you can use to facilitate the development of Java code. This chapter highlights some of those techniques. We'll continue our discussion of the Eclipse JDT in Chapter 4, which takes an in-depth look at refactoring, searching, building, and launching applications.

3.1   Speeding Up the JDT Editor

Problem

As you enter code in the JDT editor, windows flash, wavy red lines appear under text, and red boxes appear in rulers, among other annoying distractions.

Solution

You can turn off many automatic syntax and problem-checking features to speed code entry.

Discussion

Although Eclipse provides a host of automatic syntax and problem-checking features, sometimes those features can be annoying. Fortunately, Eclipse is almost endlessly customizable. Here are some of the more common auto-checking features people find distracting, along with tips for dealing with them:

Problem indicators that appear while you're typing

Turn off by selecting Window → Preferences → Java → Editor → Annotations, and then uncheck all checkboxes.

The overview ruler

Hide by selecting Window → Preferences → Java → Editor → Appearance → Show Overview Ruler, and then uncheck the appropriate checkbox.

Outline synchronization

Turn off by selecting Window → Preferences → Java → Editor → Appearance → Synchronize Outline Selection on Cursor Move, and then uncheck the appropriate checkbox.

Eclipse 3.0

Smart insert mode is another automatic feature, new in Eclipse 3.0, which you can turn on and off. This is the mode in which Eclipse does things for you automatically as you type, such as adding a closing quote to strings, adding closing braces, and so on. You can toggle smart insert mode on and off in Eclipse 3.0 by pressing the Insert key, which cycles you through the overwrite and insert modes (which Eclipse 3.0 shares with Eclipse 2.x) as well as the Eclipse 3.0 smart insert mode. You can see the smart insert mode cursor, which looks like a left bracket, in the JDT editor in Figure 3-1.

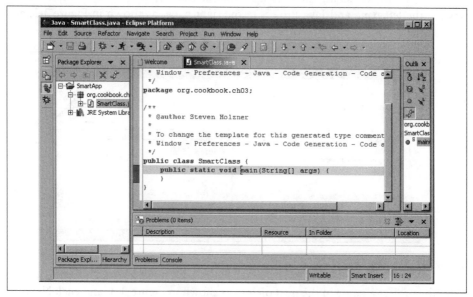

Figure 3-1. Smart insert in Eclipse 3.0

To configure whether the JDT editor closes strings for you, adds braces, and so on, as well as to configure smart insert mode in Eclipse 3.0, select Window → Preferences → Java → Editor → Typing.

3.2   Creating a Java Project

Problem

You want to begin programming, so you need to create a new Java project.

Solution

Select File → New → Project, or right-click the Package Explorer in the Java perspective, and select New → Project.

Discussion

All Java code has to go into a project of some kind in Eclipse. Although we covered the basics of creating a new project in Chapter 1, we'll take a more in-depth look at the process here.

To create a Java project, open the New Project dialog by selecting File → New → Project or by right-clicking the Package Explorer and selecting New → Project. Select Java in the left pane and Java Project in the right pane, as shown in Figure 3-2, and click Next.

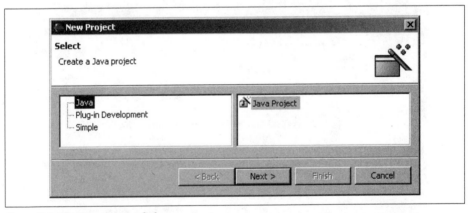

Figure 3-2. The New Project dialog

Give the project a name in the next dialog, as shown in Figure 3-3, and click Next.

The "Project contents" box shown in Figure 3-3 is where you specify the location of the project. It can be very useful to store the project where other software, such as the Tomcat web server, can find it. To select a custom location for the project, uncheck the "Use default" checkbox, and browse to a new directory.

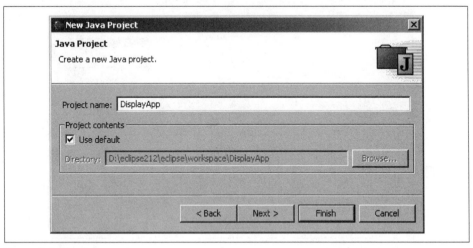

Figure 3-3. Naming a project

The final dialog in this sequence, shown in Figure 3-4, contains four tabs; here's what they do:

Source
> Enables you to specify source folders (discussed shortly)

Projects
> Enables you to specify other projects on the build path

Libraries
> Enables you to specify JAR files and other folders for the build path

Order and Export
> Enables you to specify the build path order and what entries to export

These tabs are particularly useful for configuring projects as you create them. For example, say you want to store the source code for your project in a folder named *src*. To do that, click the Source tab, click Add Folder, click Create New Folder, type the letters src, and then click OK twice. Eclipse will ask you if you want to use this new folder as your source folder instead of the default project folder, and whether you want to use an output build folder named *bin*, as shown in Figure 3-5. Click Yes if you want to set up the *src* folder to your project's source code and if you want the *bin* folder to hold the compiled output.

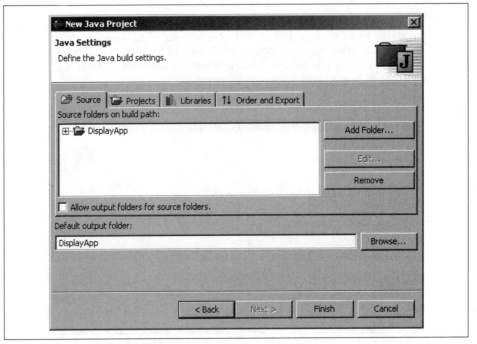

Figure 3-4. Setting project options

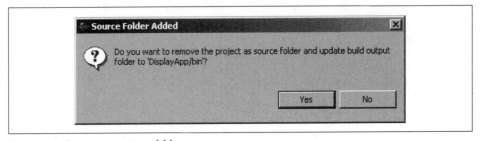

Figure 3-5. Creating an output folder

See Also

Chapter 2 of *Eclipse* (O'Reilly).

3.3   Creating Java Packages

Problem

You want to put your code into a Java package.

Solution

Select File → New → Package, or right-click the Package Explorer in the Java perspective and select New → Package. Alternatively, you can specify the package when you create a new class.

Discussion

In all but the most trivial projects, you usually put your Java code into a package. To create a new package, select a project in the Package Explorer and then select File → New → Package, or right-click the Package Explorer and select New → Package. The New Java Package dialog appears, as shown in Figure 3-6. Enter the name of the new package, and click Finish. The new package will be added to the project in the Package Explorer.

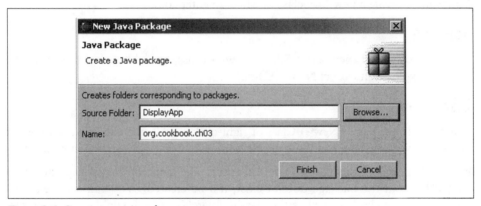

Figure 3-6. Creating a new package

When the new package appears in the project, you can add classes to it by right-clicking it and selecting New → Class.

> Although you *can* create packages this way in Eclipse, usually you would create a package when you create a class (unless you're purposely breaking up your project into multiple package.) Recipe 3.4 covers the process of creating a package when creating a class.

When you access a class in another package, you must import it using that class's fully qualified name in your code:

```
import org.cookbook.ch03.DisplayApp;

public class DisplayApp {

    public static void main(String[] args){
        DisplayApp display = new DisplayApp();
```

```
        display.print( );
    }
}
```

 Some code you want to work with might be in another project entirely. When you create a project, you can specify other projects you want included in the build path (see Recipe 3.4). Alternatively, in an existing project you can specify which other projects should be in the build path by selecting Project → Properties → Java Build Path.

3.4   Creating a Java Class

Problem

You want to create a new Java class in which to enter code.

Solution

Select a project and then select File → New → Class, or right-click a project in the Package Explorer and select New → Class.

Discussion

When you select File → New → Class or right-click a project in the Package Explorer and select New → Class, you'll see the New Java Class dialog, as shown in Figure 3-7.

Note the options in this dialog. You can specify the name of the package this class should be in (if the package doesn't exist, it'll be created). You can set the access modifier for the class, as well as the class's superclass, which enables you to implement inheritance. You can also specify what interfaces you want the class to implement, as well as a set of method stubs to create: main, a constructor, and inherited abstract methods.

 If you want to enclose one class within another, you can enter the name of the enclosing class in the "Enclosing type" box in the New Java Class dialog. If you right-click the enclosing class in the Package Explorer and select New → Class, the enclosing class's name will appear in the "Enclosing type" text box when this dialog opens; however, it won't be used unless you check the checkbox next to that text box.

Creating an anonymous inner class

In Eclipse 3.0, code assist (also called content assist) can help when you want to create an anonymous inner class. Place the cursor after the opening brace of a class instance creation and press Ctrl-Space (or select Edit → Content Assist). Code assist automatically creates the body of the anonymous inner class, including all the

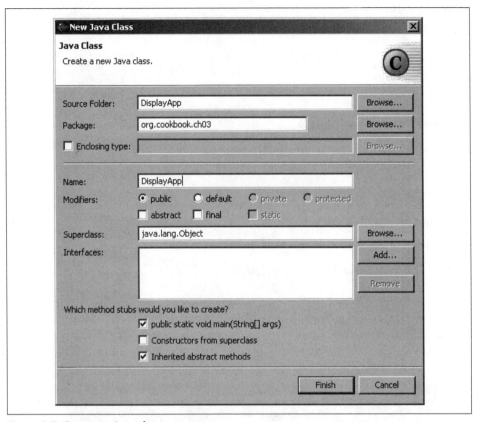

Figure 3-7. Creating a Java class

methods you need to implement. Very cool. (For more information on code assist, see Chapter 2.)

3.5   Creating a Java Method

Problem

You want to create a Java method to run your code.

Solution

Enter the method's code yourself in the JDT editor, or let code assist help out.

Discussion

Java code must be in a method to be run. Eclipse, with code assist, can help out. Say you want to create the code you see in Example 3-1, which includes a new method named display.

Example 3-1. The DisplayApp.java example

```java
public class DisplayApp
{
    public static void main(String[] args)
    {
        display();
    }

    private static void display()
    {
        System.out.println("No problem.");
    }
}
```

To see what code assist can do for you, create the *DisplayApp* project, and let Eclipse generate a main method for you:

```java
public class DisplayApp {

    public static void main(String[] args) {
    }
}
```

Instead of typing in the display method by hand, use code assist. Move the cursor beneath the main method, and enter the word private to make display a private method. Then, press Ctrl-Space to open code assist, as shown in Figure 3-8.

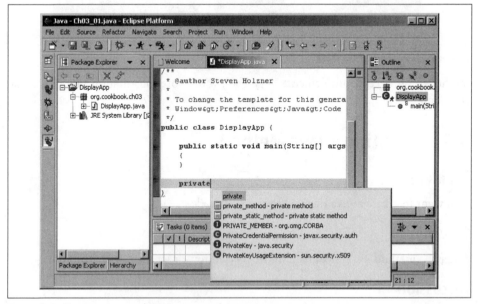

Figure 3-8. Creating a new method

Select the private static method item, and code assist will create the method template for you, as shown in Figure 3-9.

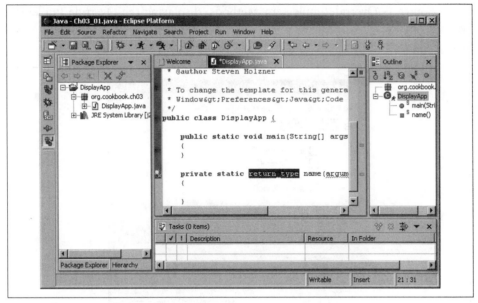

Figure 3-9. A new method template

Fill in the return_type, name, and arguments items to give you the code in Example 3-1; save the file; and run the project by selecting Run → Run As → Java Application. You should see "No problem." in the Console view.

> Eclipse also can create methods for you automatically if your code calls them. To see how that works, delete or comment out the display method in your code. Click the Quick Fix light bulb that appears next to the call to display in the main method, and select Create method 'display(...)'. Using the signature of the method you're calling, Eclipse will create a method skeleton for you.

3.6   Overriding a Java Method

Problem

You want to override the methods of a class, but first you need to know which methods are available to override.

Solution

Select Source → Override/Implement Methods.

Discussion

To see what methods you can override, open a class derived from another class, and select Source → Override/Implement Methods, displaying the Override/Implement Methods dialog shown in Figure 3-10. Selecting the methods and clicking OK will make Eclipse create method stubs for those methods automatically.

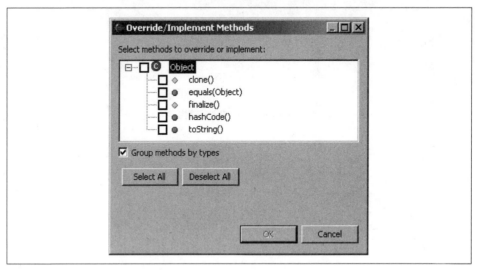

Figure 3-10. Overriding methods

3.7 Getting Method Parameter Hints

Problem

You want to call a method, but you forget what its parameters are, and you would like some hints.

Solution

Place the cursor in the method's argument list and press Ctrl-Shift-Space, or select Edit → Parameter Hints.

Discussion

When you place the cursor in a method's argument list, you will see a list of parameter hints. In the JDT editor, press Ctrl-Shift-Space, or select Edit → Parameter Hints. A tool tip will appear, showing the method's parameters.

3.8   Inserting Method Parameter Names

Problem

You forgot the parameters of a method you want to call, and instead of receiving hints in tool tips (see the previous recipe), you want Eclipse to fill in the parameter names in your code for you.

Solution

Select Window → Preferences → Java → Editor → Code Assist, and check the "Fill argument names on method completion" and "Guess filled argument names" checkboxes.

Discussion

When you check these checkboxes, code assist automatically fills in names of the parameters passed to that method in your code. For example, say you've typed `java.util.Arrays.fill`, and you press Ctrl-Space to invoke code assist, then you select one of the methods code assist offers you. Code assist will insert names for each parameter into your code, and as you tab between them, it displays their type in a tool tip, as shown in Figure 3-11.

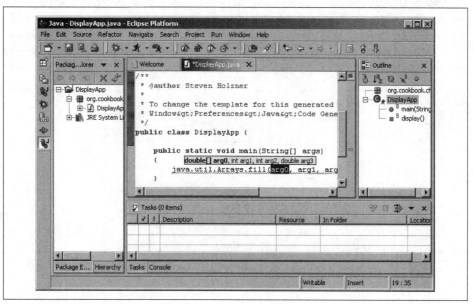

Figure 3-11. Auto-naming of parameters

3.9   Creating Getter/Setter Methods

Problem

You need to create getter/setter methods for a field (for example, when creating properties in a JavaBean™), and you are looking for a shortcut.

Solution

Select Source → Generate Getter and Setter.

Discussion

Say your code uses a field named text to store the text it displays:

```
public class DisplayApp {

    static String text = "No problem.";

    public static void main(String[] args)
    {
        System.out.println(text);
    }
}
```

Instead of storing that data in a simple field, you can create getter and setter methods for that data, making access to the data from outside the class more secure. To automatically create getter and setter methods, select Source → Generate Getter and Setter, opening the dialog shown in Figure 3-12. Select the field for which you want a getter and setter, as well as the methods to create, and click OK.

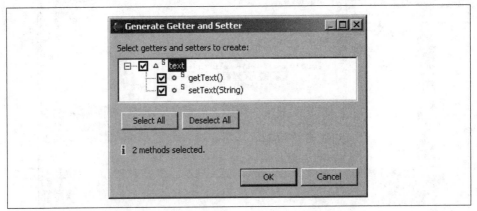

Figure 3-12. Creating getter/setter methods

This creates the new getter and setter methods shown here:

```
public class DisplayApp {

    static String text = "No problem.";

    public static void main(String[] args)
    {
        System.out.println(getText());
    }
    /**
     * @return
     */
    public static String getText() {
        return text;
    }

    /**
     * @param string
     */
    public static void setText(String string) {
        text = string;
    }

}
```

3.10   Creating Delegate Methods

Problem

You want to create a delegate method for a field.

Solution

Select the field's declaration, and then select Source → Generate Delegate Methods.

Discussion

When you select Source → Generate Delegate Methods, you'll see a list of methods for which the field will create delegates, as shown in Figure 3-13. Selecting various methods and clicking OK creates delegates for those methods and inserts them in your code.

3.11   Surrounding Code with do/for/if/try/while Blocks

Problem

You want to enclose a section of code in a try/catch block or in a do/for/if/while construct.

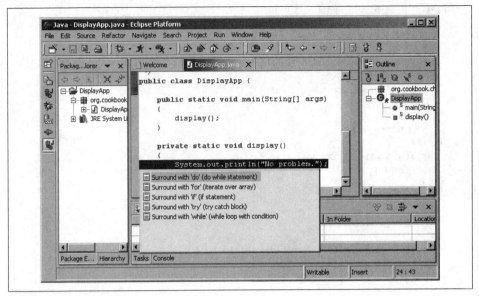

Figure 3-13. Creating delegate methods

Solution

Select the lines to surround, press Ctrl-1 (or select Edit → Quick Fix) to list all the possibilities, and select one of them.

Discussion

Figure 3-14 shows the possibilities that appear when you select code and press Ctrl-l. When you select one of these possibilities, the selected code becomes surrounded with the construct you've chosen.

 One of the great things here is that if you surround your code with a try/catch block in this way, Eclipse automatically figures out all the possible exceptions and catches them for you.

See Also

Chapter 2 of *Eclipse* (O'Reilly).

3.12   Finding the Matching Brace

Problem

Your code is getting long, and it's hard to find the closing curly brace matching an opening brace, or vice versa.

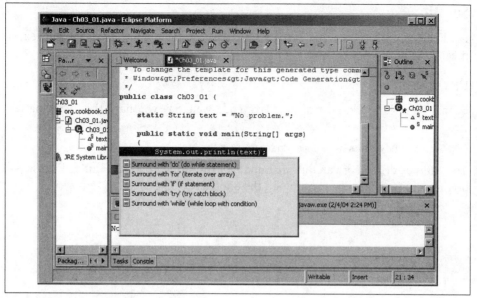

Figure 3-14. Surrounding code in a block

Solution

Select the opening or closing brace and press Ctrl-Shift-P (or select Navigate → Go To → Matching Bracket).

Discussion

This is a useful tip for long code listings. To match an opening brace with the corresponding closing brace, just select the opening brace and press Ctrl-Shift-P. Eclipse will highlight the line with the closing brace.

 You also can double-click before an opening or after a closing brace, which selects the text between the two braces automatically, thereby enabling you to locate the closing brace quickly. This technique works not only with braces, but also with parentheses.

3.13   Automatically Wrapping Strings

Problem

Your text strings are getting too long for the width of the screen, and you're getting tired of scrolling to the ends of the strings to edit them.

Solution

Let Eclipse break the strings for you. Just position the cursor in the quoted text to break, and press Enter.

Discussion

Eclipse handles breaking strings in Java code well. Say you have the following text string:

```
String text = "This is a long string of text.";
```

You can put the cursor caret in the middle of the string and press Enter; Eclipse will do the right Java thing by splitting up the quoted text like so:

```
String text = "This is a long " +
    "string of text.";
```

 You can customize this behavior in the Typing page, which you access by selecting Window → Preferences → Java → Editor → Typing.

3.14   Creating a Constructor

Problem

You want Eclipse to add a constructor to a class, including a call to the superclass's constructor.

Solution

Select Source → Add Constructor from Superclass.

Discussion

For example, if you have this code:

```
public class DisplayApp {

    static String text = "No problem.";

    public static void main(String[] args)
    {
        System.out.println(text);
    }
}
```

and you select Source → Add Constructor from Superclass, Eclipse will give you this:

```
public class DisplayApp {

    static String text = "No problem.";
```

```
/**
 *
 */
public DisplayApp( ) {
    super( );
    // TODO Auto-generated constructor stub
}

public static void main(String[] args)
{
    System.out.println(text);
}
}
```

You also can create constructors automatically when you create a class.

Eclipse 3.0

In Eclipse 3.0, you can create a constructor that will assign values to one or more fields. Select Source → Generate Constructor using Fields, opening the dialog shown in Figure 3-15.

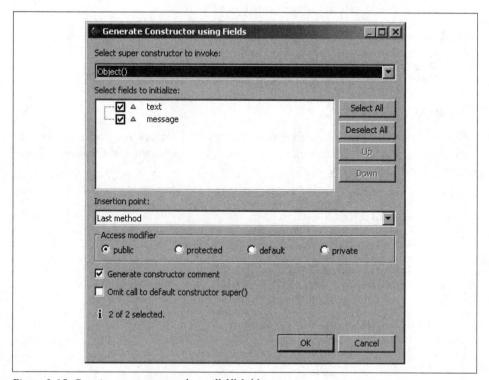

Figure 3-15. Creating a constructor that will fill fields

Selecting the two String fields, text and message, creates this constructor:

```
public DisplayApp(String text, String message) {
    super();
    this.text = text;
    this.message = message;
}
```

See Also

Chapter 2 of *Eclipse* (O'Reilly).

3.15   Converting Constructors to Factory Methods

Problem

You want to convert a constructor to a factory method.

Solution

In Eclipse 3.0, select a constructor declaration or a call to the constructor in the JDT editor, and then select Refactoring → Introduce Factory.

 This is an Eclipse 3.0-only solution. No equivalent solution exists for versions of Eclipse prior to 3.0.

Discussion

Eclipse 3.0 enables you to convert constructors into factory methods. To do that, you select a constructor declaration or a call to the constructor and then select Refactoring → Introduce Factory.

For example, say you had this call to a class's constructor:

```
public class DisplayApp {

    private String text;

    public static void main(String[] args) {
        DisplayApp DisplayApp = new DisplayApp("Hello");
    }

    public DisplayApp(String text) {
        super();
        this.text = text;
    }
}
```

Selecting the constructor call and then selecting Refactoring → Introduce Factory opens the Introduce Factory dialog. Here, Eclipse 3.0 will suggest the factory name createDisplayApp. Click OK to accept that name. Eclipse then creates that new factory method, replaces the call to the constructor with a call to that method, and makes the original constructor private:

```java
public class DisplayApp {

    private String text;

    public static void main(String[] args) {
        DisplayApp DisplayApp = createDisplayApp("Hello");
    }

    public static DisplayApp createDisplayApp(java.lang.String text) {
        return new DisplayApp(text);
    }

    /**
     * @param text
     */
    private DisplayApp(String text) {
        super();
        this.text = text;
    }
}
```

3.16   Commenting Out a Section of Code

Problem

You want to comment out a long section of code.

Solution

Select Source → Comment.

Discussion

All you have to do is to select the lines to comment out and then select Source → Comment. A single-line comment, //, will appear in front of all the lines. To uncomment them, just select Source → Uncomment.

Eclipse 3.0

Eclipse 3.0 also enables you to surround code in a block comment (/*...*/). Just select Source → Add Block Comment. To remove the comment, select Source → Remove Block Comment.

See Also

Chapter 2 of *Eclipse* (O'Reilly).

3.17   Creating Working Sets

Problem

The Package Explorer is getting crowded with projects.

Solution

Create a working set, and in the Package Explorer, select only the projects in that working set.

Discussion

In Chapter 1, you learned how to delete projects without deleting their contents, enabling you to import them back into the Package Explorer at a later time. Well, you also can customize the Package Explorer by creating *working sets*, which are sets of projects you can handle as a group in the Package Explorer.

For example, say you have four projects, *DisplayApp*, *DisplayApp2*, *DisplayApp3*, and *DisplayApp4*, as shown in Figure 3-16. However, you want to work with only two projects, *DisplayApp* and *DisplayApp2*.

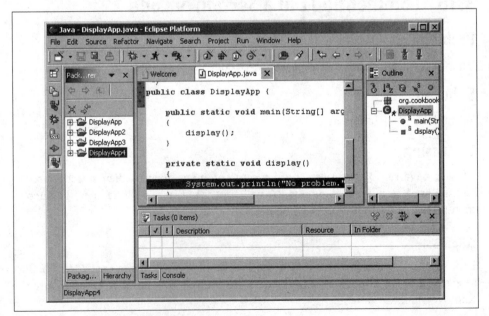

Figure 3-16. Four projects in the Package Explorer

To create a working set consisting of only those two projects, click the Package Explorer's pull-down menu (the inverted black triangle at the top of the view) and choose Select Working Set, opening the Select Working Set dialog. To create a new working set, click the New button. This opens the New Working Set dialog. In the "Working set type" box, choose Java, and then click the Next button. Now select the projects for this working set, as shown in Figure 3-17, name the working set (here, it's called Two Projects), and click Finish.

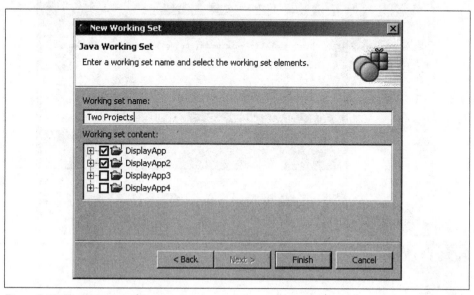

Figure 3-17. Creating a working set

When you click the Finish button, the Select Working Set dialog reappears, showing the Two Projects working set, as shown in Figure 3-18.

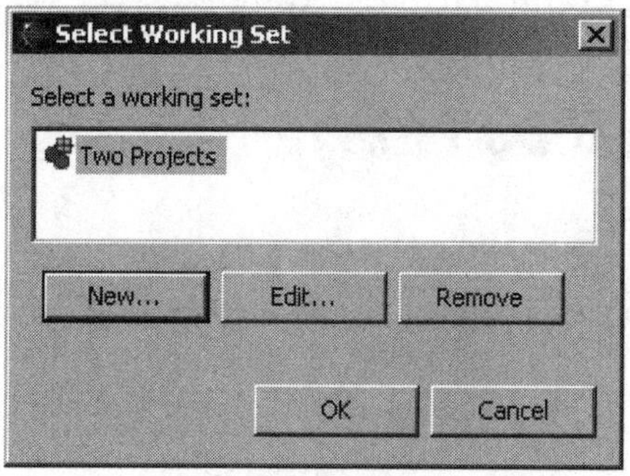

Figure 3-18. Selecting a working set

Select this new working set, and click OK. Only the two projects in the selected working set appear in the Package Explorer, as shown in Figure 3-19. In this way, you can clear out what's going on in the Package Explorer.

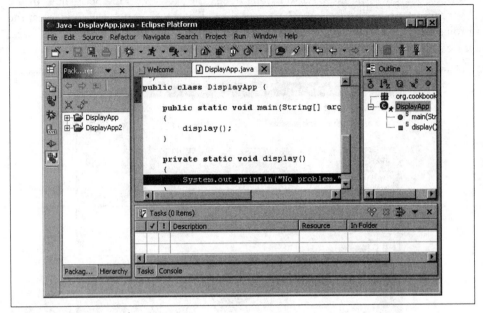

Figure 3-19. Using a working set

 Notice that although the working set determines what projects appear in the Package Explorer, you still can see all four projects in the Navigator view.

To deselect a working set, choose Deselect Working Set from the view's pull-down menu. To edit the members of a working set, choose Edit Active Working Set.

3.18   Creating TODO Tasks

Problem

You want to use annotations to keep track of everything you still have to do in your code.

Solution

Add TODO comments to your code; they'll appear in the Tasks view.

Discussion

Just including the text TODO in a single-line comment will add that comment's text to the Tasks view, enabling you to keep track of tasks in one location. You can see an example in Figure 3-20.

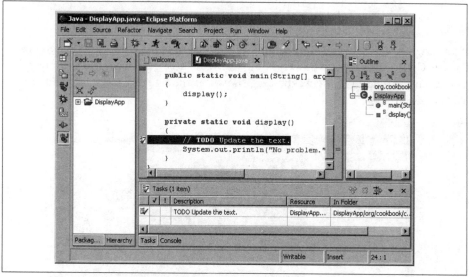

Figure 3-20. TODO comments in the Tasks view

Eclipse 3.0

The Problems view replaced the Tasks view in Eclipse 3.0, so the Tasks view doesn't appear in the Java perspective by default in this version of Eclipse. To show it, select Window → Show View → Other → Basic → Tasks.

3.19 Customizing Code Assist

Problem

Code assist is great, but some of its features don't fit your coding style.

Solution

Customize code assist by selecting Window → Preferences → Java → Code Formatter.

Discussion

One common issue with code assist is that it puts curly braces on the same line as other code.

```
public void display( ) {
    System.out.println("No problem.");
}
```

Some programmers, however, prefer that curly braces appear on separate lines:

```
public void display( )
{
    System.out.println("No problem.");
}
```

You can customize the location of curly braces by selecting Window → Preferences →
Java → Code Formatter, as shown in Figure 3-21. Here, check the "Insert a new line
before an opening brace" checkbox, as shown in the figure; the sample code below
will change to match.

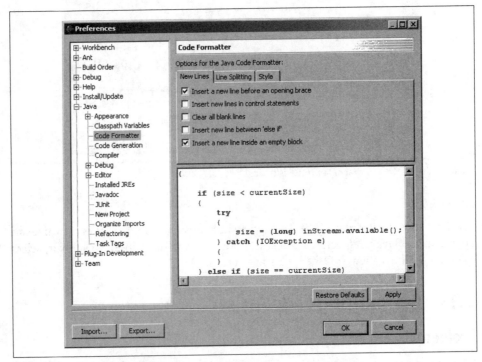

Figure 3-21. Customizing code assist

You also can create new code assist items in Eclipse. Say you want to create a shortcut to print the current date. To do that, select Window → Preferences → Java → Editor → Templates. In this case, we're going to create a new shortcut named datem to
print the date, as shown in Figure 3-22. We'll use the code:

```
System.out.println("${date}");
```

to print the date.

Besides ${date}, you can use other terms, such as ${cursor}, which indicates where to position the cursor after the insertion has been performed. When you type ${ in the New Template dialog, code assist displays the possible values you can use in code assist expressions.

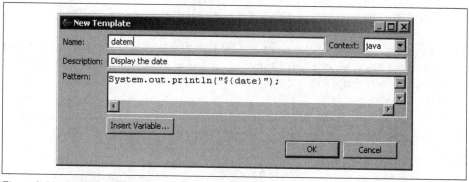

Figure 3-22. Creating a new shortcut for code assist

Now when you type datem in your code and press Ctrl-Space, code assist will enter the code needed to print the current date, as shown in Figure 3-23. In fact, if you type d and then press Ctrl-Space, code assist lists all options that begin with the letter "d," including datem.

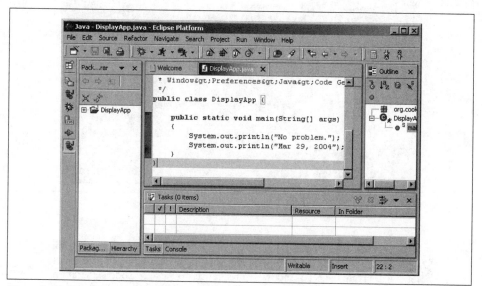

Figure 3-23. Using the new code assist shortcut

You can customize code assist in other ways as well. For example, when you create a new Java code file, the following comment is inserted automatically:

```
/*
 * Created on Feb 4, 2004
 *
 * To change the template for this generated file go to
 * Window&gt;Preferences&gt;Java&gt;Code Generation&gt;Code and Comments
 */
```

You can change the code in this comment by selecting Window → Preferences → Java → Code Generation → Code and Comments → Code → New Java Files, as shown in Figure 3-24. Then simply edit the template used to create this comment so that it reads the way you want it.

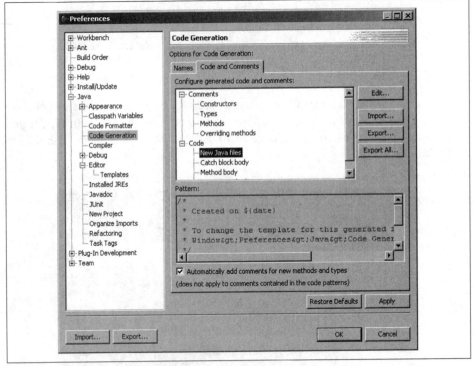

Figure 3-24. Configuring code assist comments

 You also can customize code assist by specifying the prefix or suffix for fields, static fields, parameters, and local variables that code assist will create. Select Window → Preferences → Java → Code Generation → Names, and then set the prefixes and suffixes for variables used in code assist, quick fix, and refactoring.

Eclipse 3.0

As you might expect, in Eclipse 3.0 you can customize code assist in numerous additional ways. For example, you can customize getter/setter code, as well as the comments used when a new field is inserted.

CHAPTER 4

Refactoring, Building, and Launching

4.0   Introduction

This chapter continues our coverage of the JDT, exploring actions such as *refactoring*, as well as searching, building, and launching applications. You perform such actions everyday in Eclipse, and they're essential skills.

We'll start this chapter with a look at how to handle refactoring in Eclipse—specifically, how to rename and move elements. One of the major advantages of using a good Java IDE such as Eclipse is that when you rename and move Java elements, the IDE automatically updates all references to those items throughout your code.

Besides renaming and moving elements, Eclipse supports many other refactoring operations. Here's the whole list:

- Rename elements
- Move elements
- Change a method's signature
- Convert an anonymous class to a nested class
- Convert a nested type to a top-level type
- Push down or pull up elements in terms of nesting level
- Convert methods and static fields to inline
- Convert local variables to fields
- Extract methods, variables, or constants
- Encapsulate fields

All of these are helpful while coding—if you know how they work and what they do.

Eclipse 3.0

In addition to the preceding list, Eclipse 3.0 adds these refactoring options:

- Move members to a new file
- Generalize types
- Create factory methods

4.1 Renaming Elements

Problem

You want to rename a variable, method, or other item in code, and you want to be sure you catch every place the element is used.

Solution

Select the element in the JDT editor and then select Refactor → Rename, or right-click the element and select Refactor → Rename. Enter the new name you want to give the item, and you're set.

Discussion

Say, for instance, that you have the code appearing in Example 4-1, and you decide that msg, the name of the variable in the main method, is too terse. Instead, you want it named message.

Example 4-1. A simple main method

```
package org.cookbook.ch04;

public class Messenger
{
    public static void main(String[] args)
    {
        String msg = "No problem.";
        System.out.println(msg);
    }

    public static void printem(String msg)
    {
        System.out.println(msg);
    }
}
```

To rename all uses of this msg variable, highlight the variable and select Refactor → Rename, or right-click the variable and select Refactor → Rename, opening the dialog shown in Figure 4-1.

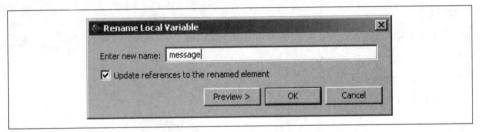

Figure 4-1. Renaming a local variable

To rename msg to message, type the word "message" in the dialog and click Preview, opening a preview of the changes, as shown in Figure 4-2.

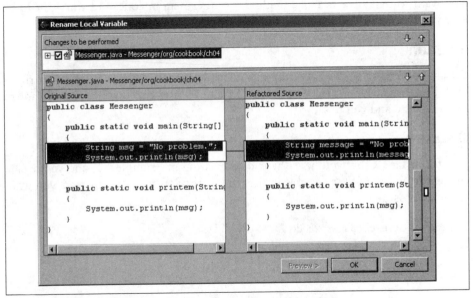

Figure 4-2. Previewing refactoring changes

Eclipse is smart enough to change only references to the variable you're renaming, not the unconnected variable of the same name in the printem method. Clicking OK changes the code in Example 4-1 so that it appears as follows:

```
package org.cookbook.ch04;

public class Messenger
{
    public static void main(String[] args)
    {
        String message = "No problem.";
        System.out.println(message);
    }

    public static void printem(String msg)
```

```
    {
        System.out.println(msg);
    }
}
```

Refactoring a method name is just as easy. For example, select the `printem` method and then select Refactor → Rename, or right-click the variable and select Refactor → Rename. This opens the Rename Method dialog shown in Figure 4-3, in which we're renaming the method to `display`. Clicking OK renames the method and all references to it.

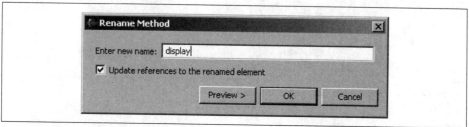

Figure 4-3. Changing a method name

Besides renaming local variables and methods, you can rename projects, resources, source folders, packages, compilation units, types (such as classes), fields, methods, and parameters with the Eclipse Refactor menu. Note also that refactoring works automatically across multiple files.

 To quickly perform a rename that doesn't require full analysis of dependencies in other files, use the "local rename" Quick Assist. In the JDT editor, place the cursor in a variable, method, or type, and press Ctrl-1 (or select Edit → Quick Fix).

Eclipse 3.0

In Eclipse 3.0, you can update references to the elements you rename not only in code, but also in string literals, comments, Javadoc comments, and even non-Java files, simply by checking the appropriate checkboxes, as shown in Figure 4-4.

See Also

Recipe 4.2 on moving elements; Recipe 4.7 on restoring elements and files from local history; Chapter 2 of *Eclipse* (O'Reilly).

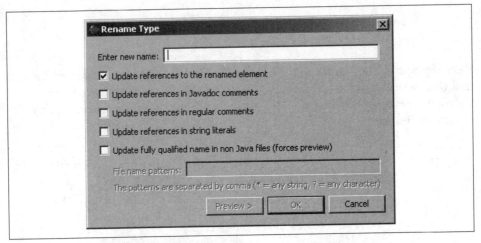

Figure 4-4. Renaming options in Eclipse 3.0

4.2 Moving Elements

Problem

You want to reorganize your code by moving an element between classes, methods, packages, or other containers.

Solution

Select the element to move, and then select Refactor → Move, or right-click and select Refactor → Move. Then use the Move dialog to move the element.

Discussion

Say you want to move the `printem` method, currently in the `Messenger` class, to another class in the project, `Messenger2`:

```
package org.cookbook.ch04;

public class Messenger
{
    public static void main(String[] args)
    {
        String msg = "No problem.";
        System.out.println(msg);
    }

    public static void printem(String msg)
    {
        System.out.println(msg);
    }
}
```

To move this method to the new class, highlight the method's name and select Refactor → Move, or right-click and select Refactor → Move, opening the Move Static Member(s) dialog shown in Figure 4-5.

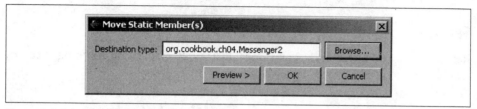

Figure 4-5. Selecting a destination

Enter the fully qualified name of the class you want to move the method to, org. cookbook.ch04.Messenger2, or browse to it, and click OK. The method is moved to the new class:

```
package org.cookbook.ch04;

public class Messenger2
{

    public static void main(String[] args)
    {
    }

    public static void printem(String msg)
    {
        System.out.println(msg);
    }
}
```

Any references to the moved method are updated automatically as well, so your code isn't broken:

```
package org.cookbook.ch04;

public class Messenger
{
    public static void main(String[] args)
    {
        String message = "No problem.";
        Messenger2.printem(message);
    }

}
```

In Eclipse, you can move a static method, static field, or instance method using refactoring.

You also can move any Java compilation units between packages using drag and drop. All missing imports will be added, and references updated.

See Also

Recipe 4.6 on comparing files against local history; Recipe 4.7 on restoring elements and files from local history; Chapter 2 of *Eclipse* (O'Reilly)

4.3   Extracting and Implementing Interfaces

Problem

You want to extract an interface from a class.

Solution

Highlight a class name and select Refactor → Extract Interface, or right-click the class name and select Refactor → Extract Interface. Enter the name of the interface you want to extract, select the members to declare in the interface, and click OK.

Discussion

Eclipse refactoring enables you to extract interfaces from classes. For example, say you have the code in Example 4-2, in which the Interfaces class includes the non-static printem method.

Example 4-2. A class from which to extract interfaces

```
package org.cookbook.ch04;

public class Interfaces
{
    public static void main(String[] args)
    {
        String msg = "No problem.";
        new Interfaces( ).printem(msg);
    }

    public void printem(String msg)
    {
        System.out.println(msg);
    }
}
```

Extracting an interface

To extract an interface from the Interfaces class, right-click that class's name in your code, and select Refactor → Extract Interface, which opens the dialog shown in Figure 4-6. Select the printem method, type in the name NewInterface, and click OK.

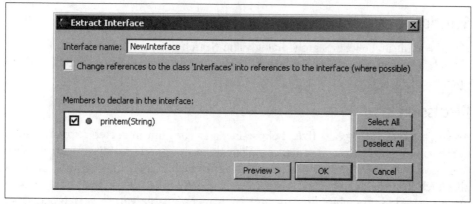

Figure 4-6. Extracting an interface

This creates a new file, *NewInterface.java*, with the new interface you've created:

```
package org.cookbook.ch04;

public interface NewInterface
{
    public abstract void printem(String msg);
}
```

 You also can create new interfaces from scratch by selecting File → New → Interface.

Implementing an interface

You can implement an interface by typing the implements keyword and the name of the interface you want to implement (e.g., public class ServletExample implements NewInterface). The JDT editor shows a Quick Fix light bulb to indicate which methods are missing. Click the light bulb (alternatively, you can press Ctrl-1 or select Edit → Quick Fix) to let Eclipse implement the missing methods.

 You don't have to implement all of the interface's methods. Eclipse will give you the option of making your class abstract.

4.4   Searching Code

Problem

You want to search a single file, or all files in a project, for some matching text.

Solution

Use the built-in Eclipse Search dialog. The Search menu contains multiple items (Search → Search, Search → File, Search → Help, and Search → Java), but all of them open the same dialog.

Discussion

As you'd expect of a good IDE, Eclipse has a lot of built-in search support. However, searching in Eclipse is not accomplished via the standard Edit → Find/Replace operation, which enables you to search the current file. Instead, searching displays all matches in the Search view so that you can select the one or ones you want to jump to. In addition, the items in the Search menu enable you to search across all files in workspaces, through the help system, all plug-ins, and more. Wildcards (* and ?) work as well.

The Search dialog appears in Figure 4-7; note the four tabs there:

File Search
> Searches specified files in a working set, the workspace, or files you select.

Help Search
> Searches the help system for matches.

Java Search
> Searches the workspace, a working set, or selected resources for matches. You can specify what you're searching for: type, method, package, constructor, or field.

Plug-in Search
> Searches for plug-ins, fragments, and extension points.

For example, take a look at the File Search tab, which enables you to search across multiple files for specified text (printem in this example). You can give the pattern(s) of the files to search, such as "*.java, *.*", and so on, in the "File name patterns" box, and set the scope of the search with the radio buttons beneath that box.

 The "Selected Resources" radio button in the "Scope" box is not enabled in this dialog by default. If you want to search only the current project or just a restricted number of projects without using a working set, select that project or those projects in the Package Explorer, then open the Search dialog and click the "Selected Resources" radio button.

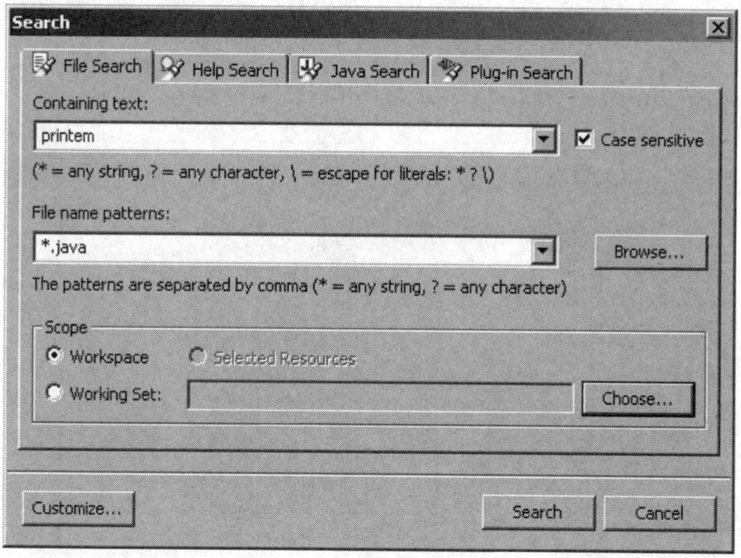

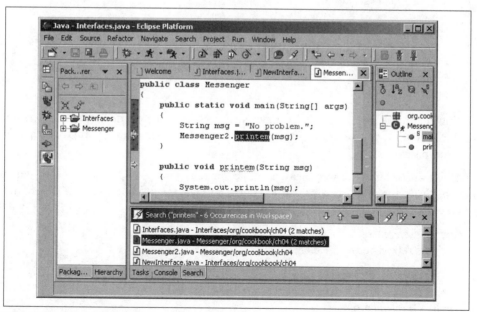

Figure 4-7. The Search dialog

When you click the Search button, the results appear in the Search view, shown in Figure 4-8. Double-clicking a match opens the match in the JDT editor with an arrow in the marker bar, as shown in the figure.

Figure 4-8. Search results

You also can perform Java searches with the Java Search tab in the Search dialog. This kind of search enables you to search for Java elements by kind—types, methods, packages, constructors, and fields, as shown in Figure 4-9. You can limit the search so that it matches only references, also shown in the figure.

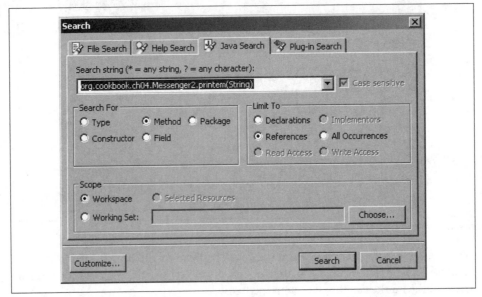

Figure 4-9. Performing a Java search

 To search for methods with a specific return type, open the Search dialog, and click the Java Search tab. Type * *<return type>* in the Search string, click the "Method" and "Declarations" radio buttons, and then click Search.

Being able to perform multifile searches such as this is one of the biggest reasons for using an IDE. If you've been writing Java with a simple text editor, you'll find there's no comparison.

Besides the Search → Search, Search → File, Search → Help, and Search → Java items in the Search menu, you also can highlight an element in your code and select the following Search menu items to do a quick search:

Search → References
 Finds references to the element

Search → Declarations
 Finds the element's declaration

Search → Implementors
 Finds implementors of the element

Search → Read Access
 Finds read accesses (fields only)

Search → Write Access
 Finds write accesses (fields only)

These items are handy for tracking down all references to a method or variable, for example; just search for the references, and double-click the results in the Search view. To limit the scope of the search, select Workspace, Hierarchy, or Working Set from each item's submenu.

 Another quick way to search for references is to highlight an identifier and select Search → Occurrences in File. This is more useful than Edit → Find/Replace because it lists all matches in the Search view, enabling you to navigate to the ones you want.

Eclipse 3.0

In Eclipse 3.0, you also can click a radio button to automatically limit the searches to the enclosing project in the File Search, Java Search, and Plug-in Search tabs. Plans are in the works to enable you to use regular expressions in searches as well.

4.5   Comparing Files

Problem

You need to see the differences between two files displayed graphically.

Solution

Select the files in a view and then select Compare With → Each Other in the view's context menu.

Discussion

One of the most common things professional developers need to do is to compare the contents of two files to see the changes made to each; the support in most operating systems for such operations is minimal.

To compare two files, highlight them in a view such as the Package Explorer and select Compare With → Each Other in the view's context menu. Eclipse will perform the comparison in an intelligent manner and display the results in a Compare Editor, as shown in Figure 4-10.

You even can edit the files, copying changes from one file to the other using the buttons in the Java Source Compare pane.

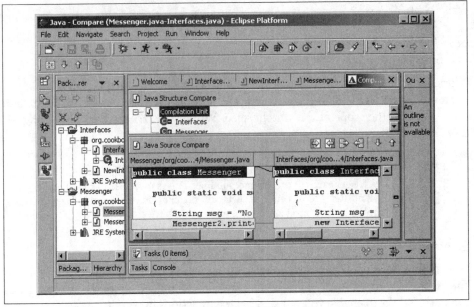

Figure 4-10. Comparing two files

 You can ignore comments and formatting changes when performing the comparisons: click the Ignore Whitespace option in the Compare Editor's toolbar button (that's the fourth button from the right in the main toolbar in Figure 4-10). This is useful when working with XML.

See Also

Recipe 4.6 on comparing files against local history; Recipe 4.7 on restoring elements and files from local history.

4.6   Comparing Files Against Local History

Problem

You need to see how a file has been changed since the last save.

Solution

Highlight the file in a view, and select Compare With → Local History in the view's context menu.

Discussion

Eclipse records changes to a file in its local history. To get an idea of how a file has been changed since it was last saved, highlight the file and right-click it, selecting Compare With → Local History. The recent changes appear in the dialog shown in Figure 4-11, graphically displayed.

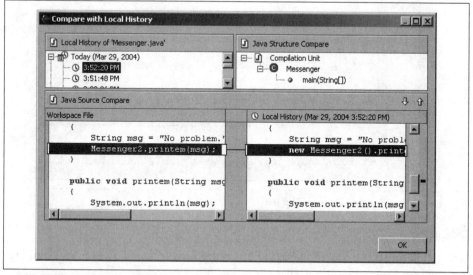

Figure 4-11. Comparing against local history

 You also can check an individual element's recent history (instead of an entire file). Right-click an element and select Local History → Compare With to see a graphical display of the recent changes.

Eclipse 3.0

Eclipse 3.0 has a built-in Quick Diff bar that enables you to compare lines individually to those stored on disk (the default), as well as to changes in a CVS repository. You can see the Quick Diff bar immediately to the left of the JDT editor in Figure 4-12. To compare a line with the most recent version of the file on disk, rest the mouse cursor over the Quick Diff bar.

 To turn off Quick Diff, right-click the Quick Diff bar and select Disable QuickDiff. To make Quick Diff compare against your code in a CVS repository, right-click the Quick Diff bar and select Set Quick-Diff Reference → Latest CVS Revision.

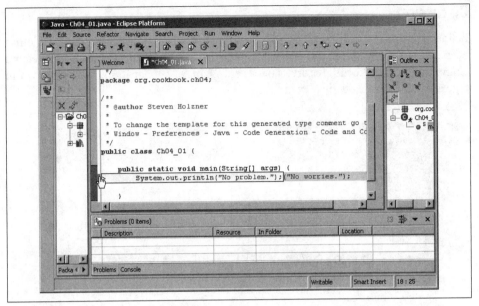

Figure 4-12. The Eclipse 3.0 Quick Diff bar

See Also

Recipe 4.5 on comparing files; Recipe Restoring Elements and Files from Local History on restoring elements and files from local history.

4.7 Restoring Elements and Files from Local History

Problem

You decide a recent change was a mistake and want to revert to a previous version.

Solution

Right-click an element and use the Local History menu, or right-click a file and use the items in the Replace With menu.

Discussion

Because it maintains a local history, Eclipse enables you to undo recent changes without having to resort to selecting Edit → Undo, which provides limited options. For example, if you've made some changes to a method that you want to undo, right-click the method's name in its declaration and select Local History → Replace With Previous.

The context menu items for the JDT editor that enable you to restore from local history are as follows:

Local History → Replace With Previous
Replaces a file with the previous version.

Local History → Replace With
Replaces an element, such as a variable, field, or method, with its version from local history. This item shows the local history graphically before the change is made.

Local History → Restore From
Restores a Java element from local history. This item shows the available choices from local history graphically before the change is made.

For example, selecting Local History → Replace With enables you to review the change before making it, as shown in Figure 4-13.

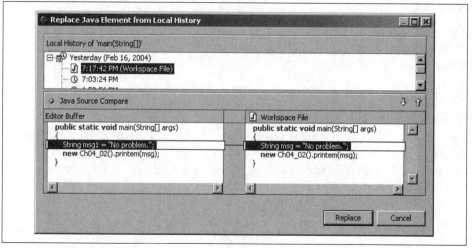

Figure 4-13. Replacing Java elements from local history

You also can revert an entire file to its previous version by right-clicking it in a view such as the Package Explorer and selecting one of the following menu items:

Replace With → Previous from Local History
Replaces the file with the previous version in local history

Replace With → Local History
Replaces the file with a version you select from local history

Restore from Local History
Restores a file from local history

Eclipse 3.0

In Eclipse 3.0, you can restore a line of code to its original version. Right-click the Quick Diff bar, and select Revert Line.

See Also

Recipe 4.5 on comparing files; Recipe 4.6 on comparing files against local history.

4.8   Selecting the Java Runtime for Builds

Problem

You want to target your code at a particular JRE, or change the default JRE that Eclipse uses.

Solution

You can specify what Java runtime you want Eclipse to use by selecting Window → Preferences, clicking Installed JREs, and choosing the JRE you want (use the Add button to add JREs and SDKs).

Discussion

When you first run Eclipse, it searches for installed Java runtimes, which means it might not use the one you want to use. For example, Eclipse might want to use the outdated JRE that came with your browser instead of the new Java SDK you've just downloaded. To specify what runtime to use, select Window → Preferences, click Installed JREs, and choose the JRE you want, as shown in Figure 4-14.

 To set a project-specific JRE (as when you want to target a project to a specific JRE), select Project → Properties → Java Build Path, click the Libraries tab, click JRE System Library, and click Edit. In the dialog that appears, select a project-specific JRE.

Setting the JVM using the -vm switch

Eclipse might not start if the JRE it finds is too old. In this case, start Eclipse from the command line and use the -vm switch, specifying the JRE you want to use. For example, you might type:

```
eclipse -vm c:\jre1.4\bin\javaw.exe
```

After Eclipse starts, set the JRE you want to use from then on.

See Also

Recipe 4.9 on running code; Chapter 2 of *Eclipse* (O'Reilly).

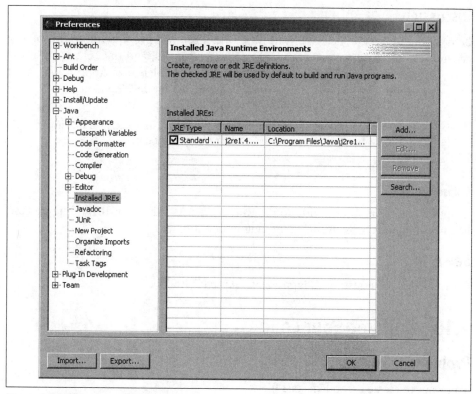

Figure 4-14. Choosing a JRE

4.9   Running Your Code

Problem

You want to run your code.

Solution

Select one of the following items in the Run menu:

Run → Run Last Launched
  Runs the last launched program

Run → Run History
  Enables you to select programs to run from a submenu

Run → Run As
  Enables you to select how to run a program—with the Java Applet, Java Application, JUnit Test (discussed in Chapter 5), or Run-time Workbench

Run → Run
  Enables you to set the launch configuration and run your code

Discussion

Before running your code, save your files, or Eclipse will prompt you to do so. The general way to run your code is to select Run → Run As, and then choose the way you want to run your code from the submenu: Java Applet, Java Application, JUnit Test, or Run-time Workbench (used to run plug-ins under development).

 The Run → Run History and Run → Run Last Launched menu items give you handy shortcuts for running recent programs.

Eclipse 3.0

Eclipse 3.0 adds another option to the Run → Run As submenu: JUnit Plug-In Test. Eclipse 3.0 makes JUnit available for plug-in development.

See Also

Chapter 5 on JUnit testing; Chapter 2 of *Eclipse* (O'Reilly).

4.10 Building Your Code

Problem

You want to create compiled *.class* files.

Solution

By default, compiled *.class* files are created or updated when you save your code. You also can perform builds manually.

Discussion

When you save a resource, *.class* files are built automatically by default. If that feature isn't turned on, select Window → Preferences → Workbench, and then check the "Perform build automatically on resource modification" checkbox, as shown in Figure 4-15. To turn off automatic building, uncheck this checkbox.

To build a project manually, select Project → Build Project.

 If a *.class* file has been moved or damaged, auto-build won't work, and you'll have to start over by rebuilding the *.class* file yourself. In this case, select Project → Build Project.

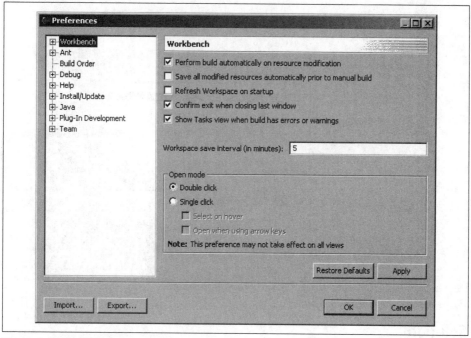

Figure 4-15. Turning on auto-build

Changing the build order

Eclipse actually does a good job setting the build order of projects by interpreting project references itself. However, you also can set the build order yourself. Select Window → Preferences → Build Order, as shown in Figure 4-16.

Building only selected projects

If you highlight a project in a view and select Project → Rebuild Project, the project you've selected is rebuilt. What's cool about this is that you can choose only certain projects and just select Project → Rebuild Project to rebuild them, without having to rebuild all projects (which Project → Rebuild All does).

4.11   Using .jar and .class Files

Problem

You need to access code in a *.jar* or *.class* file in your project, but Eclipse can't find these files.

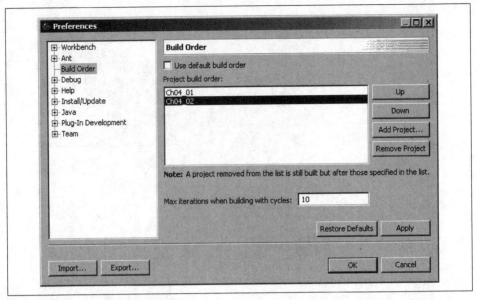

Figure 4-16. Setting the build order

Solution

Select the project in the Package Explorer, and then select Project → Properties to open the Properties dialog. Click the Libraries tab in this dialog, click Add External JARs for *.jar* files or Add Class Folder for *.class* files, navigate to the *.jar* file or to the folder containing *.class* files, and click OK.

Discussion

Often you need other code in the build path, such as *.class* or *.jar* files. For instance, say you're developing a Java servlet, as shown in Example 4-3.

Example 4-3. A simple servlet

```
package org.cookbook.ch04;

import java.io.*;
import javax.servlet.*;
import javax.servlet.http.*;

public class ServletExample extends HttpServlet {

    public void doGet(HttpServletRequest request,
        HttpServletResponse response)
        throws IOException, ServletException
    {
```

Example 4-3. A simple servlet (continued)

```
        response.setContentType("text/html");
        PrintWriter out = response.getWriter();
        out.println("<HTML>");
        out.println("<HEAD>");
        out.println("<TITLE>");
        out.println("Using Servlets");
        out.println("</TITLE>");
        out.println("</HEAD>");
        out.println("Using Servlets");
        out.println("</BODY>");
        out.println("</HTML>");
    }
}
```

A lot of the support for servlets is in *servlet.jar*. Eclipse can't find *servlet.jar* by itself, so a lot of wavy red lines will appear when it comes to the imports, as shown as in Figure 4-17.

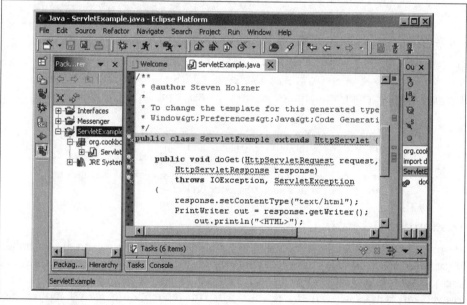

Figure 4-17. Missing the servlet.jar file

To add *servlet.jar* to the build path, select Project → Properties, and click the Libraries tab. Then click Add External JARs, navigate to *servlet.jar*, and click OK. Doing so adds *servlet.jar* to the build path, as shown in Figure 4-18. Click OK to close the Properties dialog, and then build the project; when you do, things will work out fine (and you'll see *servlet.jar* in the Package Explorer).

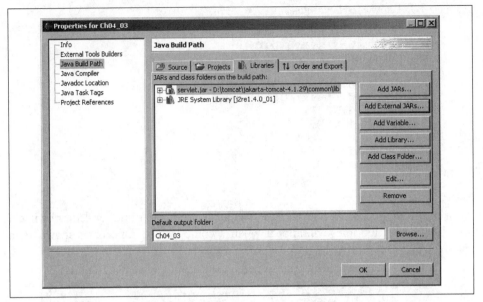

Figure 4-18. servlet.jar in the build path

If you add multiple .jar files to the classpath, you also can indicate the order in which you want them searched. Just click the Order and Export tab in the Properties dialog, and change the order of imported items by using the Up and Down buttons.

If you know you're going to be using a .jar file such as *servlet.jar* when you first create the project, you can add that .jar file to the project's classpath in the third pane of the New Project dialog. You'll see the same tabs there as you do in Figure 4-18. Just click the Libraries tab, and add the .jar files you want to the project.

Creating classpath variables

If you know you're going to be using a .jar file such as *servlet.jar* often, you might want to create a *classpath variable*. Doing so will save you time when you want to include items in a project's build path. Using classpath variables like this is not only convenient, but also it centralizes your classpath references for easy handling. For example, if you want to use a new version of *servlet.jar* across multiple projects, all you have to do is to update one classpath variable.

To create a classpath variable, select Window → Preferences → Java → Classpath Variables, as shown in Figure 4-19. Click New, enter the new variable's name—we'll use SERVLET_JAR here—enter its path (or browse to its location), and then click OK. You can see this new variable in the figure.

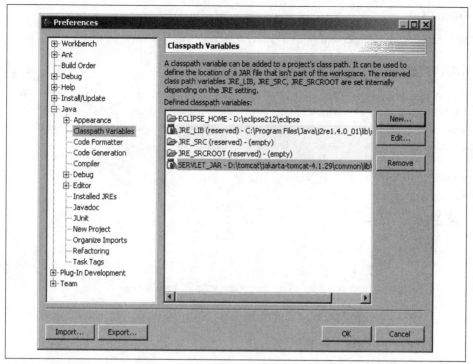

Figure 4-19. Creating a classpath variable

Using classpath variables

When you want to add this classpath variable to a project's classpath, open the project's Properties dialog, click the Libraries tab, click the Add Variable button (shown in Figure 4-18), and select the variable you want to add to the classpath.

See Also

Recipe 1.5 on creating a Java project.

4.12   Setting the Launch Configuration

Problem

You want to pass command-line arguments to your code, or select a JRE for the current project only, or pass arguments to the JVM.

Solution

Set the project's launch configuration by selecting Run → Run.

Discussion

Say you're trying to run the code in Example 4-4, *Launcher.java*, which reads command-line arguments, concatenates them, and displays the results. If you don't pass any command-line arguments to this code, you get a `java.lang.ArrayIndexOutOf-BoundsException` exception.

Example 4-4. Concatenation sample

```
package org.cookbook.ch04;

public class Launcher
{
    public static void main(String[] args)
    {
        String text ="";
        for (int loopIndex = 0; loopIndex <args.length; loopIndex++){
            text += args[loopIndex] + " ";
        }

        System.out.println(text);
    }

}
```

You can supply command-line arguments in the launch configuration for this project by highlighting *Launcher.java* in the Package Explorer, selecting Run → Run to open the Run dialog, and clicking the New button to create a new launch configuration for this project, as shown in Figure 4-20. The Main tab in this dialog enables you to select the main class in a project. The Arguments tab enables you to specify command-line and JVM arguments. The JRE tab enables you to select the JRE for the project. And the Source tab enables you to connect source code to your project for the debugger.

Type the words No problem. in the "Program arguments" box, as shown in Figure 4-20. Then click Run, and the code will read that command-line argument and display it, as shown in Figure 4-21.

See Also

Recipe 4.8 on selecting the Java runtime; Recipe 4.9 on running your code.

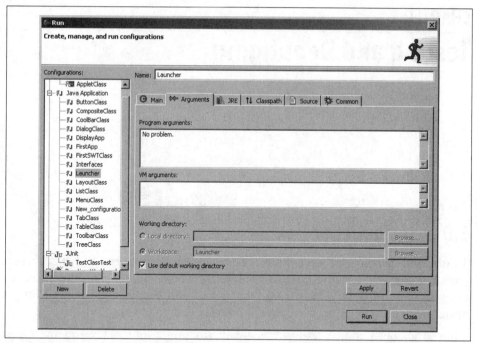

Figure 4-20. Setting a launch configuration

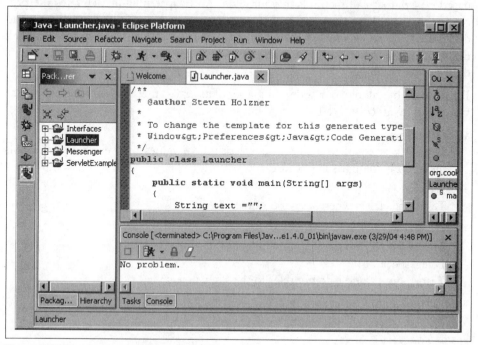

Figure 4-21. Passing command-line arguments

CHAPTER 5
Testing and Debugging

5.0 Introduction

Testing and debugging code is a fact of life for Java developers, and this chapter focuses on the testing and debugging facilities that come with Eclipse. Often, you can test your code using the JUnit package that comes with Eclipse, and you can debug it using the built-in debugger. We'll look at both facilities in this chapter.

JUnit is an open source testing framework (for more information on the Open Source Initiative, visit *www.opensource.org*). You use it to test the results of JUnit-based classes that call methods in your code. An Eclipse plug-in facilitates the process of running JUnit tests. Using JUnit, you can create a standard set of tests and distribute them to everyone working on your code; if someone edits your code, all that person needs to do is to run the tests with a few mouse clicks to make sure he didn't break anything.

JUnit works by calling your code using a set of assertion methods that test the return values from your code. Here are the JUnit tests:

assertEquals(a, b)
: Tests if a is equal to b (a and b are primitive values or must have an equals method for comparison purposes)

assertFalse(a)
: Tests if a is false, where a is a Boolean value

assertNotNull(a)
: Tests if a is not null, where a is either an object or null

assertNotSame(a, b)
: Tests if both a and b do not refer to the same object

assertNull(a)
: Tests if a is null, where a is either an object or null

assertSame(a, b)
: Tests if both a and b refer to the same object

```
assertTrue(a)
```
   Tests if a is true, where a is a Boolean value

When you run a JUnit application using the JUnit plug-in in Eclipse, it opens its own view to give you immediate feedback on which tests have passed and which have failed.

5.1   Installing JUnit

Problem

You want to install JUnit so that you can use it in Eclipse.

Solution

Add *junit.jar* to your project's classpath.

Discussion

In Eclipse 2.1.x and in the current versions of Eclipse 3.0, you can find *junit.jar* in *eclipse/plugins/org.junit_3.8.1/junit.jar*.

If you're going to be using JUnit regularly, it helps to create a new classpath variable; I named mine JUNIT. Select Window → Preferences → Java → Classpath Variables, and click the New button to open the New Variable Entry dialog; now enter the name of the new variable—JUNIT—and the path to *junit.jar*.

You also can let Eclipse know where JUnit's source code is; this is a useful step for debugging, giving Eclipse access to a JAR file's code so that it can display it as needed. Note that this is an optional step because you don't need to see the JUnit code. To create a new variable for the JUnit source, which we'll call JUNIT_SRC, connect that variable to *eclipse/plugins/org.eclipse.jdt.source_x.y.z/src/org.junit_3.8.1/junitsrc.zip*, where *x.y.z* is your version of Eclipse. Then right-click your project, click Properties, click the Java Build Path node and the Libraries tab, and then expand the node for the JUNIT entry, as shown in Figure 5-1.

When you expand a JAR file's node, you can specify where to find the associated source code and Javadoc. To use JUNIT_SRC for the source code here, select "Source attachment" in the expanded node, and click Edit to open the Source Attachment Configuration dialog. Click the Variable button, double-click JUNIT_SRC, and click OK to close this dialog. You can see the results in Figure 5-2, in which we've made the source for JUnit accessible to Eclipse. Click OK to close the Properties dialog.

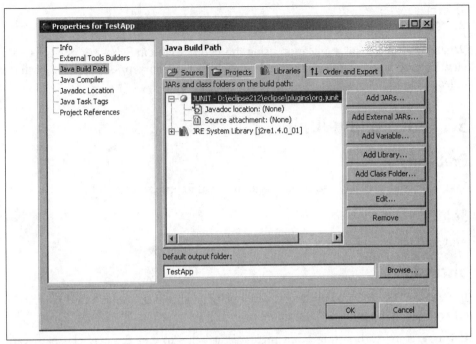

Figure 5-1. Making source code accessible to Eclipse

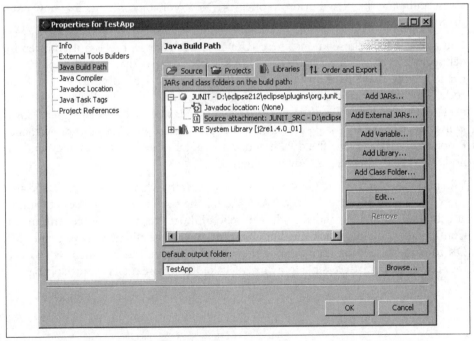

Figure 5-2. Connecting source code to a .jar file

This is the way you're *supposed* to do things—i.e., adding *junit.jar* to the build path yourself. But it turns out that if you don't do it this way, you haven't lost much. As soon as you try to build a JUnit test case, the JUnit plug-in will ask you if you want to add *junit.jar* to the build path automatically if you haven't already done so. In this case, the plug-in will do all the work for you.

See Also

Recipe 4.11 on using *.jar* and *.class* files; Recipe 5.2 on testing an application with JUnit; the JUnit section of the *Java Extreme Programming Cookbook* (O'Reilly).

5.2   Testing an Application with JUnit

Problem

You want to create a JUnit test case.

Solution

Create a JUnit-based class, and implement the tests you want to run. Then use the JUnit plug-in to see your test results immediately.

Discussion

As an example, we're going to test the application *TestApp*, shown in Example 5-1, which uses a class named TestClass. This application has two methods: get, which returns a string, and set, which returns a confirming value of true if the value you pass is 0 or greater.

Example 5-1. A simple Java class

```
package org.cookbook.ch05;

public class TestClass
{
    public String get( ) {
        return "Test String";
    }

    public boolean set(int index) {
        if (index < 0) {
            return false;
        } else {
            return true;
        }
    }
}
```

To test this application, use the JUnit Wizard plug-in to create a new class in the project that extends the JUnit TestCase class. To invoke the wizard, right-click the class you want to test, TestClass here, and select New → Other to open the New dialog shown in Figure 5-3.

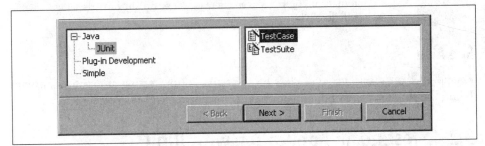

Figure 5-3. Creating a new JUnit TestCase-based class

Expand the Java node in the left pane, and select JUnit. In the right pane, select TestCase. Click Next, displaying the dialog shown in Figure 5-4.

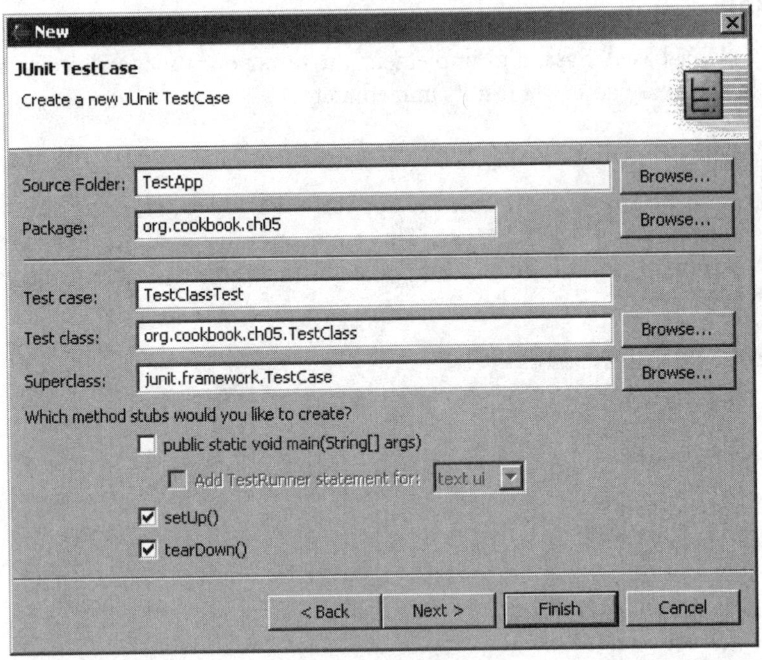

Figure 5-4. Configuring a JUnit test class

The JUnit convention is to name test cases by adding "Test" to the name of the class you're testing. In our example, JUnit suggests a test case name of TestClassTest. Be sure to check the setUp and tearDown method checkboxes, as shown in Figure 5-4.

These methods enable you to set up and clean up after data and/or objects in the test case (the JUnit term for these items is *fixtures*). Click Next to open the next dialog, shown in Figure 5-5.

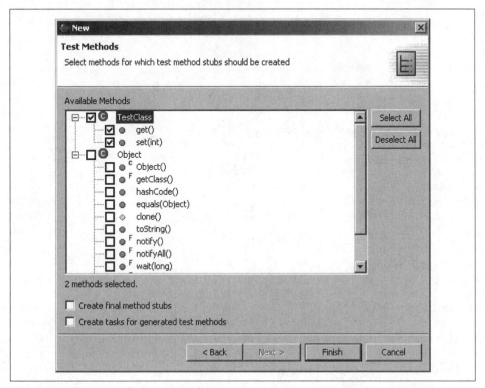

Figure 5-5. Selecting methods to test with JUnit

In this dialog you select the methods you want to test so that the JUnit Wizard can create stubs for them. In this case, we want to test the set and get methods, so select them, as shown in Figure 5-5, and click Finish.

This creates the TestClassTest class, shown in Example 5-2. You can see method stubs in the TestClassTest class to test the set and get methods; these stubs are named testSet and testGet.

Example 5-2. Testing TestClass

```
package org.cookbook.ch05;

import junit.framework.TestCase;

public class TestClassTest extends TestCase
{
```

Example 5-2. Testing TestClass (continued)

```java
/**
 * Constructor for TestClassTest.
 * @param arg0
 */
public TestClassTest(String arg0)
{
    super(arg0);
}

/*
 * @see TestCase#setUp( )
 */
protected void setUp( ) throws Exception
{
    super.setUp( );
}

/*
 * @see TestCase#tearDown( )
 */
protected void tearDown( ) throws Exception
{
    super.tearDown( );
}

public void testGet( )
{
}

public void testSet( )
{
}
}
```

To test your code, add code to these JUnit stubs that calls the methods you want to test. To call the nonstatic get and set methods in our code, you'll need an object of the TestClass class, which we'll name testClassObject. We'll create that object in the JUnit setUp method, called before each JUnit test starts:

```java
public class TestClassTest extends TestCase
{
    TestClass testClassObject;

        .
        .
        .

    protected void setUp( ) throws Exception
    {
        super.setUp( );
        testClassObject = new TestClass( );
    }
```

Now that we've created this object, `testClassObject`, let's get to work. In the `testGet` method, you can test the `TestClass` class's get method, which is supposed to return a `String` object. Here's how to check that return value:

```
public void testGet() {
    assertEquals(testClassObject.get(), "Test String");
}
```

The set method is supposed to return true if it's been successful, so let's test it with an `assertTrue` call like so:

```
public void testSet() {
    assertTrue(testClassObject.set(-1));
}
```

After adding this test code, highlight the `TestClassTest` class in the Package Explorer and select Run → Run As → JUnit Test, opening the view shown at left in Figure 5-6.

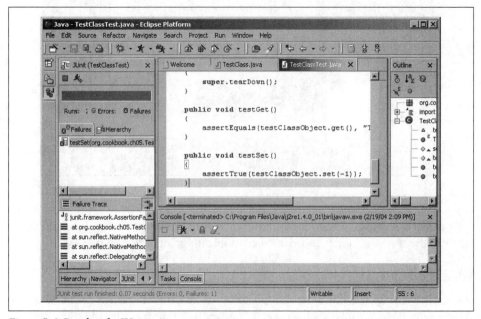

Figure 5-6. Results of a JUnit test

The red bar at the top of this view (which appears in black and white in the figure) indicates that there was an error, and if you look under the Failures tab in the JUnit view, you'll see that the testSet test failed. That's because the set method returns true only if you pass it a non-negative value, but we passed it a value of -1, which means that running assertTrue on the return value will fail:

```
public void testSet() {
    assertTrue(testClassObject.set(-1));
}
```

Change that code by passing set a value of 1 instead:

```
public void testSet() {
    assertTrue(testClassObject.set(1));
}
```

Now rerun the test, and you'll see a green bar for success, as displayed in glorious black and white in Figure 5-7. Congratulations—the tests passed. All systems are go.

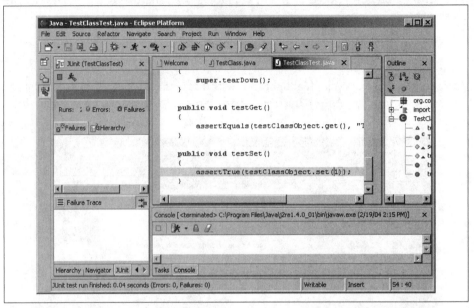

Figure 5-7. A successful JUnit test

You can see how this works; when you (or anyone) make(s) changes to your code, just run the test case again, and you'll get an instant green if things are OK.

Eclipse 3.0

As of this writing, the JUnit process is similar in Eclipse 3.0, except that in 3.0, you have a few more options, such as specifying whether you want to add a constructor to your test case in addition to the setUp and tearDown methods.

See Also

Recipe 5.1 on installing JUnit; the JUnit section of the *Java Extreme Programming Cookbook* (O'Reilly); Chapter 3 of *Eclipse* (O'Reilly).

5.3 Starting a Debugging Session

Problem

Your code isn't running as you want it to, and it's time to debug.

Solution

Start a new debugging session with the items in the Run menu. Then use the various debugging options, such as single-stepping, setting breakpoints, and more.

Discussion

Say you want your code to display this output:

```
3...
2...
1...
Houston, we have liftoff.
```

Your first attempt at the code might look like that shown in Example 5-3, in the class DebugClass in an application named *DebugApp*.

Example 5-3. The DebugApp example

```
package org.cookbook.ch05;

public class DebugClass
{
    public static void main(String[] args)
    {
        for(int loopIndex = 3; loopIndex > 0; loopIndex--)
        {
            System.out.println(loopIndex + "...");
            if(loopIndex == 0)
            {
                System.out.println("Houston, we have liftoff.");
            }
        }
    }
}
```

Unfortunately, the code in Example 5-3 gives you this result:

```
3...
2...
1...
```

It's time to debug. To start a debugging session, use one of the following items in the Run menu:

Run → Debug History
> Enables you to select a recently run project to debug

Run → Debug As

Enables you to select the type of session to run (Java Applet, Java Applications, JUnit Test, or Run-time Workbench) from a submenu

Run → Debug

Enables you to set the launch configuration for a debugging session

To start debugging the code in *DebugApp*, select Run → Debug As → Java Application, which opens and runs your code in the Debug perspective, as shown in Figure 5-8.

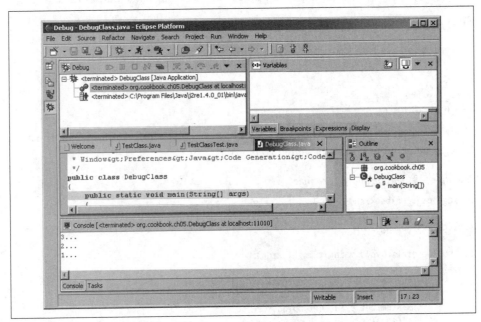

Figure 5-8. First attempt at debugging

Take a look at the Debug perspective in Figure 5-8. You can see entries for the program(s) you're debugging in the Debug view at upper left. Next to the word Debug in the Debug view are five buttons. The names of the buttons are, from left to right, Resume (start executing code again), Suspend (pause code, as when you've got a runaway infinite loop), Terminate (stop debugging), Disconnect (disconnect from the debug session), and Remove All Terminated Launches.

 As you can see in Figure 5-8, the Debug view displays all terminated launches of your code. That view can fill up fast. To clear those terminated launches, click the Remove All Terminated Launches button in the view's toolbar. In general, the terminated sessions are retained in case you want to go back to them at some point to compare what's happening now with what happened previously.

To the right of the Debug view is a set of stacked views: Variables, Breakpoints, Expressions, and Display.

The Debug perspective's Variables view enables you to examine the value of local variables. You can edit these values (which we'll do later in this chapter) as you debug your code. In this way, you can edit what's going on in your program interactively.

 To indicate when the value of a variable in the Variables view has changed, Eclipse changes the color of the variable's entry to red.

The Debug perspective's Breakpoints view enables you to manage breakpoints in your code by right-clicking them in the list and selecting Disable, Enable, Remove, or Remove All from the context menu.

The Debug perspective's Expressions view enables you to evaluate expressions, as discussed in Recipe 5.12 . When you right-click an expression in the editor, and then click Inspect, the expression is evaluated in the Expressions view. Similarly, when you click Display on the context menu, the results appear in the Display view.

The editor under the Debug perspective is much like the JDT editor; you can examine the values of elements simply by hovering your mouse over those elements.

Next to the editor is the Outline view, as shown in Figure 5-8, which is the same as the Outline view in the Java perspective. Below the editor is the standard Console view, which, like its counterpart in the Java perspective, displays program output.

Figure 5-8 shows that the code has run and terminated with the same results as before, without displaying the expected Houston, we have liftoff. message. To watch the program as it executes, take a look at Recipe 5.4 on setting breakpoints.

 When you end a debug session, you are still in the Debug perspective. You can switch back to the Java perspective by selecting Window → Open Perspective → Java, but during the debugging cycle it's easier to switch perspectives by clicking the shortcut icons shown at extreme left in Figure 5-8.

Eclipse 3.0

Eclipse 3.0 also adds a Run → Debug As → JUnit Plug-in Test item to the options for starting a debugging session. By default, the Breakpoints view appears in its own window under the Outline view; it doesn't appear stacked above it.

See Also

Recipe 5.12 on evaluating expressions; Recipe 5.4 on setting a breakpoint; Recipe 5.5 on stepping through code; Chapter 3 of *Eclipse* (O'Reilly).

5.4   Setting a Breakpoint

Problem

You need to watch your code while it's executing to pinpoint a problem.

Solution

Set a breakpoint and start a debug session, which executes your code until the breakpoint is encountered. When execution halts, you can see what's going on as your code executes.

Discussion

Breakpoints give you the chance to stop your code and take a look around as your program runs. To set a breakpoint in the JDT editor, double-click the marker bar next to the line of executable code to which you want to add a breakpoint (alternatively, highlight the line and select Run → Add/Remove Breakpoint to toggle breakpoints). To remove the breakpoint later, just double-click it again.

To see how this works, we'll set a breakpoint in the code we've been developing:

```java
public class DebugClass
{
    public static void main(String[] args)
    {
        for(int loopIndex = 3; loopIndex > 0; loopIndex--)
        {
            System.out.println(loopIndex + "...");
            if(loopIndex == 0)
            {
                System.out.println("Houston, we have liftoff.");
            }
        }
    }
}
```

The breakpoint icon (in the shape of a small circle) appears to the left of this line in the JDT editor, as shown in Figure 5-9.

Now select Run → Debug As → Java Application, and you'll see your application stopped at the breakpoint, as shown in Figure 5-10.

Letting the cursor rest on top of the loopIndex variable, as shown in Figure 5-10, indicates that the variable holds the value 3, which is appropriate for the beginning of the loop in the code. So, what do you do from here? You can step through your code, watching it being executed. See Recipe 5.5 for more details.

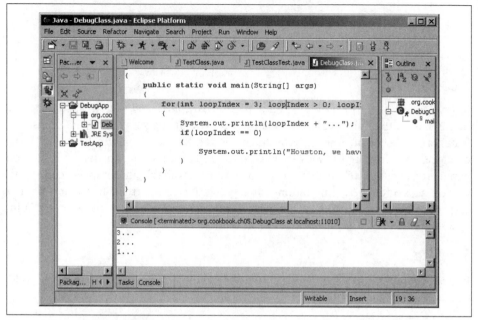

Figure 5-9. A new breakpoint

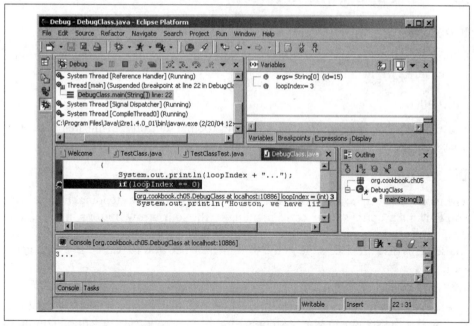

Figure 5-10. Halting at a breakpoint

To terminate a debugging session, such as when you're paused at a breakpoint, just click the Terminate button in the Debug view (the red button shaped like a square), or select Run → Terminate.

Eclipse 3.0

In Eclipse 3.0, you can set breakpoints in *external source code*—that is, source code that is not on the build path of a Java project. The debugger's display in Eclipse 3.0 features a number of other improvements as well; for example, in Eclipse 3.0, the debugger uses invented names such as `arg1`, `arg2`, and so on, to stand for method parameter variables when the real names are not available in compiled code. This version also offers new annotations for highlighting the current instruction pointer and frames in the execution call stack (which you can configure by selecting Window → Preferences → Java → Editor → Annotations).

See Also

Recipe 5.3 on starting a debugging session; Recipe 5.5 on stepping through code; Chapter 3 of *Eclipse* (O'Reilly).

5.5   Stepping Through Your Code

Problem

Your code is stopped at a breakpoint, and you want to execute it line by line, or until it encounters the next breakpoint.

Solution

Use the code-stepping options available via toolbar buttons, menu items, or keyboard shortcuts.

Discussion

The most basic way to move through paused code is by single-stepping. Eclipse gives you four main options here, corresponding to the four arrow buttons in the Debug view toolbar, beginning with the double-headed arrow and moving to the right (these items also are accessible in the Run menu when you're paused in a debugging session):

Step With Filters (also Shift-F5)
    Steps into the selected statement using predefined filters, or filters you've created. If the statement you're stepping into is a method call, execution continues inside the called method unless you've filtered out the method.

Step Into (also F5)
> Steps into the selected statement. If that statement is a method call, execution continues inside the called method.

Step Over (also F6)
> Steps over the selected statement. Does not step into method calls.

Step Return (also F7)
> Executes until the end of the current method and then returns, pausing after the method returns (or when a breakpoint is encountered).

In our example, clicking the Step Into button makes the debugger move to the next line of executable code. Because we were paused at the line if(loopIndex == 0) in the previous recipe, and because loopIndex is equal to 3, not 0, the body of the if statement is not executed. Instead, we move to the next iteration of the enclosing for loop, as shown in Figure 5-11.

Note the display in the Debug view at upper left, which displays your location in the code. Here, we're executing code in the main thread, and we are in the DebugClass.main *stack frame* (stack frames are marked by icons composed of three horizontal bars). Knowing where you are in a stack frame is very useful when the code you're debugging contains many levels of method calls. To resume debugging in any stack frame, just select that stack frame in the Debug view.

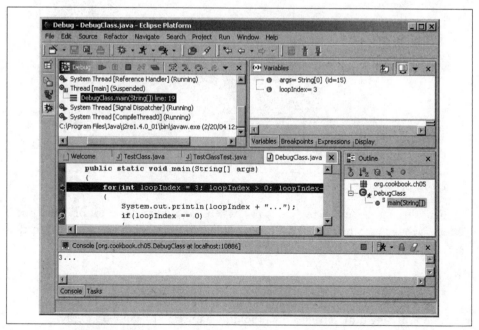

Figure 5-11. Single-stepping through code

When you're stepping through your code, you also can use *step filters*, which enable you to specify code to avoid (or to filter out) while single-stepping. For example, filtering out the code in a class or package means you won't step through that code when you select Step With Filters.

You can set step filters by selecting Window → Preferences → Java → Debug → Step Filtering, as shown in Figure 5-12. If you want to filter out code, use the checkboxes next to the predefined filters you see in the figure, or create a new filter by clicking the Add Filter button.

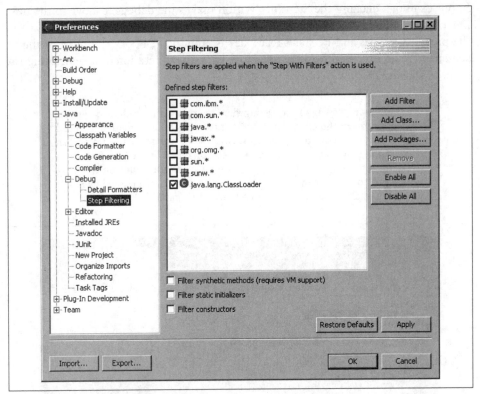

Figure 5-12. Specifying step filters

Stepping through code line by line is fine when you don't have a lot of code. But if you are debugging a few hundred lines of code, you need something faster. In that case, take a look at Recipe 5.6 on running until a breakpoint is encountered.

See Also

Recipe 5.3 on starting a debugging session; Recipe 5.4 on setting a breakpoint; Recipe 5.6 on running until hitting a breakpoint; Chapter 3 of *Eclipse* (O'Reilly).

5.6   Running Until Encountering a Breakpoint

Problem

You don't want to single-step through many lines of code while debugging. Rather, you want to step through breakpoints only.

Solution

While paused at a breakpoint, click the Resume button in the Debug view or select Run → Resume. Execution continues until the next breakpoint is encountered.

Discussion

If you don't want to keep single-stepping through your code, you have other options. For example, you can simply let your code execute until it reaches a breakpoint. To do that, just click the Resume button in the Debug view (the arrow button to the right of the word Debug in the Debug view), or select Run → Resume.

In the previous recipe, we stopped at a breakpoint and then single-stepped to the next line of executable code. Clicking Resume resumes program execution until the breakpoint is encountered for a second time, and the index loopIndex will hold a value of 2, as shown in Figure 5-13.

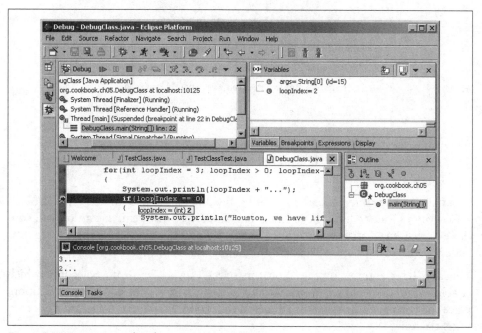

Figure 5-13. Running to a breakpoint

Clicking Resume again takes us to the next iteration, where `loopIndex` holds 1. Clicking `loopIndex` one more time makes the code execute until the program terminates, which is unexpected because we're waiting for `loopIndex` to equal 0.

Getting an unexpected result is an indication you've found your bug; the problem is in the line in which we've set up the `for` loop incorrectly:

```java
public class DebugClass
{
    public static void main(String[] args)
    {
        for(int loopIndex = 3; loopIndex > 0; loopIndex--)
        {
            System.out.println(loopIndex + "...");
            if(loopIndex == 0)
            {
                System.out.println("Houston, we have liftoff.");
            }
        }
    }
}
```

The `for` loop should be written like this instead:

```java
public class DebugClass
{
    public static void main(String[] args)
    {
        for(int loopIndex = 3; loopIndex >= 0; loopIndex--)
        {
            System.out.println(loopIndex + "...");
            if(loopIndex == 0)
            {
                System.out.println("Houston, we have liftoff.");
            }
        }
    }
}
```

That fixes the problem, as shown in Figure 5-14, where the debugged code operates as it should.

In addition to resuming execution until a breakpoint is encountered, you also can select Run → Run to Line. Just click a line and select this item; execution will continue to that line. This option is often extremely useful while debugging to skip over large sections of code and to set ad hoc breakpoints on the fly.

You also have another option. You can select Run → Step Into Selection, which enables you to indicate where you want to step into. In the current line of execution, place the cursor on the name of a method that you want to step into, and click Step into Selection.

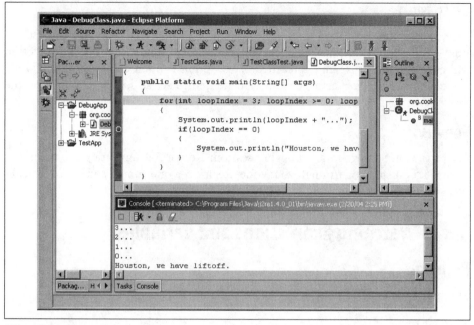

Figure 5-14. The working code

Eclipse 3.0

In Eclipse 3.0, the Step into Selection command is no longer restricted to the line currently executing (which was very annoying in previous versions of Eclipse).

See Also

Recipe 5.3 on setting up a debugging session; Recipe 5.4 on setting a breakpoint; Recipe 5.5 on stepping through your code; Recipe 5.7 on running until a specific line number is reached.

5.7 Running to a Line of Code You Select

Problem

You want to stop execution at a specific line of code that doesn't have a breakpoint.

Solution

Select Run → Run to Line.

Discussion

Besides resuming execution until a breakpoint is encountered, you also can use the Run → Run to Line option. Just click a line, and select Run → Run to Line; execution will continue until that line is reached. This option is often extremely useful while debugging to skip over large sections of code and to set ad hoc breakpoints on the fly.

See Also

Recipe 5.3 on setting up a debugging session; Recipe 5.4 on setting a breakpoint; Recipe 5.5 on stepping through your code; Recipe 5.6 on running code until a breakpoint is encountered.

5.8 Watching Expressions and Variables

Problem

You need to watch the value of a variable or expression as your code executes.

Solution

Highlight the variable or expression while debugging, right-click it, and select Watch, or select Run → Watch. The variable or expression, along with its value, will appear in the Expressions view from then on.

Discussion

You can see an example in Figure 5-15, where we added the value of the variable named loopIndex to the Expressions view. As you execute your code in the debugger, the current value of loopIndex always appears in the Expressions view, unless you right-click it in the Expressions view and select Remove.

5.9 Setting a Hit Count for Breakpoints

Problem

You want to break only after a breakpoint has been encountered a specified number of times.

Solution

Breakpoints can be enabled after a specified number of hits, called a *hit count*. To set a breakpoint's hit count, right-click the breakpoint in the Breakpoints view and click Properties, opening the Java Line Breakpoint Properties dialog. Check the "Enable Hit Count" checkbox, and enter the hit count you want.

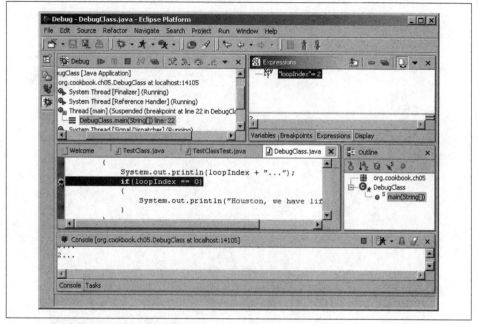

Figure 5-15. Watching a variable's value

Discussion

You can see an example in Figure 5-16, in which the hit count of a breakpoint is set to 3.

Click OK to close this dialog, and then restart the debugging session (you can end the session by clicking the Terminate button, or by selecting Run → Terminate and starting the debugging session again). When you do, execution will be suspended the third time that breakpoint is encountered.

> You also can set a breakpoint's hit count by right-clicking the breakpoint in the Breakpoints view, clicking Hit Count, and entering the hit count you want in the dialog that opens.

See Also

Recipe 5.10 on configuring breakpoint conditions.

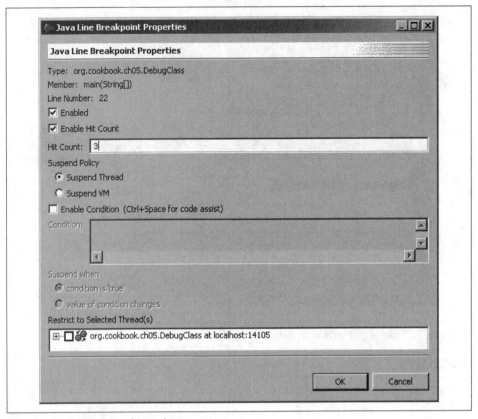

Figure 5-16. Setting a breakpoint hit count

5.10 Configuring Breakpoint Conditions

Problem

You want to halt a program when a certain condition occurs in your code, such as when a variable contains a certain value.

Solution

Configure your breakpoint to respond to the condition you specify. You do that by right-clicking the breakpoint in the Breakpoints view, clicking Properties, checking the "Enable Condition" checkbox, and entering the condition you want to use (such as loopIndex == 2).

Discussion

To demonstrate how this works, we're setting the condition for a breakpoint to loopIndex == 2 in Figure 5-17.

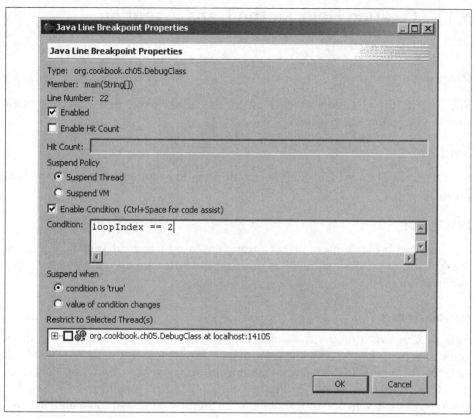

Figure 5-17. Setting a breakpoint's condition

Now the breakpoint will be active when it's encountered, *and* when the value in loopIndex equals 2.

You also can break when the value of a condition changes. For example, if some part of your code is changing the value in a variable named loopIndex and it shouldn't, you can type that variable name into the Condition box and check the "value of condition changes" checkbox. (You can use any valid expression in the Condition box, not just variable names.)

See Also

Recipe 5.9 on setting hit counts for breakpoints; Recipe 5.8 on watching expression and variable values.

5.11 Creating Field, Method, and Exception Breakpoints

Problem

You need to stop execution when a field or method is about to be accessed, or when a certain exception occurs.

Solution

Set a field, method, or exception breakpoint using the appropriate items in the Run menu.

Discussion

The standard breakpoints we've been using are called *line breakpoints*; besides line breakpoints, the JDT supports three other types of breakpoints: field, method, and exception breakpoints.

Field breakpoints

Field breakpoints, also called *watchpoints*, suspend execution when your code is going to access and/or modify the value of a field (watchpoints cannot be set on local variables, only on fields). This is different from when you set a condition on a standard breakpoint; this breakpoint happens every time a field is going to be accessed in any way. Using a watchpoint is often much easier than trying to catch all the possible points in your code in which the field you want to watch might be modified.

To set a watchpoint, highlight a field in a Java view and select Run → Add/Remove Watchpoint. The new watchpoint will appear in the Breakpoints view, and you can configure it by right-clicking it and then clicking Breakpoint Properties, which opens the Java Watchpoint Properties dialog shown in Figure 5-18. Note in particular that you can check two checkboxes here—"Access" and "Modification"—that enable you to indicate whether you want to suspend execution when the field is accessed and/or when it is modified.

Method breakpoints

Method breakpoints suspend execution when you enter or leave a method, depending on how you configure the breakpoints. You usually use these breakpoints on methods for which you do not have source code. To set a method breakpoint, highlight the call to that method in a Java view, and select Run → Add/Remove Method Breakpoint. You can configure these breakpoints by right-clicking them in the Breakpoints view, which opens the Java Method Breakpoint Properties dialog shown in Figure 5-19. You can select whether the breakpoint happens on entry into the method, exit from the method, or both, using the checkboxes in this dialog.

Figure 5-18. Setting watchpoint properties

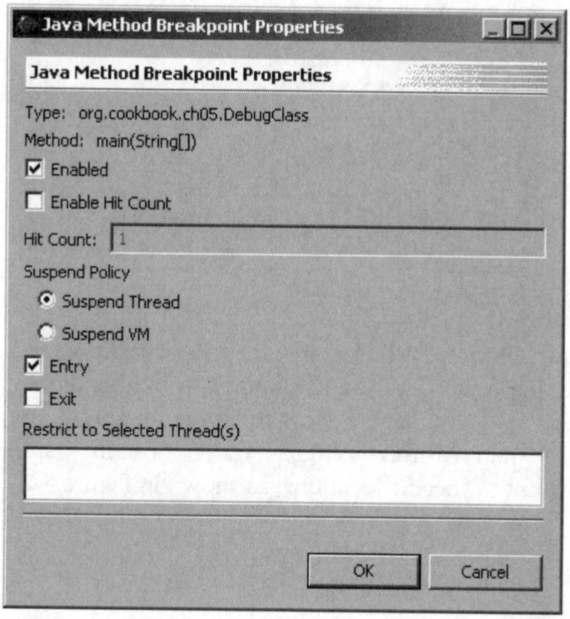

Figure 5-19. Setting up a method breakpoint

Exception breakpoints

You also can work with *exception breakpoints*, which enable you to suspend execution when an exception occurs. This is very useful if your code throws unexpected exceptions, such as a NullPointerException. You can suspend execution and see what's going on with your code when a thrown exception is caught or not caught.

To set an exception breakpoint, select Run → Add/Remove Exception Breakpoint, which opens the dialog shown in Figure 5-20 that enables you to select which breakpoint(s) you are interested in, as well as whether you want to break when they are caught or not caught, or both.

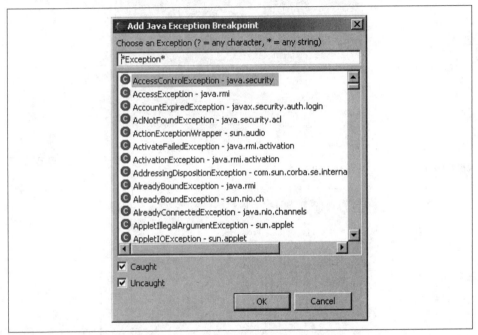

Figure 5-20. Setting up an exception breakpoint

You can configure the properties for an exception breakpoint as you can for any other breakpoint. Just right-click the breakpoint in the Breakpoints view, and click Properties. For example, you can see how to configure an exception breakpoint for uncaught java.lang.NullPointerException exceptions in Figure 5-21. You can restrict the breakpoint to specific locations, as shown in Figure 5-21, and even use hit counts.

Eclipse 3.0

The process for creating breakpoints in Eclipse 3.0 is the same as in earlier versions. However, the Add/Remove Watchpoint menu item is called Toggle Watchpoint in

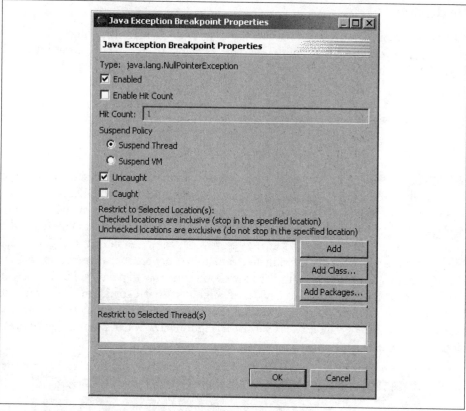

Figure 5-21. Setting properties for a Java exception breakpoint

Eclipse 3.0. In addition, the breakpoint properties dialogs are laid out differently (but so far they contain the same items).

See Also

Recipe 5.10 on configuring breakpoint conditions; Chapter 3 of *Eclipse* (O'Reilly).

5.12   Evaluating Expressions

Problem

You want to evaluate an expression while debugging.

Solution

Enter the expression you want to evaluate in the Debug perspective's Expressions view, right-click it, and click Inspect.

Discussion

During a debugging session, it can be very useful to evaluate the values of expressions. Say, for example, that your code has a variable named temperature, set to 72 degrees Fahrenheit:

```
public class DebugClass
{
    public static int temperature = 72;
        .
        .
        .
```

While you're debugging your code to check the interface to that new code you got from Europe, you suddenly realize you'll need that temperature in Celsius. How can you convert it on the fly? To open temperature in the Expressions view while you're debugging, highlight it in your code, right-click it, and click Inspect. You'll see the current value of temperature, 72, in the Expressions view, as shown in Figure 5-22. Now enter the expression you want to evaluate to convert the temperature to Celsius, (temperature - 32) * 5 / 9, in the Expressions view *detail pane*, which appears at the bottom of the Expressions view. Then highlight that expression, right-click it, and click Inspect. The expression is added to the list of items in the Expressions view along with its current value, 22, as shown in Figure 5-22. What's more, that expression's value will be kept updated as you execute your code.

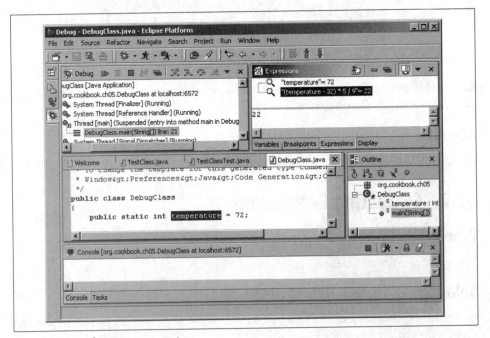

Figure 5-22. Evaluating an expression

Eclipse 3.0

In Eclipse 3.0, the detail pane appears to the right of the Expressions view by default, not at the bottom.

See Also

Recipe 5.3 on starting a debugging session; Recipe 5.13 on assigning values to variables during a debugging session.

5.13 Assigning Values to Variables While Debugging

Problem

You want to change the values of variables while debugging to run tests on those new values.

Solution

Just double-click a field or variable name in the Variables view, and enter a new value in the dialog that opens.

Discussion

The Variables view displays the currently available variables and their values, as you can see at upper right in Figure 5-23.

To change a variable's value, just double-click it, and enter a new value. For example, to change the value in loopIndex from 3 to 2, double-click loopIndex in the Variables view, enter 2 in the dialog that opens (shown in Figure 5-24), and click OK.

Note, however, that monkeying with data in a running program can break your code.

Eclipse 3.0

In Eclipse 3.0, some Java types, such as collections and maps, can be displayed in a more compact and meaningful form using variable *filters*. These filters are controlled with a toggle button in the Variables view.

See Also

Recipe 5.12 on evaluating expressions.

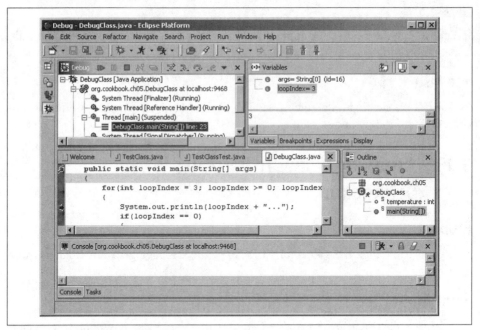

Figure 5-23. Debugging with the Variables view

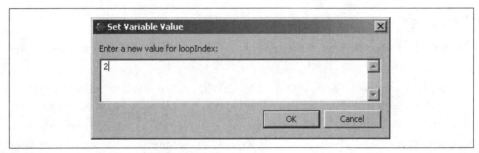

Figure 5-24. Changing a variable on the fly

5.14 Changing Code on the Fly

Problem

You see a code error, and you want to fix it and test the fix, all without restarting the debugging session.

Solution

If you have Java Version 1.4 or later, just edit your code as you're debugging and save it (provided the auto-build on save capability is turned on), and you can keep debugging.

Discussion

The process of editing code while debugging is called *hot code replacement*, and you'll need Java Version 1.4 or later to use it. Make sure the "auto-build on save" capability is turned on (it's on by default). If it isn't, turn it on by selecting Window → Preferences → Workbench, and check the "Perform build automatically on resource modification" checkbox.

Now debug your code until execution stops at a breakpoint. At this point, you're free to edit your code. After editing, save the code and resume execution.

 If you don't want to turn on the "auto-build on save" capability, simply rebuild your code manually after editing it by selecting Project → Rebuild Project or Project → Rebuild All, and then resume execution.

Note that you have to use Java Version 1.4 or later to support hot code replacement. If you're targeting an earlier version of Java with the actual code you're developing, in Eclipse you can use different JREs to run and debug your code. If you want to set the debug launch configuration so that it uses a different JRE, select Run → Debug, then click the JRE tab and select the JRE you want to use for debugging.

See Also

Recipe 4.8 on selecting the Java runtime.

CHAPTER 6

Using Eclipse in Teams

6.0   Introduction

Professional developers frequently work in teams, and Eclipse is up to the task. Eclipse supports the Concurrent Versions System (CVS) for this purpose. If you're working in a team, you have to coordinate your development work with others to avoid conflicts. You're all sharing the same code, which means your work of genius might be destroyed unintentionally by someone else's thoughtless efforts.

Source control precludes those kinds of problems because it controls access to shared code in a well-defined way. Besides controlling access to code, source control maintains a history of changes so that you can restore the code from earlier versions. Because it maintains a history of your code, not only can you restore code against earlier versions, but you can also compare the current code to earlier versions to see the differences at a glance.

Like much else in the Java world, CVS is an open source project. CVS first appeared in 1986, when it was a set of Unix shell scripts; it wasn't until 1989 that dedicated CVS software first appeared. Today, CVS is available on many operating systems across the board, from Unix and Linux to Windows.

 For details on CVS, take a look at *http://www.cvshome.org*.

The CVS *repository* is where developers store code files to be shared. To retrieve a file from the repository, you check that file out of the repository. When you want to store your newly changed version of the file, you commit it to the repository. Refreshing your copy of the code from the repository is called *updating* it.

CVS also has slightly different terminology than Eclipse; what's a *project* to Eclipse is a *module* to CVS. Each module gets its own directory in the repository, making it easier to separate modules. Standard projects also are called *physical modules*, while *logical* or *virtual modules* are collections of related resources.

How many copies of your code are available to be checked out at once? That depends on which repository model you use. Here are the options:

Pessimistic locking

> Sequential access. With this type of locking, only one developer can check out a file at a time. When the file is checked out, the file is locked. It's possible for someone else to check out read-only copies of the file, but not to change the original. Access is sequential.

Optimistic locking

> Random access. With this type of locking, developers can check out and modify files freely. When you commit changed files, the repository software *merges* your changes automatically. If the merge operation has issues, the software will flag them and ask you to resolve the problems.

CVS uses optimistic locking by default (some CVS software also supports pessimistic locking). We'll be using optimistic locking here, which is what Eclipse supports. You use a CVS server to handle the actual file manipulation, as we'll do in this chapter.

CVS also automatically assigns a version number to each file when it's committed. When you first commit a file, it's version 1.1 (1.0 on some CVS installations). The next time, the version number is 1.2, and so on. When you update your code locally, Eclipse doesn't just overwrite your local version of a file. Instead, it merges the changes with your local file in an intelligent way. If conflicts exist, it'll insert special CVS markup to make the conflicting lines stand out, and those conflicts will have to be handled before running the code. Usually updates are smooth, but if there are a lot of conflicts because there's been a lot of work on the file or you haven't updated in some time, it can take a while to unravel.

CVS also enables you to support multiple development streams, called *branches*, in the same module. The main development stream in a module is called the *head*, and branches are forks that can diverge from that main stream. For example, a branch can represent a beta version of the project, or some new capability you're adding to your code that you want to test first.

6.1 Getting a CVS Server

Problem

You want to start working with CVS and need to install a CVS server.

Solution

You might already have a CVS server installed; if not, you can download one.

Discussion

Today, most Linux and Unix installations come with a CVS server as part of their standard distribution. To check if you have a working CVS installation, type cvs --help on the command line; you should see a list of help prompts. If you can't find a CVS server, download one from *http://www.cvshome.org*. On larger systems, talk to the support techs if you can't find a CVS installation.

If you're running Windows, you can find a number of CVS servers available for download. For example, the venerable CVSNT is available for free from *http://www. cvsnt.org*. Just run the executable to install it.

 A variety of CVS servers are available, and they all come with their own installation instructions. I'm not going to reproduce those installation instructions here, having been burned by that in the past as new versions—with totally different installation instructions—appeared. Usually, installation is not difficult once you've downloaded the server you want. Just check the instructions that come with the download. And bear in mind that if the install is too complex, and things aren't working, other CVS servers are always available.

See Also

Chapter 4 of *Eclipse* (O'Reilly).

6.2   Creating a CVS Repository

Problem

You need to create a CVS repository to store code to share with others.

Solution

In Linux and Unix, use the command cvs -d *path* init, where *path* gives the location of the directory you want to use as the repository. In Windows CVSNT, use the Repository tab's Add button to add a new repository.

Discussion

After installing a CVS server, you need to create a repository in which to store shared code. In Linux and Unix, you can enter cvs -d *path* init at the command prompt, where *path* is the location of the repository.

When creating a repository, bear in mind that the permissions and ownership for *path* have to allow access to all members of the development team.

In Windows, CVSNT runs as a Windows service. You start it from the Start menu, selecting the Service control panel item from whatever program group you've added it to. This opens the CVSNT control panel shown in Figure 6-1. Click the Repositories tab in the CVSNT control panel, click the Add button, enter the path of the new repository directory, and click OK. In the figure, we're using the directory *c:/repository* as the CVS repository.

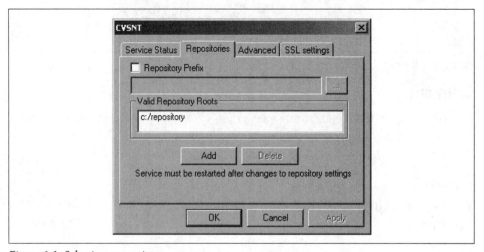

Figure 6-1. Selecting a repository

You start the server by selecting the Service control panel item from the program group to which you've added CVSNT, opening the CVSNT control panel. Click the Start button in both the "CVS Service" and "CVS Lock Service" boxes, which will make CVSNT display the word Running in both of those boxes, as shown in Figure 6-2.

See Also

Recipe 6.4 on storing a project in a CVS repository.

6.3 Connecting Eclipse to a CVS Repository

Problem

You want to connect Eclipse to a CVS repository.

Figure 6-2. Running CVSNT

Solution

In Eclipse, open the Repositories view, right-click that view, and select New → Repository Location, opening the Add CVS Repository dialog. Enter the required information, and click OK.

Discussion

You have to establish a connection from Eclipse through the CVS server to the CVS repository before working with that repository. First, make sure your CVS server is running.

To connect Eclipse to the CVS repository, select Window → Open Perspective → Other, and select the CVS Repository Exploring perspective. After you do this the first time, Eclipse adds this perspective to the Window → Open Perspective submenu and also adds a shortcut for this perspective to the other perspective shortcuts at the extreme left of the Eclipse window.

When the CVS Repository Exploring perspective opens, right-click the blank CVS repositories view at left, and select New → Repository Location, opening the Add CVS Repository dialog shown in Figure 6-3.

In the Add CVS Repository dialog, enter the name of the CVS server, often the name of the machine hosting the CVS server, and the path to the CVS repository. To connect to the CVS server, you'll also need to supply a username and password, as shown in Figure 6-3 (in this case we're using integrated Windows NT security, so no password is needed). You can use two connection protocols with CVS servers, SSH (secure shell) and pserver. We'll use pserver here.

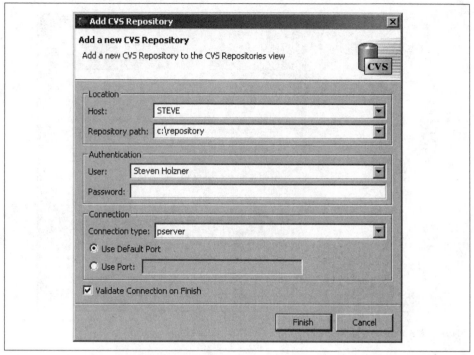

Figure 6-3. Connecting Eclipse to a CVS repository

pserver is a CVS client/server protocol that uses its own password files and connections. It's more efficient than SSH but less secure. If security is an issue, go with SSH.

Click Finish after configuring the connection. The new connection to the CVS server should appear in the CVS Repositories view, as shown in Figure 6-4.

A public CVS server is available that gives you access to the code for Eclipse; go to *:pserver:anonymous@dev.eclipse.org:/home/eclipse*.

If you wish, you can see what commands Eclipse sends to the CVS server. To do so, open the CVS console by selecting Window → Show View → Other → CVS → CVS Console. The CVS Console view will appear (this view overlaps the standard Console view).

Eclipse 3.0

Eclipse 3.0 also supports CVS SSH2 in addition to the pserver and SSH protocols. You can enable SSH2 in the SSH2 Connection Method preference page (right-click a project and select Team → CVS → SSH2 Connection Method). All CVS server connections of type extssh will use SSH2 from that point on.

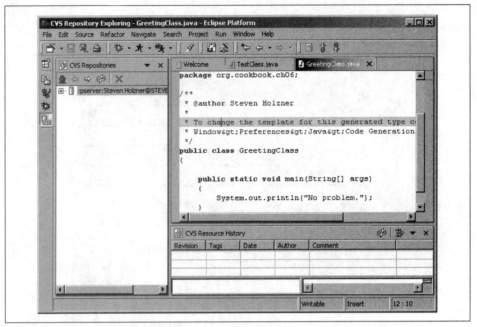

Figure 6-4. A new repository created in the CVS Repositories view

See Also

Chapter 4 of *Eclipse* (O'Reilly).

6.4   Storing an Eclipse Project in a CVS Repository

Problem

You have an Eclipse project you want to store in a CVS repository to make it available to other developers.

Solution

Right-click the project you want to share, and select Team → Share Project. Follow the directions in the Share Project with CVS Repository dialog.

Discussion

As an example, we'll create a project here and add it to a CVS repository. The code for this example project, *GreetingApp*, appears in Example 6-1. All this code does is display the message No problem..

Example 6-1. The GreetingApp project

```
package org.cookbook.ch06;

public class GreetingClass
{

    public static void main(String[] args)
    {
        System.out.println("No problem.");
    }
}
```

To add this project to the CVS repository, open the Java perspective, right-click the project, and select Team → Share Project. This displays the Share Project with CVS Repository dialog, as shown in Figure 6-5.

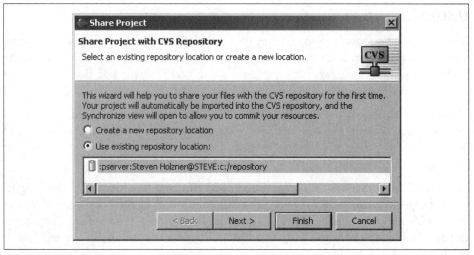

Figure 6-5. Sharing a project with a CVS repository

Make sure the "Use existing repository location" radio button is selected, and select the repository you want to use. Click Finish to add the project to the CVS repository. This creates a CVS module with the same name as the Eclipse project.

 If you want to give the created CVS module a different name, click Next instead of Finish, enter the name of the CVS module you want to create, enter a new module name, and click Finish.

This adds the project to the CVS repository and also opens a Synchronize view in Eclipse which overlaps with the Console view (more on how to work with the Synchronize view later in this chapter; because there's nothing to synchronize with at this point, it's not of much use to us now).

See Also

Recipe 6.5 on committing files to the CVS repository.

6.5   Committing Files to the CVS Repository

Problem

You've edited a file, saved your changes, and want to send it to the CVS repository so that others can access it.

Solution

Right-click a file, and select Team → Commit.

Discussion

In Recipe 6.4, you saw how to add a project to a CVS repository. To share your code, you have to check in code files. This requires two steps: first, you add a file to the CVS repository, which registers the file with the CVS server but doesn't actually upload it; then you commit the file, which uploads it to the repository.

Technically, the way to send files to the CVS repository is to add them to Eclipse's version control and then commit them. You do that by right-clicking the files and selecting Team → Add to Version Control. Then select Team → Commit to commit the files.

However, Eclipse gives you a shortcut here. To commit all the files in a project, right-click the project, and select Team → Commit. When you do, Eclipse displays the Add to CVS Version Control dialog. Click the Details button and check the check-boxes matching the files you want to add to CVS version control; Eclipse will list all the files in the project, including your Java source files and the *.project* and *.classpath* files. Then click Yes.

 If you want to check in and check out projects as Eclipse projects, be sure to commit the *.project* and *.classpath* files.

Eclipse will prompt you for a comment for the set of files you're committing, giving you the chance to label those files. In this case, just enter some text, such as The Greeting App, as shown in Figure 6-6, and click OK.

You also can simply right-click an individual file and select Team → Commit. If the file is not yet under version control, Eclipse will ask if you want to add it; click Yes. Eclipse will display the same Commit dialog shown in Figure 6-6, enabling you to enter a comment for the file before it's committed.

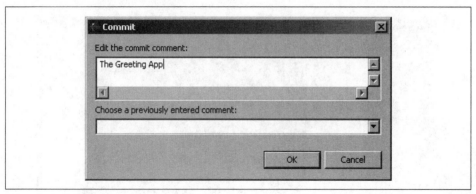

Figure 6-6. Committing files

When the file is committed, it's uploaded to the CVS repository and given a version number. Eclipse also will use a special decoration for files under version control if you tell it to do so; see Recipe 6.6.

See Also

Recipe 6.6 on visually labeling files under version control; Chapter 4 of *Eclipse* (O'Reilly).

6.6   Visually Labeling Files Under Version Control

Problem

You want to see at a glance what files in a project are under version control.

Solution

Turn on CVS decorations by selecting Window → Preferences → Workbench → Label Decorations, check the CVS checkbox, and click OK.

Discussion

To make Eclipse indicate which files are under version control, you turn on CVS label decorations. Select Window → Preferences → Workbench → Label Decorations to open the Preferences dialog, then check the "CVS" checkbox, and click OK. This makes Eclipse add a gold cylinder to the icons of files under CVS version control, as shown in the *GreetingApp* project in Figure 6-7. Note also that files in the repository will have a CVS version number showing; that version is 1.1 here.

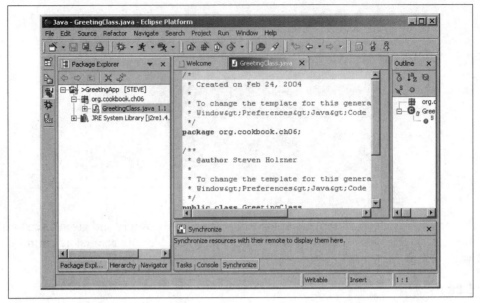

Figure 6-7. Files under version control

See Also

Chapter 4 of *Eclipse* (O'Reilly).

6.7 Examining the CVS Repository

Problem

You want to explore the CVS repository from inside Eclipse.

Solution

Use the CVS Repository Exploring perspective. Open this perspective by selecting
Window → Open Perspective → Other → CVS Repository Exploring. Or, if you've
opened this perspective in the past—which means Eclipse will have added it to the
Open Perspective menu—select Window → Open Perspective → CVS Repository
Exploring.

Discussion

The CVS Repository Exploring perspective enables you to see what's inside the CVS
repository. For example, you can see the entire *GreetingApp* project, all the way
down to the *GreetingClass.java* file, in the CVS Repositories view at left in
Figure 6-8.

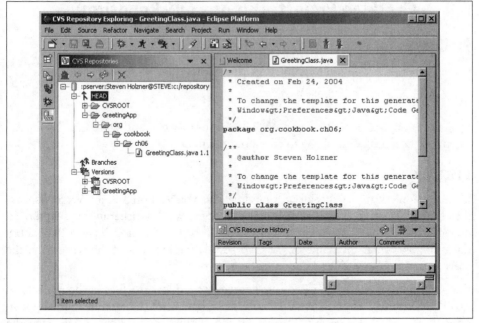

Figure 6-8. The CVS repository perspective

This project, *GreetingApp*, is in the repository's HEAD section, which is the main development stream.

Also note the *CVSROOT* directory, which holds CVS administrative data; the Branches node, which holds any files in other branches of development; and the Versions node, which holds explicitly labeled versions.

Eclipse 3.0

In Eclipse 3.0, you can determine who's responsible for a bug. You right-click a file and select Team → Show Annotation to open a CVS Annotation view showing the selected file in the CVS Repositories view. When you select a line in the editor, the CVS Annotation view reveals who released that edit to the file.

See Also

Recipe 6.8 on checking projects out of a CVS repository; Recipe 6.13 on creating CVS branches; Chapter 4 of *Eclipse* (O'Reilly).

6.8   Checking Projects Out of a CVS Repository

Problem

Someone wants to check out a project of yours from the CVS repository.

Solution

In Eclipse, right-click a file in the CVS Repositories view, and click Check Out As. Then use the Check Out dialog to check out the item.

Discussion

If other people want to check out a module that you've stored in a CVS repository, they have to create a connection to the repository as we did earlier in this chapter. To do this, they should right-click the CVS Repositories view; select New → Repository Location; and enter the name of the CVS server, the location of the repository, the username, the password, and the type of connection.

They can then open the CVS Repositories view to explore the files in the repository. To check out the *GreetingApp* module, they can right-click the module in the Repositories view and click Check Out As from the context menu. Eclipse will open the New Project dialog and automatically create a new project corresponding to the CVS module.

If you're sharing an Eclipse project, and each CVS module has its own Eclipse .*project* file, you can select Check Out As Project from the Repositories view's context menu, which checks out an Eclipse project and adds it to the Package Explorer. Note that if your code isn't in a project of a kind that Eclipse can recognize, it will ask you what type of project to create.

See Also

Chapter 4 of *Eclipse* (O'Reilly).

6.9   Updating Your Code from a CVS Repository

Problem

You want to update your local code with the code in a CVS repository.

Solution

Right-click the file, and select Team → Update, then resolve any conflicts. Alternatively, if you just want to replace your version with what's in the CVS repository, right-click the file and select Replace With → Latest From HEAD.

Discussion

For example, say that someone checked out your code and changed this line:

```
public static void main(String[] args)
{
    System.out.println("No problem.");
}
```

to this:

```
public static void main(String[] args)
{
    System.out.println("No problems at all.");
}
```

When she makes these changes in his version of Eclipse, a > character appears in front of files that haven't yet been committed, as shown in Figure 6-9.

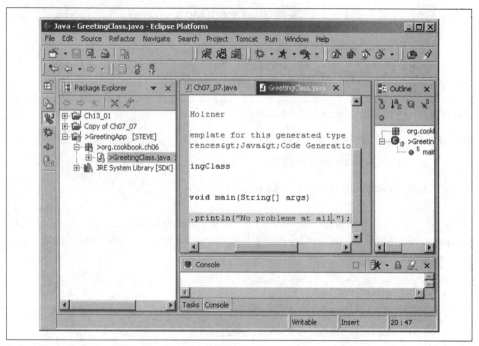

Figure 6-9. Outgoing changes ready

When she commits her changes, the latest version of *GreetingClass.java* in the CVS repository changes from 1.1 to 1.2, as shown in Figure 6-10.

To update your code with the most recent version of the code in the repository (which is now Version 1.2, as stored by the other developer), right-click the project or file in your version of Eclipse and select Team → Update. Doing so upgrades your version of the project's files to version 1.2—if there's no conflict.

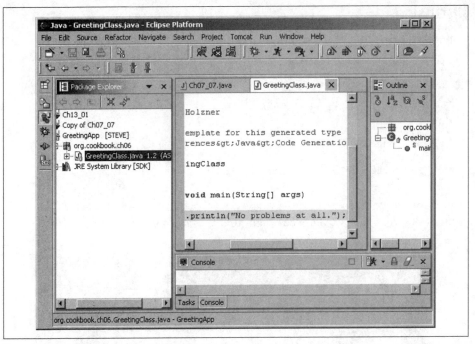

Figure 6-10. A new version in the CVS repository

If you've changed this line of code yourself to something such as this:

```
public static void main(String[] args)
{
    System.out.println("No problems here.");
}
```

there will be a conflict with the new line in the new version, version 1.2, of the file. Eclipse will mark that conflict by listing both versions in your code with some added CVS markup such as this:

```
public static void main(String[] args) {
<<<<<<< GreetingClass.java
    System.out.println("No problems here.");
=======
    System.out.println("No problems at all.");
>>>>>>> 1.2
    }
}
```

It's up to you to handle these conflicts in your code (Eclipse is not going to compile your code until the CVS markup has been dealt with and removed). Letting Eclipse handle updates like this is one way to handle updates from the CVS repository, but if the changes are substantial, it's best to *synchronize* with the repository, an issue we discuss in Recipe 6.10.

Note that if you just want to *replace* your version of a file with the latest version of the file in the main development stream for the project in the CVS repository, right-click the file and select Replace With → Latest From HEAD.

6.10 Synchronizing Your Code with the CVS Repository

Problem

You've got a lot of changes from the version of a file in the CVS repository and want to get your code up to speed.

Solution

Right-click the project and select Team → Synchronize with Repository. Then take a look at the synchronization issues that Eclipse displays side by side.

Discussion

Synchronizing with the repository enables you to compare changes that have been made side by side in an easier format than the update merge format. For instance, say that the version of the code in the repository uses this code:

```
public static void main(String[] args)
{
    System.out.println("No problems at all.");
}
```

But you've changed that line of code to this:

```
public static void main(String[] args)
{
    System.out.println("No problems here.");
}
```

To synchronize your code with the version of the file in the repository, right-click the project and select Team → Synchronize with Repository. Then double-click the *GreetingClass.java* node in the Structure Compare view to take a look at the synchronization issues for that file. You can see the results in Figure 6-11.

Note the side-by-side comparison going on at the bottom of Figure 6-11, where your local file is being compared to that in the CVS repository. As shown in the figure, lines appear connecting the differences in the files.

You can use the up and down arrow buttons at right in the Java Source Compare view to navigate between changes. You also can use the two arrow buttons next to the navigation buttons to accept or make changes. The button with the left-facing arrow copies the current change from the repository to your local code, and the button with the right-facing arrow copies the current change from your local file to the

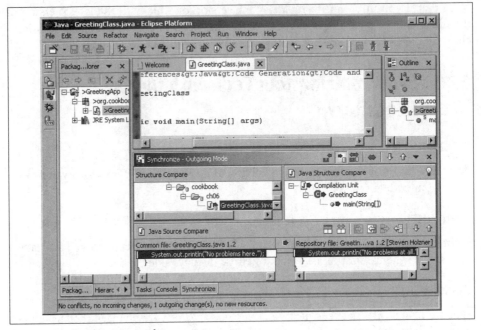

Figure 6-11. Synchronizing code

repository. After you've synchronized your version of the code with that in the repository, commit your changes to the repository.

Eclipse 3.0

Eclipse 3.0 has a handy way to look at changes in the local document as compared to the version of that document in the CVS repository. Right-click the Quick Diff ruler, and set the Set QuickDiff Reference item to CVS Repository. This makes the Quick-Diff bar compare recent changes to those in the CVS repository—very handy.

See Also

Recipe 4.6 on comparing files against local history; Recipe 4.7 on restoring elements and files from local history; Recipe 6.9 on updating code from a repository; Chapter 4 of *Eclipse* (O'Reilly).

6.11 Creating Code Patches

Problem

You need to coordinate your development with another team of developers using a patch they can install to update their code.

Solution

Create a code patch so that they can update their code. (Note that this is a *code patch*, not a binary patch. Eclipse can use this patch to update source code to match another version.)

Discussion

Say your version of the code displays the text "No problems here.":

```
public static void main(String[] args)
{
    System.out.println("No problems here.");
}
```

But the code the other team is using from the CVS repository displays "No problems at all.":

```
public static void main(String[] args)
{
    System.out.println("No problems at all.");
}
```

To update the other developers without changing version numbers, you can create a code patch. To create a code patch, Eclipse compares your local code to what's in the repository and creates a patch file holding the differences.

To create a code patch using your local version of a file as the version to which the patch will update the version in the repository, save your file locally, right-click it, and select Team → Create Patch, opening the dialog shown in Figure 6-12.

In this example, we'll save the file named *patch* in the current workspace, as shown in Figure 6-12. Click the Finish button to save the patch.

This creates the text file named *patch*. Here's what that file looks like; you can see the line to remove marked with a - and the line to add marked with a +:

```
Index: GreetingClass.java
===================================================================
RCS file: c:/repository/GreetingApp/org/cookbook/ch06/GreetingClass.java,v
retrieving revision 1.2
diff -u -r1.2 GreetingClass.java
--- GreetingClass.java     25 Feb 2004 16:34:07 -0000     1.2
+++ GreetingClass.java     25 Feb 2004 18:12:18 -0000
@@ -17,6 +17,6 @@

  public static void main(String[] args)
  {
-     System.out.println("No problems at all.");
+     System.out.println("No problems here.");
  }
}
```

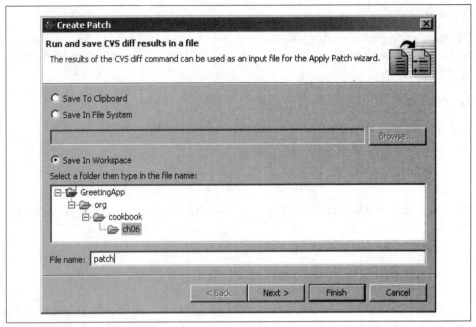

Figure 6-12. Creating a new patch

To apply the new patch to code that has not yet been patched, right-click the file to be updated in Eclipse and select Team → Apply Patch, opening the dialog shown in Figure 6-13.

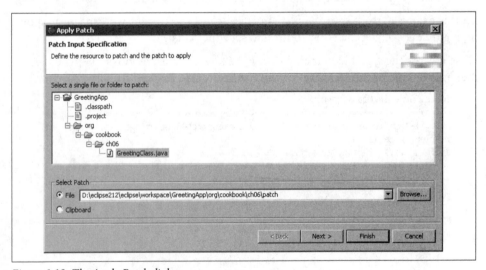

Figure 6-13. The Apply Patch dialog

Click Next to open the dialog shown in Figure 6-14. In this dialog you can review the changes the patch will create in the local version of the file. As shown in the figure, Eclipse will change the line:

```
System.out.println("No problems at all.");
```

to:

```
System.out.println("No problems here.");
```

To apply the patch, click Finish.

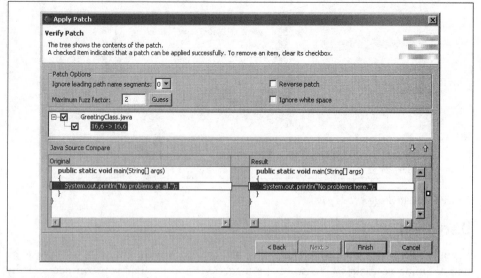

Figure 6-14. Accepting a patch

Applying the patch makes this change to the code in the other team's installation of Eclipse, as shown in Figure 6-15. Note that the version number of the file was not changed, but the file was updated with the new code.

6.12 Naming Code Versions

Problem

You've got a milestone build of your project, and you want to save it by name in the CVS repository for easy reference later on.

Solution

Tag the project with a version name by right-clicking it and selecting Team → Tag As Version.

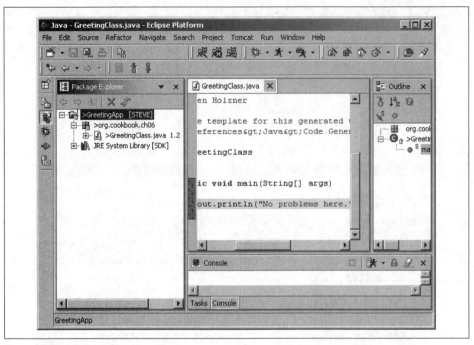

Figure 6-15. Applying a code patch

Discussion

If you've created a milestone build of your project, you might want to save it by name. Doing so makes CVS store the tagged version so that you can access it by name later.

Right-clicking a project under version control, and selecting Team → Tag As Version opens the dialog shown in Figure 6-16. In this case, we're going to name our current version of the project Gold_Edition, as shown in the figure.

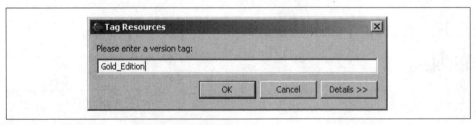

Figure 6-16. Tagging a version of your code

Note that version labels must start with a letter, and they cannot include spaces or these characters: `` `$,.:;@|' ``. After tagging the current version with this name, you can find it in the Versions node in the CVS Repositories view, as shown in Figure 6-17.

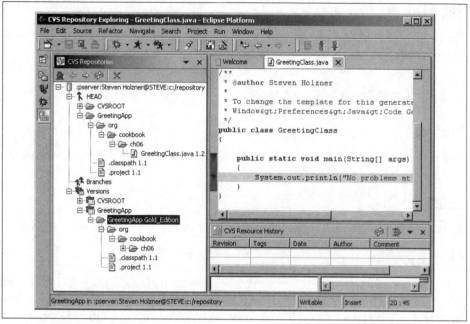

Figure 6-17. A new tagged version

You can check out a tagged version of a module by right-clicking it in the CVS Repositories view and selecting context menu items such as Check Out as Project, as with any other CVS module. Alternatively, you can right-click a project in the Package Explorer and select Replace With → Another Branch or Version, opening the dialog shown in Figure 6-18. Select the version with which you want to replace the current project, and click OK.

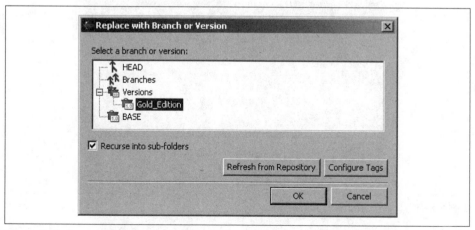

Figure 6-18. Accessing a milestone build

See Also

Recipe 6.4 on storing an Eclipse project in CVS; Recipe 6.5 on committing files to the repository.

6.13 Creating CVS Branches

Problem

You want to develop a new version of your code, such as a beta version, by creating a new branch in your development tree.

Solution

Add a new branch to your project's development tree by selecting Team → Branch.

Discussion

CVS also enables you to create new branches in your code's development tree. Such branches can act as alternate streams of development for your code; e.g., you might want to develop a new version of your code that uses prompts in another language.

To create a branch, right-click a project and select Team → Branch, which opens the Create a new CVS Branch dialog shown in Figure 6-19. In this example, we'll name the new branch Spanish_Version, as shown in the figure. At the same time, you can create a new version name for your code that will act as a reference, giving Eclipse a reference point for merging the branch into the main stream if you want to do that; Eclipse will suggest the name Root_Spanish_Version here.

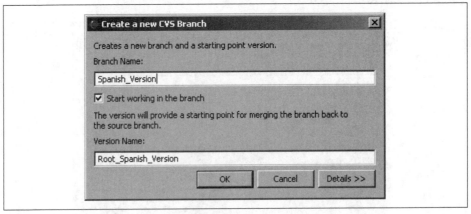

Figure 6-19. Creating the Spanish_Version branch

Clicking OK here opens the new branch in Eclipse, as shown in Figure 6-20 (note the project name in the Package Explorer).

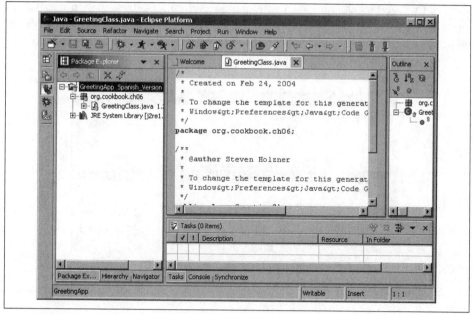

Figure 6-20. A new branch

You can check out the new branch from the CVS Repositories view, as shown in Figure 6-21.

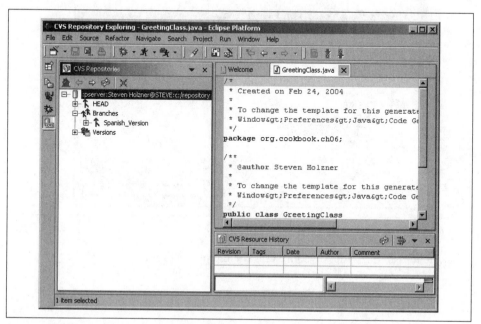

Figure 6-21. The new branch in the CVS Repositories view

You can merge branches back into the main development stream when needed. To do that, right-click the branch in the Package Explorer, and select Team → Merge, which opens the Merge dialog shown in Figure 6-22. Select the merge point for this operation—in this case, Root_Spanish_Version—and click Next.

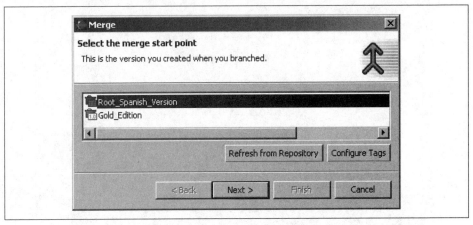

Figure 6-22. Selecting a root version to merge to

The next dialog enables you to select the branch from which you want to merge. In this case, select Spanish_Version, as shown in Figure 6-23.

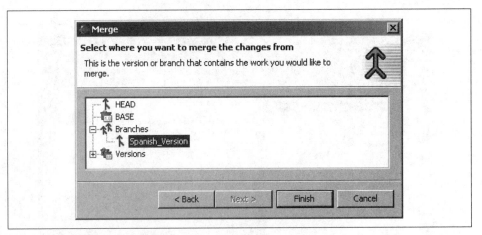

Figure 6-23. Merging a branch

Clicking Finish in this dialog completes the merge operation.

CHAPTER 7

Eclipse and Ant

7.0   Introduction

Eclipse is a great Java IDE, and it excels at enabling you to edit, debug, share, compile, and run your code. However, advanced projects can demand more from the build process. For example, you might want to compile multiple files, copy your compiled files to a specific location, create *.jar* files, delete previous build files, and more.

All these things are possible with the well-known Ant build tool from Apache (see *http://ant.apache.org/*). Ant has a great deal of power built in. It enables you to automate the build process—compile, move, copy, and delete files, create and delete directories, and more. And now Ant comes built into Eclipse. If your project requires more than just compiling one or two files, this is the chapter for you.

 This chapter discusses how to use Ant from Eclipse, but it doesn't discuss how to use Ant in detail, which would take a book by itself. For more information on how to work with this tool, see *Ant: The Definitive Guide* (O'Reilly).

7.1   Connecting Ant to Eclipse

Problem

You want to start working with Ant from Eclipse, but you need to know how to connect Ant to Eclipse.

Solution

All you have to do is to add a *build.xml* file to an Eclipse project. Eclipse will know that a file with that name should be treated as an Ant build file.

Discussion

As an example, we'll create an Ant build file, *build.xml*, that builds an Eclipse project, storing the resulting *.class* file in a *.jar* file stored in the directory we want. To follow along, create a Java Eclipse project named *AntProject*.

Store the source for this project in a folder named *src* and the output in a folder named *bin*. In the third step of the New Project dialog, the Java Setting dialog, click the Source tab and the Add Folder button. Then click the Create New Folder button to open the New Folder dialog. Enter src in the Folder name box and click OK twice. Eclipse will ask:

```
Do you want to remove the project as source folder and update build output folder to
'AntProject/bin'?
```

Click Yes, which gives you the results shown in Figure 7-1. Click Finish to finish creating the project, which now includes *src* and *bin* folders.

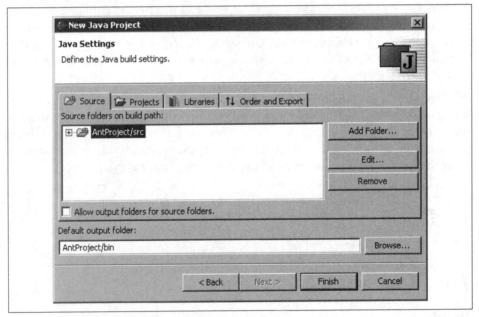

Figure 7-1. Creating the AntProject project

Add a new class, AntClass, in the org.cookbook.ch07 package. We're just going to use some sample code in this class to display a message, as shown in Example 7-1.

Example 7-1. Simple Ant test class

```
package org.cookbook.ch07;

public class AntClass
{
```

Example 7-1. Simple Ant test class (continued)

```
    public static void main(String[] args)
    {
        System.out.println("This code is stored in a JAR file.");
    }
}
```

Add a file named *build.xml* to the project by right-clicking the project in the Package Explorer and selecting New → File. Enter build.xml in the File name box, and click Finish, which creates the file and opens it in the Ant editor, as shown in Figure 7-2. Note that Eclipse knows this is an Ant build file already, and gives it an ant icon in the Package Explorer.

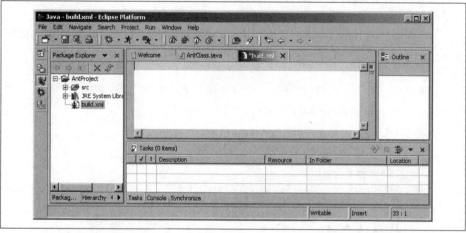

Figure 7-2. Creating build.xml

This file, *build.xml*, is the XML file Ant uses to build the project. Begin this file with the standard XML declaration and an Ant project element:

```
    <?xml version="1.0" encoding = "UTF-8"?>
    <project name="AntProject" default="Build" basedir=".">
            .
            .
            .
    </project>
```

You can set properties in Ant build files both to centralize the definitions of terms you'll use later in a build file and to interact with Ant. In this case, we're going to specify that Ant should use the same compiler that we use in the JDT by setting the build.compiler property to org.eclipse.jdt.core.JDTCompilerAdapter like so:

```
    <?xml version="1.0" encoding = "UTF-8"?>
    <project name="AntProject" default="Build" basedir=".">
```

```
    <property name="build.compiler"
        value="org.eclipse.jdt.core.JDTCompilerAdapter"/>
        .
        .
        .
</project>
```

We'll also add the following properties to the build file that correspond to the various build paths used in this project:

srcDir
> The directory that holds the source code, *src* here

binDir
> The binary output directory, *bin* here

jarDir
> The directory for the created *.jar* file; we'll use a directory named *lib* in the *bin* directory

jarFile
> The name of the *.jar* file we'll create—in this case, *AntProject.jar*

Enter these properties into *build.xml* in the Eclipse editor:

```
<?xml version="1.0" encoding = "UTF-8"?>
<project name="AntProject" default="Build" basedir=".">

    <property name="build.compiler"
        value="org.eclipse.jdt.core.JDTCompilerAdapter"/>
    <property name="srcDir" location="src"/>
    <property name="binDir" location="bin"/>
    <property name="jarDir" location="${binDir}/lib"/>
    <property name="jarFile" location="${jarDir}/AntProject.jar"/>
        .
        .
        .
</project>
```

Ant build files are constructed around Ant *targets*. In this example, the first target will delete everything currently in the output directory, *bin*, and in the *.jar* file output directory, *bin/lib*, and then reconstruct those directories. We'll do that in a target named Initialization:

```
<?xml version="1.0" encoding = "UTF-8"?>
<project name="AntProject" default="Build" basedir=".">

    <property name="build.compiler"
        value="org.eclipse.jdt.core.JDTCompilerAdapter"/>
    <property name="srcDir" location="src"/>
    <property name="binDir" location="bin"/>
    <property name="jarDir" location="${binDir}/lib"/>
    <property name="jarFile" location="${jarDir}/AntProject.jar"/>
```

```
    <target name="Initialization">
        <delete dir="${binDir}"/>
        <delete dir="${jarDir}"/>
        <mkdir dir="${binDir}"/>
        <mkdir dir="${jarDir}"/>
    </target>
          .
          .
          .
</project>
```

The next Ant target, Compilation, will compile the source file and put the resulting .
class file into the *bin* directory. Note that this target depends on the Initialization
target having been built successfully:

```
<?xml version="1.0" encoding = "UTF-8"?>
<project name="AntProject" default="Build" basedir=".">

    <property name="build.compiler"
        value="org.eclipse.jdt.core.JDTCompilerAdapter"/>
    <property name="srcDir" location="src"/>
    <property name="binDir" location="bin"/>
    <property name="jarDir" location="${binDir}/lib"/>
    <property name="jarFile" location="${jarDir}/AntProject.jar"/>

    <target name="Initialization">
        <delete dir="${binDir}"/>
        <delete dir="${jarDir}"/>
        <mkdir dir="${binDir}"/>
        <mkdir dir="${jarDir}"/>
    </target>

    <target name="Compilation" depends="Initialization">
        <javac srcdir="${srcDir}"
            destdir="${binDir}">
        </javac>
    </target>
          .
          .
          .
</project>
```

The Jar target compresses *AntProject.class* into a *.jar* file and stores that file as
${jarfile}. Note that this target depends on the Initialization and Compilation tar-
gets having already been built.

```
    <target name="Jar" depends="Initialization, Compilation">
        <jar destfile="${jarFile}" basedir="${binDir}"/>
    </target>
```

Now create the main target for this build file, called Build. This target coordinates all
the other targets by requiring them to have been completed, and it displays a message, Ant is building your project.. The following shows how the Build target looks.

```
<target name="Build" depends="Initialization, Compilation, Jar">
    <echo message="Ant is building your project."/>
</target>
```

Finally, we'll make the Build target the default target of the build file in the <project> element so that Ant knows to begin with it. You can see how this works in the complete build file in Example 7-2.

Example 7-2. Completed build.xml

```
<?xml version="1.0" encoding = "UTF-8"?>
<project name="AntProject" default="Build" basedir=".">

    <property name="build.compiler"
        value="org.eclipse.jdt.core.JDTCompilerAdapter"/>
    <property name="srcDir" location="src"/>
    <property name="binDir" location="bin"/>
    <property name="jarDir" location="${binDir}/lib"/>
    <property name="jarFile" location="${jarDir}/AntProject.jar"/>

    <target name="Initialization">
        <delete dir="${binDir}"/>
        <delete dir="${jarDir}"/>
        <mkdir dir="${binDir}"/>
        <mkdir dir="${jarDir}"/>
    </target>

    <target name="Compilation" depends="Initialization">
        <javac srcdir="${srcDir}"
            destdir="${binDir}">
        </javac>
    </target>

    <target name="Jar" depends="Initialization, Compilation">
        <jar destfile="${jarFile}" basedir="${binDir}"/>
    </target>

    <target name="Build" depends="Initialization, Compilation, Jar">
        <echo message="Ant is building your project."/>
    </target>

</project>
```

When you enter this XML into *build.xml*, you can see its properties and targets in the Outline view, as shown in Figure 7-3.

The next step is to use this build file to build the application, a process we'll discuss in the following recipe.

 Eclipse can create some Ant build files for you automatically. If your project uses an XML-based manifest file of the type used to build plugins (see Chapter 12), all you have to do is right-click that file and click Create Ant Build File.

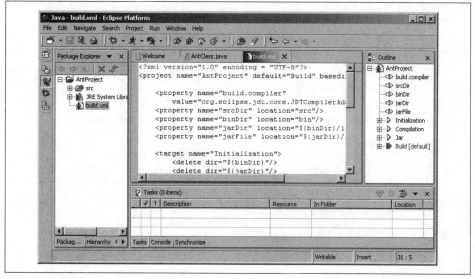

Figure 7-3. build.xml in Eclipse

Eclipse 3.0

In Eclipse 3.0, the Ant editor has more support for Ant. It includes tool tips for properties, targets, and referenced objects (such as paths). You can also now reformat an Ant build file using the Format command (Ctrl-Shift-F) from the Ant editor context menu.

See Also

Recipe 7.2 on building with Ant from Eclipse; Recipe 7.4 on building with a build file other than *build.xml*; *Ant: The Definitive Guide* (O'Reilly); the *Java XP Cookbook* (O'Reilly); Chapter 5 of *Eclipse* (O'Reilly).

7.2   Building an Eclipse Application Using Ant

Problem

You have an Ant build file, and you want to build your application.

Solution

Right-click the build file, click Run Ant, choose the Ant target(s) to execute, and click Run.

Discussion

You created a *build.xml* file for an Eclipse project in the previous recipe; to run that file in the version of Ant that comes with Eclipse, right-click *build.xml*, and click Run Ant. Doing so displays the AntProject *build.xml* dialog shown in Figure 7-4. You can see the Ant targets created there with the default Build target already selected. You can select targets to run independently, but in this case just leave Build selected, and click Run to execute all the targets in the build file and build the project.

> You also can start an Ant build by highlighting the project in the Package Explorer and selecting Run → External Tools → Run As → Ant Build. If you want to select the targets to run, you also can select Run → External Tools → External Tools → Targets, select the targets you want to run, and click Run.

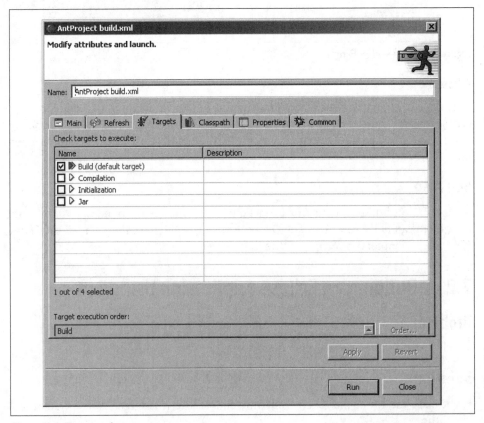

Figure 7-4. Running Ant

The results appear in Eclipse in Figure 7-5. Note the message we made Ant echo to the Console view here, Ant is building your project., followed by the message BUILD SUCCESSFUL.

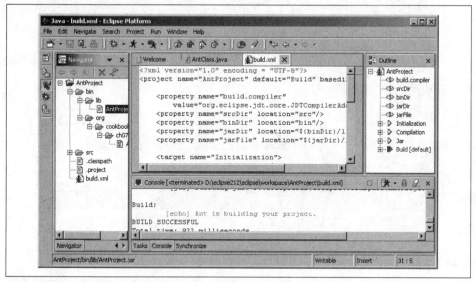

Figure 7-5. A successful Ant build

Here's the text that appears in the Console view as Ant executes each target:

```
Buildfile: D:\eclipse212\eclipse\workspace\AntProject\build.xml

Initialization:
  [delete] Deleting directory D:\eclipse212\eclipse\workspace\AntProject\bin
  [mkdir] Created dir: D:\eclipse212\eclipse\workspace\AntProject\bin
  [mkdir] Created dir: D:\eclipse212\eclipse\workspace\AntProject\bin\lib

Compilation:
  [javac] Compiling 1 source file to D:\eclipse212\eclipse\workspace\AntProject\bin
  [javac] Compiled 22 lines in 381 ms (57.7 lines/s)
  [javac] 1 .class file generated

Jar:
  [jar] Building jar: D:\eclipse212\eclipse\workspace\AntProject\bin\lib
    \AntProject.jar

Build:
  [echo] Ant is building your project.
BUILD SUCCESSFUL
Total time: 922 milliseconds
```

If you switch to the Navigator view, you can see the new *lib* directory containing the *.jar* file, *AntProject.jar*, as shown in Figure 7-6.

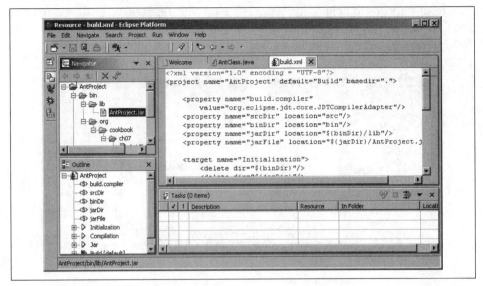

Figure 7-6. The new .jar file

Eclipse 3.0

By default in Eclipse 3.0, Ant executes in the JVM that is running Eclipse. That means you *don't* have to set the `build.compiler` property, as we have in this example, to use the same JVM as Eclipse is using. In Eclipse 3.0, you can set what JVM Ant should use when by right-clicking *build.xml,* clicking the JRE tab, and then clicking Run Ant.

See Also

Chapter 5 of *Eclipse* (O'Reilly).

7.3   Catching Ant Build File Syntax Problems

Problem

You have a problem with a build file, and you would like to track it down.

Solution

The current version of Ant displays syntax errors for Ant scripts only when you try to run them. However, Eclipse 3.0 does catch and display syntax errors as they're created.

This is an Eclipse 3.0-only solution.

Discussion

Eclipse does offer some support for catching syntax errors when you write Ant scripts. However, the Eclipse editor catches syntax errors only if your XML documents are not well formed in the XML sense (e.g., nesting errors, omitting quotes for attribute values, etc.). You can see an example in Figure 7-7, where we've omitted the quote in front of the text jarFile, which is being assigned to an attribute in the <property> element.

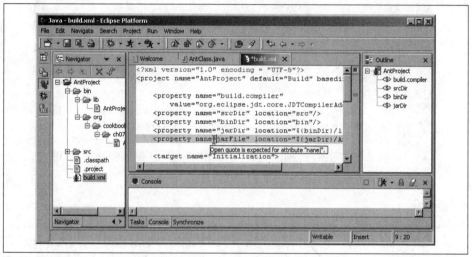

Figure 7-7. An XML error in an Ant script

Note, however, that although the Ant editor indicated that the XML was not well formed, it entirely missed the fact that the <property> element's name attribute is misspelled as nane, as shown in the figure.

On the other hand, when you try to run this script, Ant will realize there's a syntax error, and you'll get the results you see in Figure 7-8, where the syntax error is indicated.

Eclipse will show you the syntax error when you try to run the script, but it's up to you from that point; no Quick Fixes are available. Nor can you interactively debug Ant scripts (yet).

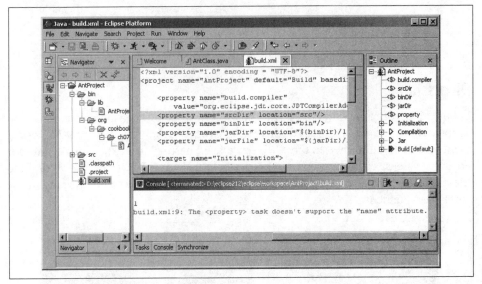

Figure 7-8. An Ant error

Actually, it's worth noting that the Ant editor *does* offer code assist for Ant build files. For example, if you enter < and pause, code assist displays a list of possible Ant build file elements, and you can select one. Code assist also lists possible attributes of Ant elements; just place the cursor inside the opening tag of an Ant element, and press Ctrl-Space.

Eclipse 3.0

Eclipse clearly knows whether syntax errors are in your Ant script (see Figure 7-8), so why can't it tell you as you're writing them? In Eclipse 3.0, it can. Now, Ant-specific errors are shown in the Ant editor with the typical wavy red lines, as shown in Figure 7-9, where the editor is catching the nane syntax error.

This is a considerable improvement. However, Eclipse developers are still awaiting interactive Ant script debugging and wizards that will enable you to create scripts visually. Maybe one day we'll see these items.

See Also

Chapter 5 of *Eclipse* (O'Reilly).

7.4   Using a Different Build File

Problem

You want to build your project using an XML build file not named *build.xml*.

176 | **Chapter 7: Eclipse and Ant**

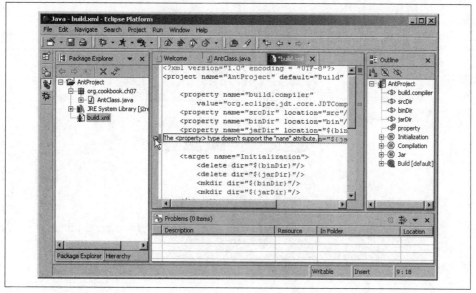

Figure 7-9. Catching a syntax error

Solution

Just select Window → Preferences → Ant and enter the name(s) of your build file(s). Then click OK.

Discussion

If you need to change the name of your build file from *build.xml* to something else, select Window → Preferences → Ant, opening the Ant Preferences page shown in Figure 7-10. Just enter the name of your build file, and click OK. If you want to list multiple names, separate them with commas (use only one of these build files per project, or else Eclipse will be confused, and you'll get an error). Note that this is a global change, so if you change the build filename here, it'll be changed for all projects.

> You also can specify the location of a build file. Right-click *build.xml*, click Run Ant, and click the Main tab in the dialog that opens. You can set the location of the build file you want to use in this dialog, as well as the base directory for the build.

Note that you also can configure Ant a little in the Window → Preferences → Ant dialog, but not much. This dialog allows you to select only the colors of Ant messages in the Console view, which isn't very impressive. More Ant configuration options are available by selecting the nodes under the Ant item; see the following few recipes for more details.

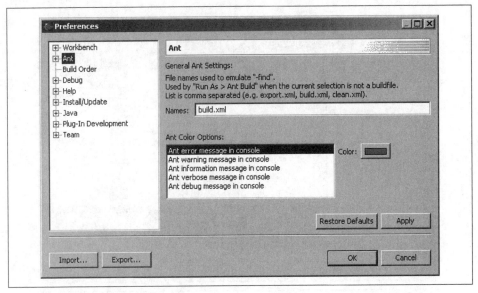

Figure 7-10. Setting the build filename

Eclipse 3.0

Eclipse 3.0 adds a little to the Window → Preferences → Ant dialog, which enables you to handle some additional warnings and errors, such as when the Ant classpath doesn't include *tools.jar*, as shown in Figure 7-11.

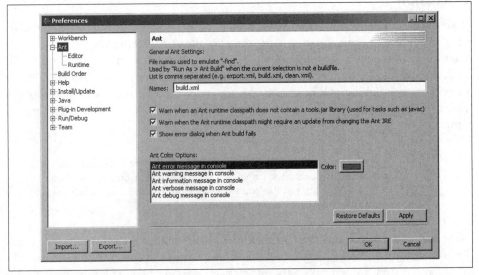

Figure 7-11. The Window → Preferences → Ant dialog in Eclipse 3.0

See Also

Recipe 7.5 on using your own version of Ant and on setting Ant's classpath; Chapter 5 of *Eclipse* (O'Reilly).

7.5 Using Your Own Version of Ant

Problem

A newer version of Ant is out, one more recent than that which comes with Eclipse, and you want to upgrade. Or you just want to use a version of Ant that's different from the one that comes with Eclipse.

Solution

Select Window → Preferences → Ant → Runtime → Classpath, and point to the new Ant *.jar* files.

Discussion

To set the version of Ant (you can get Ant directly from Apache at *http://ant.apache.org*), just select Window → Preferences → Ant → Runtime → Classpath. All you have to do is to point to the new Ant *.jar* files *ant.jar* and *optional.jar*, shown in Figure 7-12.

 The Ant *.jar* files *ant.jar* and *optional.jar* are specific to Ant 1.5.3, which is the version of Ant that comes with Eclipse 2.1.2. Different versions of Ant might have different names for these files, or include more *.jar* files.

Eclipse 3.0

The current build of Eclipse 3.0 comes with Ant 1.6.0 and has classpath entries for 29 Ant *.jar* files—not just the two of earlier versions. Also, by default, now you are warned if you attempt to execute Ant without a *tools.jar* file on the Ant classpath; you are warned when Ant is configured to run in the same JVM as Eclipse (which you might not want in case you're targeting your build at another version of Java); and you are warned when the Xerces packages (which no longer are needed) are included in the Ant classpath.

See Also

Recipe 7.10 on using Ant as an external tool.

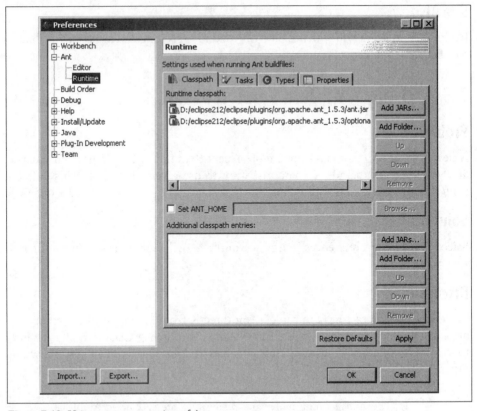

Figure 7-12. Using your own version of Ant

7.6 Setting Types and Global Properties

Problem

You want to create tasks and types for an Ant build, or set global Ant properties.

Solution

Select Window → Preferences → Ant → Runtime, and click the Tasks, Types, or Properties tabs.

Discussion

If you click the Tasks and Types tabs, you can add new Ant tasks and types. Those tasks and types then will be available to build files without having to use Ant <taskdef> or <typedef> elements. Eclipse also enables you to set global Ant properties, across all projects, if you click the Properties tab in this dialog. To add a new global property, just click the Add button in the Properties tab, and enter a name and value for the new property.

7.7   Setting Ant Editor Options

Problem

You want to customize the Ant editor's appearance.

Solution

Select Window → Preferences → Ant → Editor, and choose from the items in that dialog.

Discussion

You have some control over the Ant editor's appearance using the Window → Preferences → Ant → Editor dialog. In Eclipse 2.1.2, the Ant editor is really little more than a simple XML editor, but you can specify such items as the colors used in syntax highlighting, and whether the editor shows an overview ruler or line numbers, as shown in Figure 7-13.

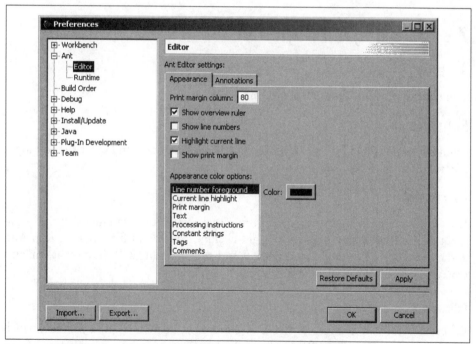

Figure 7-13. Setting options for the Ant editor

For example, turning on line numbers makes the Ant editor display them, as shown in Figure 7-14.

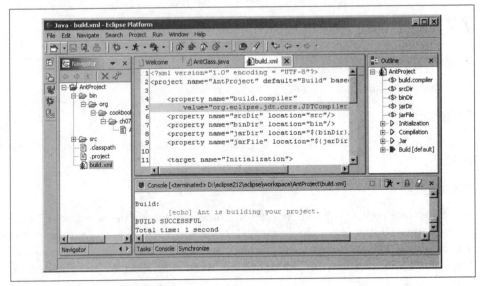

Figure 7-14. Line numbers in the Ant editor

7.8   Setting Ant Arguments

Problem

You need to pass some arguments to Ant.

Solution

Right-click your build file, click Run Ant, click the Main tab, and enter the Ant arguments you want to use. No problem.

Discussion

If you want to pass arguments to Ant, you can enter those arguments in the Arguments box of the dialog opened by right-clicking your build file, clicking Run Ant, and clicking the Main tab. You can see that dialog in Figure 7-15 (note that you also can set the build file location and base directory here).

Eclipse 3.0

Eclipse 3.0 adds another tab to the dialog shown in Figure 7-15, the JRE tab, which enables you to select which JVM to use with Ant.

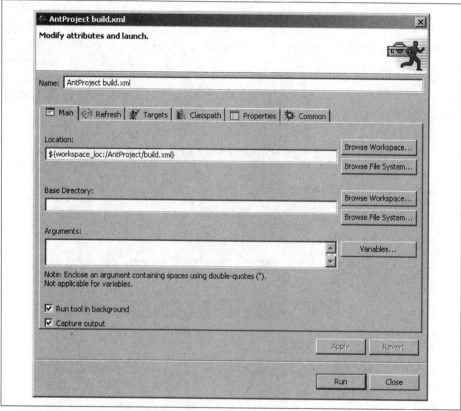

Figure 7-15. The Ant build.xml dialog

7.9   Using the Ant View

Problem

You want an easier way to build Ant targets.

Solution

Open the Ant view by selecting Window → Show View → Other → Ant. When you want to build a target, just double-click it in the Ant view, or right-click it and click Run.

Discussion

The relatively new Ant view can make things a little more convenient, especially if you just want to double-click targets to build them. To open this view, select

Window → Show View → Other → Ant (or Window → Show View → Ant if you've opened this view before).

As shown in Figure 7-16, this view gives you an Ant-based overview of build files. To add a build file to this view, right-click the view, select Add Buildfile, and navigate to the build file you want to display. The view will display the targets in the build file; you can build various Ant targets by double-clicking them, or by right-clicking them and clicking Run.

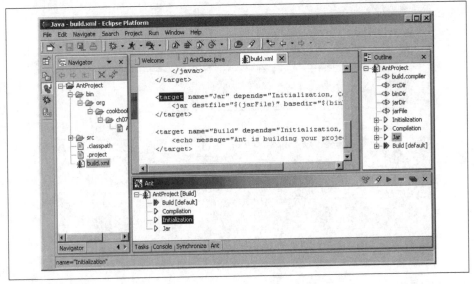

Figure 7-16. The Ant view

Eclipse 3.0

In Eclipse 3.0, you also can add build files to the Ant view via drag-and-drop. Plus, the Ant view now shows a toggle button that allows internal build targets to be filtered out.

7.10 Using Ant as an External Tool

Problem

You want to run Ant as an external tool.

Solution

Select Run → External Tools → External Tools, click Program, click New, and enter the required information to install Ant as an external tool. Then click Run to execute the build file.

Discussion

Eclipse can launch and run external tools as easily as internal ones. You can run Ant as an external tool if you want to: select Run → External Tools → External Tools, click Program, click New, and enter the name you want to give to the external version of Ant. As for the Location field, click Browse File System, and find the correct file for your operating system to run Ant (for example, that's *ant.bat* in the Ant *bin* folder in Windows). In the Working Directory field enter the directory of your build file, and enter any arguments you want to pass to Ant in the Arguments directory. Then click Run to execute your build file and perform the build.

 External tools now can be run in the background, by a separate thread. Just check the "Run tool in background" checkbox in the Run → External Tools → External Tools dialog. Doing so means that you can let an Ant build run or launch an external program and still continue to work in Eclipse.

See Also

Recipe 7.5 on using your own version of Ant.

CHAPTER 8
SWT: Text, Buttons, Lists, and Nonrectangular Windows

8.0 Introduction

IBM created the Standard Widget Toolkit (SWT) as a replacement for the Abstract Windowing Toolkit (AWT) and Swing in Java. The SWT is a fully featured GUI API, and it comes built into Eclipse. There's a lot to cover in this and in the following two chapters. We're going to see some impressive code.

Java has had a long history of supporting GUIs. One of the early efforts was Java applets, and you can see an example in an Eclipse project, *Applet*, in Example 8-1.

Example 8-1. An example applet

```
package org.cookbook.ch08;

import java.applet.Applet;
import java.awt.*;

public class AppletClass extends Applet {

    public void init()
    {
        setBackground(Color.white);
    }

    public void start()
    {
    }

    public void paint(Graphics g)
    {
        g.drawString("Greetings from Applets.", 40, 100);
    }

    public void stop()
    {
    }
```

Example 8-1. An example applet (continued)

```
    public void destroy( )
    {
    }
}
```

Launch this applet from Eclipse by selecting Run → Run As → Java Applet. You can see the results in Figure 8-1.

Figure 8-1. A Java applet launched from Eclipse

As an early GUI offering, Sun wrote the AWT in a few weeks and it was quite a success in its time. The AWT was easy to use and enabled Java developers to create rudimentary GUIs.

The AWT used the underlying operating system's controls. In Windows, for example, you'd see a Windows text box; on the Macintosh, you'd see a Mac text box. In fact, because the control sets in various operating systems differed, Sun only implemented a set of controls common to all platforms. And the AWT ended up being very limited for developers' needs.

To meet those growing needs, Sun created Swing, a GUI API that includes support for nonnative implementations of specialized controls such as trees and tables. You can see a Swing example in Example 8-2, the *SwingApp* Eclipse project, which you can find at this book's O'Reilly site in the Examples section.

Example 8-2. A Swing application

```
package org.cookbook.ch08;

import javax.swing.*;
import java.awt.*;
import java.awt.event.*;

public class SwingClass extends JFrame {

    Panel panel;
```

Example 8-2. A Swing application (continued)

```java
    public SwingClass()
    {
        super("Swing Example");

        Container contentPane = getContentPane();
        panel = new Panel();
        contentPane.add(p);
    }

    public static void main(String args[])
    {
        final JFrame frame = new SwingClass();

        frame.setDefaultCloseOperation(DISPOSE_ON_CLOSE);
        frame.setBounds(100, 100, 280, 250);
        frame.setVisible(true);

        frame.addWindowListener(new WindowAdapter() {
            public void windowClosing(WindowEvent e) {
                System.exit(0);
            }
        });
    }
}

class Panel extends JPanel
{
    Panel()
    {
        setBackground(Color.white);
    }

    public void paintComponent (Graphics g)
    {
        super.paintComponent(g);
        g.drawString("Greetings from Swing", 70, 100);
    }
}
```

Launching a Swing application from Eclipse is no different from launching the applications we've already run. Just select Run → Run As → Java Application; you can see the results in Figure 8-2.

Swing gives you a lot of power, but the results are Java-specific, at least visually. Sun tried adding an operating system-specific "look-and-feel" as an option, but in the end, Sun couldn't keep up with the rapid changes to all the operating systems. Also, Swing response times were slow compared to native implementations.

SWT comes to the rescue in many ways here. It supports a set of widgets that use native controls when such controls are available for use. If such controls aren't available, SWT uses its own widgets. SWT is a bold move on IBM's part; designed as it is

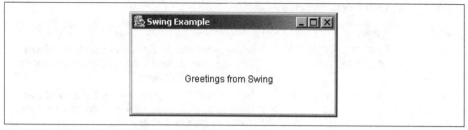

Figure 8-2. A Swing application launched from Eclipse

to utterly replace AWT and Swing. And as you'd expect, SWT provides depth and a rich set of features.

8.1   Working with SWT Widgets

Problem

You want to work with SWT, but you need to know what widgets are available to work with.

Solution

See Table 8-1, which lists all the SWT widgets, as well as their styles and events.

Discussion

As a starting point for our work on SWT, Table 8-1 provides a reference for all the SWT widgets.

Table 8-1. The SWT widgets

Widget	Styles	Events
Button	BORDER, CHECK, PUSH, RADIO, TOGGLE, FLAT, LEFT, RIGHT, CENTER, ARROW (with UP, DOWN)	Dispose, FocusIn, FocusOut, Help, KeyDown, KeyUp, MouseDouble-Click, MouseDown, MouseEnter, MouseExit, MouseHover, MouseUp, MouseMove, Move, Paint, Resize, Selection
Canvas	BORDER, H_SCROLL, V_SCROLL, NO_ BACKGROUND, NO_FOCUS, NO_MERGE_PAINTS, NO_REDRAW_RESIZE, NO_RADIO_GROUP	Dispose, FocusIn, FocusOut, Help, KeyDown, KeyUp, MouseDouble-Click, MouseDown, MouseEnter, MouseExit, MouseHover, MouseUp, MouseMove, Move, Paint, Resize
Caret		Dispose
Combo	BORDER, DROP_DOWN, READ_ONLY, SIMPLE	Dispose, FocusIn, FocusOut, Help, KeyDown, KeyUp, MouseDouble-Click, MouseDown, MouseEnter, MouseExit, MouseHover, MouseUp, MouseMove, Move, Paint, Resize, DefaultSelection, Modify, Selection

Table 8-1. The SWT widgets (continued)

Widget	Styles	Events
Composite	BORDER, H_SCROLL, V_SCROLL	Dispose, FocusIn, FocusOut, Help, KeyDown, KeyUp, MouseDouble-Click, MouseDown, MouseEnter, MouseExit, MouseHover, MouseUp, MouseMove, Move, Paint, Resize
CoolBar	BORDER	Dispose, FocusIn, FocusOut, Help, KeyDown, KeyUp, MouseDouble-Click, MouseDown, MouseEnter, MouseExit, MouseHover, MouseUp, MouseMove, Move, Paint, Resize
CoolItem	DROP_DOWN	Dispose
Group	BORDER, SHADOW_ETCHED_IN, SHADOW_ETCHED_OUT, SHADOW_IN, SHADOW_OUT, SHADOW_NONE	Dispose, FocusIn, FocusOut, Help, KeyDown, KeyUp, MouseDouble-Click, MouseDown, MouseEnter, MouseExit, MouseHover, MouseUp, MouseMove, Move, Paint, Resize
Label	BORDER, CENTER, LEFT, RIGHT, WRAP, SEPARATOR (with HORIZONTAL, SHADOW_IN, SHADOW_OUT, SHADOW_NONE, VERTICAL)	Dispose, FocusIn, FocusOut, Help, KeyDown, KeyUp, MouseDouble-Click, MouseDown, MouseEnter, MouseExit, MouseHover, MouseUp, MouseMove, Move, Paint, Resize
List	BORDER, H_SCROLL, V_SCROLL, SINGLE, MULTI	Dispose, FocusIn, FocusOut, Help, KeyDown, KeyUp, MouseDouble-Click, MouseDown, MouseEnter, MouseExit, MouseHover, MouseUp, MouseMove, Move, Paint, Resize, Selection, DefaultSelection
Menu	BAR, DROP_DOWN, NO_RADIO_GROUP, POP_UP	Dispose, Help, Hide, Show
MenuItem	CHECK, CASCADE, PUSH, RADIO, SEPARATOR	Dispose, Arm, Help, Selection
ProgressBar	BORDER, INDETERMINATE, SMOOTH, HORIZONTAL, VERTICAL	Dispose, FocusIn, FocusOut, Help, KeyDown, KeyUp, MouseDouble-Click, MouseDown, MouseEnter, MouseExit, MouseHover, MouseUp, MouseMove, Move, Paint, Resize
Sash	BORDER, HORIZONTAL, VERTICAL	Dispose, FocusIn, FocusOut, Help, KeyDown, KeyUp, MouseDouble-Click, MouseDown, MouseEnter, MouseExit, MouseHover, MouseUp, MouseMove, Move, Paint, Resize, Selection
Scale	BORDER, HORIZONTAL, VERTICAL	Dispose, FocusIn, FocusOut, Help, KeyDown, KeyUp, MouseDouble-Click, MouseDown, MouseEnter, MouseExit, MouseHover, MouseUp, MouseMove, Move, Paint, Resize, Selection
ScrollBar	HORIZONTAL, VERTICAL	Dispose, Selection
Shell	BORDER, H_SCROLL, V_SCROLL, CLOSE, MIN, MAX, NO_TRIM, RESIZE, TITLE (see also SHELL_TRIM, DIALOG_TRIM)	Dispose, FocusIn, FocusOut, Help, KeyDown, KeyUp, MouseDouble-Click, MouseDown, MouseEnter, MouseExit, MouseHover, MouseUp, MouseMove, Move, Paint, Resize, Activate, Close, Deactivate, Deiconify, Iconify

Table 8-1. The SWT widgets (continued)

Widget	Styles	Events
Slider	BORDER, HORIZONTAL, VERTICAL	Dispose, FocusIn, FocusOut, Help, KeyDown, KeyUp, MouseDouble-Click, MouseDown, MouseEnter, MouseExit, MouseHover, MouseUp, MouseMove, Move, Paint, Resize, Selection
TabFolder	BORDER	Dispose, FocusIn, FocusOut, Help, KeyDown, KeyUp, MouseDouble-Click, MouseDown, MouseEnter, MouseExit, MouseHover, MouseUp, MouseMove, Move, Paint, Resize, Selection
TabItem		Dispose
Table	BORDER, H_SCROLL, V_SCROLL, SINGLE, MULTI, CHECK, FULL_SELECTION, HIDE_SELECTION	Dispose, FocusIn, FocusOut, Help, KeyDown, KeyUp, MouseDouble-Click, MouseDown, MouseEnter, MouseExit, MouseHover, MouseUp, MouseMove, Move, Paint, Resize, Selection, DefaultSelection
TableColumn	LEFT, RIGHT, CENTER	Dispose, Move, Resize, Selection
TableItem		Dispose
Text	BORDER, SINGLE, READ_ONLY, LEFT, CENTER, RIGHT, WRAP, MULTI (with H_SCROLL, V_SCROLL)	Dispose, FocusIn, FocusOut, Help, KeyDown, KeyUp, MouseDouble-Click, MouseDown, MouseEnter, MouseExit, MouseHover, MouseUp, MouseMove, Move, Paint, Resize, DefaultSelection, Modify, Verify
ToolBar	BORDER, FLAT, WRAP, RIGHT, SHADOW_OUT, HORIZONTAL, VERTICAL	Dispose, FocusIn, FocusOut, Help, KeyDown, KeyUp, MouseDouble-Click, MouseDown, MouseEnter, MouseExit, MouseHover, MouseUp, MouseMove, Move, Paint, Resize,
ToolItem	PUSH, CHECK, RADIO, SEPARATOR, DROP_DOWN	Dispose, Selection
Tracker	LEFT, RIGHT, UP, DOWN, RESIZE	Dispose, Move, Resize
Tree	BORDER, H_SCROLL, V_SCROLL, SINGLE, MULTI, CHECK	Dispose, FocusIn, FocusOut, Help, KeyDown, KeyUp, MouseDouble-Click, MouseDown, MouseEnter, MouseExit, MouseHover, MouseUp, MouseMove, Move, Paint, Resize, Selection, DefaultSelection, Collapse, Expand
TreeItem		Dispose

Eclipse 3.0

Eclipse 3.0 also adds a browser widget to the list of SWT widgets.

See Also

Chapter 7 of *Eclipse* (O'Reilly).

8.2   Creating an SWT Application

Problem

You want to create a new SWT application.

Solution

Import the SWT classes, create an SWT shell, and add the widgets you want to use to that shell. Then use the shell's open method to display it.

Discussion

In this example, we're going to create an SWT window and display text in it. To follow along, create a new Java Eclipse project named *FirstSWTApp*. Add a class, FirstSWTClass, in the org.cookbook.ch08 class. We'll need to import the SWT classes:

```
package org.cookbook.ch08;

import org.eclipse.swt.widgets.*;
import org.eclipse.swt.*;
    .
    .
    .
```

In the main method, you create a new SWT Display object, and you use that object to create a Shell object that corresponds to an SWT window. Here are some of the most popular Shell methods:

void addShellListener(ShellListener listener)
: Adds the listener to the collection of listeners who will be notified when operations are performed on the shell

void close( )
: Closes the shell

void dispose( )
: Disposes of the operating system resources associated with the shell

Rectangle getClientArea( )
: Returns the shell's client area

boolean isDisposed( )
: Returns true if the shell has been disposed, false otherwise

void open( )
: Opens the shell on the screen

void setLocation(int x, int y)
: Sets the shell's location (measurements are in pixels)

void setText(String s)
: Sets the shell's titlebar text

void setSize(int width, int height)
: Sets the shell's size

We'll customize the shell by setting its title and size using the setText and setSize methods:

```
package org.cookbook.ch08;

import org.eclipse.swt.widgets.*;
import org.eclipse.swt.*;

public class FirstSWTClass {

    public static void main(String [] args) {
        Display display = new Display( );
        Shell shell = new Shell(display);
        shell.setText("First SWT Application");
        shell.setSize(250, 250);
           .
           .
           .
```

To display text, we'll create an SWT Label object, displaying in it the text Greetings from SWT. Label widgets are designed simply to display text, and you can use the setText and getText methods to work with that text. Like other widgets, you can use the setBounds method to set the bounds of a label widget; in this case, we'll make the label correspond to the shell's entire client area:

```
package org.cookbook.ch08;

import org.eclipse.swt.widgets.*;
import org.eclipse.swt.*;

public class FirstSWTClass {

    public static void main(String [] args) {
        Display display = new Display( );
        Shell shell = new Shell(display);
        shell.setText("First SWT Application");
        shell.setSize(250, 250);
        Label label = new Label(shell, SWT.CENTER);
        label.setText("Greetings from SWT");
        label.setBounds(shell.getClientArea( ));
           .
           .
           .
```

To open the window, you call the Shell object's open method. To manage the window, you use the Shell object's isDisposed method to determine when it's been closed. If the window is still open, you call the application's message pump with the Display object's readAndDispatch method. If the shell is closed, you dispose of it with its dispose method, as shown in Example 8-3.

When you're done with a resource in SWT, you should deallocate it with the Widget.dispose method.

Example 8-3. FirstSWTClass.java

```
package org.cookbook.ch08;

import org.eclipse.swt.widgets.*;
import org.eclipse.swt.*;

public class FirstSWTClass {

    public static void main(String [] args) {
        Display display = new Display();
        Shell shell = new Shell(display);
        shell.setText("First SWT Application");
        shell.setSize(250, 250);
        Label label = new Label(shell, SWT.CENTER);
        label.setText("Greetings from SWT");
        label.setBounds(shell.getClientArea());
        shell.open();
        while(!shell.isDisposed()) {
            if(!display.readAndDispatch()) display.sleep();
        }
        display.dispose();
    }
}
```

That completes the code, but if you enter it as it stands, you'll see a lot of squiggly red lines because we haven't added the SWT *.jar* file to the build path. To give Eclipse access to the SWT classes it needs, see the next recipe.

See Also

Recipe 8.3 on adding SWT JAR files to the build path; Recipe 8.4 on launching an SWT application; Chapter 7 of *Eclipse* (O'Reilly).

8.3   Adding the Required SWT JAR Files to the Build Path

Problem

To run an SWT application, Eclipse needs to know where to find the SWT classes.

Solution

Add *swt.jar* to the build path.

Discussion

To make an SWT application such as the one whose code we created in the previous recipe work, you need to satisfy the imports:

```
package org.cookbook.ch08;

import org.eclipse.swt.widgets.*;
import org.eclipse.swt.*;
    .
    .
    .
```

All you have to do is to include *swt.jar* in your build path. As you know, SWT is operating system-dependent, so a different *swt.jar* will exist for different operating systems.

To add *swt.jar* to a project, select the project in the Package Explorer, right-click it, and click Properties. In the Properties dialog, click Java Build Path, and click the Add External JARs button. Then navigate to *swt.jar*, which you'll find in one of the following directories, depending on your operating system (*HOMEDIR* is the directory in which you installed Eclipse):

Win32
  HOMEDIR\eclipse\plugins\org.eclipse.swt.win32_2.1.2\ws\win32\swt.jar

Linux GTK
  HOMEDIR/eclipse/plugins/org.eclipse.swt.gtk_2.1.2/ws/gtk/swt.jar

Linux Motif
  HOMEDIR/eclipse/plugins/org.eclipse.swt.motif_2.1.2/ws/motif/swt.jar

Solaris Motif
  HOMEDIR/eclipse/plugins/org.eclipse.swt.motif_2.1.2/ws/solaris/sparc/swt.jar

AIX Motif
  HOMEDIR/eclipse/plugins/org.eclipse.swt.motif_2.1.2/ws/aix/ppc/swt.jar

HPUX Motif
  HOMEDIR/eclipse/plugins/org.eclipse.swt.motif_2.1.2/ws/hpux/PA_RISC/swt.jar

Photon QNX
  HOMEDIR/eclipse/plugins/org.eclipse.swt.photon_2.1.2/ws/photon/swt.jar

Mac OS X
  HOMEDIR/eclipse/plugins/org.eclipse.swt.carbon_2.1.2/ws/carbon/swt.jar

You might have to update these paths for your version of Eclipse, such as changing 2.1.2 to 2.1.3. The current milestone build of Eclipse 3.0 uses 3.0.0.

Browse to *swt.jar*, click Open, and then click OK.

Some operating systems, such as Linux GTK, need more than one *.jar* file; in Linux GTK you use *swt.jar* and *swt-pi.jar*. You'll find all the required *.jar* files in the same folder.

See Also

Recipe 8.2 on creating an SWT application; Recipe 8.4 on launching an SWT application.

8.4   Launching an SWT Application

Problem

You want to launch your SWT application.

Solution

You need to tell the JVM where to find the Java Native Interface (JNI) code support for SWT when launching an SWT application. Here's the argument you supply when you run an SWT application (as before, *HOMEDIR* is the directory in which you installed Eclipse, and you should update these paths to match your version of Eclipse. For example, 2.1.2 should become 2.1.3 or some other version number):

Win32
```
-Djava.library.path=HOMEDIR\eclipse\plugins\org.eclipse.swt.win32_2.1.2\
os\win32\x86
```

Linux GTK
```
-Djava.library.path=HOMEDIR/eclipse/plugins/org.eclipse.swt.gtk_2.1.2/os/
linux/x86
```

Linux Motif
```
-Djava.library.path=HOMEDIR/eclipse/plugins/org.eclipse.swt.motif_2.1.2/
os/linux/x86
```

Solaris Motif
```
-Djava.library.path=HOMEDIR/eclipse/plugins/org.eclipse.swt.motif_2.1.2/
os/solaris/sparc
```

AIX Motif
```
-Djava.library.path=HOMEDIR/eclipse/plugins/org.eclipse.swt.motif_2.1.2/
os/aix/ppc
```

HPUX Motif
```
-Djava.library.path=HOMEDIR/eclipse/plugins/org.eclipse.swt.motif_2.1.2/
os/hpux/PA_RISC
```

Photon QNX
```
-Djava.library.path=HOMEDIR/eclipse/plugins/org.eclipse.swt.photon_2.1.2/
os/qnx/x86
```

Mac OS X
```
-Djava.library.path=HOMEDIR/eclipse/plugins/org.eclipse.swt.carbon_2.1.2/
os/macosx/ppc
```

Discussion

Even after you've compiled as SWT application, you still need to complete another step before you're ready to roll. You have to tell the JVM where to find the native code support for SWT with an argument to the JVM.

To launch the SWT application we've been developing in the previous two recipes, select the class you want to run, FirstSWTClass, in the Package Explorer, and select Run → Run to set up a launch configuration.

In the Launch Configurations dialog, select Java Application, and click the New button. The Name, Project, and Main class boxes should be filled in automatically; if they aren't, fill them in. Then click the Arguments tab. In the "VM arguments" box, enter the JVM argument as shown earlier (see Figure 8-3).

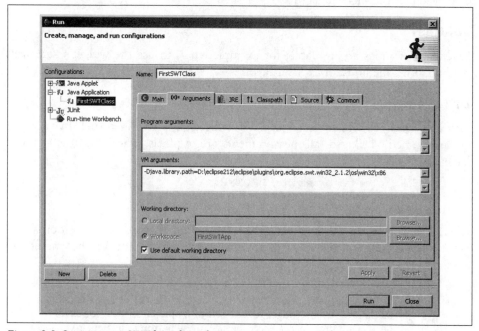

Figure 8-3. Setting up an SWT launch configuration

Then click the Apply button, followed by the Run button. You should see this new example at work, as shown in Figure 8-4.

Congratulations—you're an SWT developer.

See Also

Recipe 8.2 on creating an SWT application; Recipe 8.3 on setting Eclipse's build path to use SWT; Chapter 7 of *Eclipse* (O'Reilly).

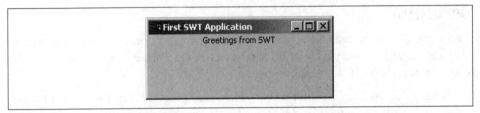

Figure 8-4. Running an SWT application

8.5 Positioning Widgets and Using Layouts

Problem

You need to position a widget in an SWT shell.

Solution

Several possibilities are available; for example, you can use the widget's setBounds method, other methods, or an SWT layout.

Discussion

You can specify where to place an SWT widget anywhere in a shell by using its setBounds method like so (all measurements are in pixels, where (0, 0) is at upper left):

```
Label label = new Label(composite, SWT.PUSH);
label.setText("Label 0");
label.setBounds(100, 100, 150, 120);
```

Alternatively, you can use the setLocation(int x, int y) method to position a widget's upper left corner, followed by the setSize(int width, int height) method to set the widget's size.

 Besides using the setSize method, you can use the widget's pack( ) method to let the widget resize itself to its preferred size (for example, for a button, pack( ) sets the size of the button to just enclose its caption).

You also can use an SWT layout to specify how to arrange your widgets. Four layout classes are built into SWT:

FillLayout
: Fills a shell's client area

FormLayout
: Arranges widgets relative to a parent composite or to another widget

GridLayout

> Arranges widgets in a grid

RowLayout

> Arranges widgets in either horizontal rows or vertical columns

Here's an example using the grid layout. In this case, we're going to create a grid of four columns, filling those columns with SWT labels. We start by creating a new GridLayout object, setting the number of columns in the layout to 4, and installing that layout in the shell with the setLayout method:

```
import org.eclipse.swt.*;
import org.eclipse.swt.layout.*;
import org.eclipse.swt.widgets.*;

public class LayoutClass {

    public static void main (String [] args) {
        Display display = new Display ();
        final Shell shell = new Shell (display);
        shell.setSize(200, 200);
        shell.setText("Layout Example");
        GridLayout gridLayout = new GridLayout();
        gridLayout.numColumns = 4;
        shell.setLayout(gridLayout);
        .
        .
        .
```

All you need to do now is to create a set of labels and add them to the layout, where they'll be arranged in a grid automatically, as shown in Example 8-4.

Example 8-4. Using SWT layouts

```
package org.cookbook.ch08;

import org.eclipse.swt.*;
import org.eclipse.swt.layout.*;
import org.eclipse.swt.widgets.*;

public class LayoutClass {

    public static void main (String [] args) {
        Display display = new Display ();
        final Shell shell = new Shell (display);
        shell.setSize(200, 200);
        shell.setText("Layout Example");
        GridLayout gridLayout = new GridLayout();
        gridLayout.numColumns = 4;
        shell.setLayout(gridLayout);

        for (int loopIndex = 0; loopIndex < 28; loopIndex++) {
            Label label = new Label(shell, SWT.SHADOW_NONE);
```

Example 8-4. Using SWT layouts (continued)

```
            label.setText("Label " + loopIndex);
        }

        shell.open ();
        while (!shell.isDisposed()) {
            if (!display.readAndDispatch()) display.sleep();
        }
        display.dispose ();
    }
}
```

You can see the results in Figure 8-5, showing the labels in a grid layout.

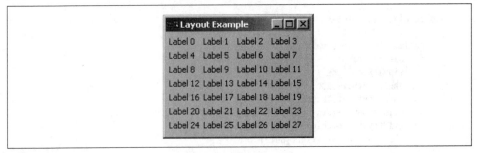

Figure 8-5. Labels in a grid layout

See Also

Recipe 8.6 on creating button and text widgets; Recipe 8.9 on creating composite widgets; Recipe 8.8 on creating list widgets; Chapter 7 of *Eclipse* (O'Reilly).

8.6   Creating Button and Text Widgets

Problem

You need to use buttons to interact with the user and to display text in your application.

Solution

Use SWT button and text widgets and use SWT listeners to catch button events.

Discussion

This example adds SWT button widgets to a shell and catches click events, displaying a message in a text widget when the button is clicked. We'll start by creating a button widget in a new project, *ButtonApp*. Here's a selection of some of the most popular button widget methods:

```
void addSelectionListener(SelectionListener listener)
```
Adds the listener to the collection of listeners who will be notified when the button is selected

```
String getText( )
```
Returns the button's text

```
void setBounds(int x, int y, int width, int height)
```
Sets the button's size and location to the area specified by the arguments

```
void setImage(Image image)
```
Sets the button's image

```
void setText(String string)
```
Sets the button's text

Creating button widgets is easy enough; just use the Button class's constructor, position the button with setBounds or a layout, and set the caption in the button with the setText method:

```
package org.cookbook.ch08;

import org.eclipse.swt.widgets.*;
import org.eclipse.swt.SWT;
import org.eclipse.swt.events.*;

public class ButtonClass {

    public static void main(String [] args) {
        Display display = new Display( );
        Shell shell = new Shell(display);
        shell.setSize(200, 200);
        shell.setText("Button Example");

        final Button button = new Button(shell, SWT.PUSH);
        button.setBounds(40, 50, 50, 20);
        button.setText("Click Me");
            .
            .
            .
```

Creating a text widget is similarly easy. Here's a selection of popular text widget methods:

```
void copy( )
```
Copies the selected text

```
void cut( )
```
Cuts the selected text

```
String getSelectionText( )
```
Gets the selected text

```
String getText( )
```
Gets the widget's text

```
void paste( )
    Pastes text from the clipboard
void setBounds(int x, int y, int width, int height)
    Sets the text widget's size and location to the area specified by the arguments
void setFont(Font font)
    Sets the font
void setText(String string)
    Sets the contents of the text widget
```

In this example, we'll give this text widget a border and add it to our shell:

```java
public class ButtonClass {

    public static void main(String [] args) {
        Display display = new Display( );
        Shell shell = new Shell(display);
        shell.setSize(200, 200);
        shell.setText("Button Example");

        final Button button = new Button(shell, SWT.PUSH);
        button.setBounds(40, 50, 50, 20);
        button.setText("Click Me");

        final Text text = new Text(shell, SWT.BORDER);
        text.setBounds(100, 50, 70, 20);
            .
            .
            .
```

That installs the button and text widgets; the next step is to handle button events, which we'll discuss in the next recipe.

See Also

Recipe 8.1 on using widgets in SWT; Recipe 8.7 on handling events from widgets; Chapter 7 of *Eclipse* (O'Reilly).

8.7   Handling SWT Widget Events

Problem

You need to catch widget events such as button clicks and respond to them in code.

Solution

Use an SWT listener. In SWT, listeners are much like listeners in AWT. Here are some of the most popular SWT listeners:

ControlListener
    Handles moving and resizing events

FocusListener
    Handles getting and losing focus events

KeyListener
    Handles keystroke events

MouseListener, MouseMoveListener, MouseTrackListener
    Handles mouse events

SelectionListener
    Handles widget selection events (including button clicks)

Discussion

To see how this works, we'll continue the example begun in the previous recipe where we want text to appear in a text widget when you click a button. You can catch button clicks by adding a SelectionListener object to the button with the addSelectionListener method. To implement the SelectionListener interface, you have to implement two methods: widgetSelected, which occurs when a selection occurs in a widget, and widgetDefaultSelected, which occurs when a default selection is made in a widget.

In this case, we're going to display the text No problem in the text widget using a SelectionListener object in an anonymous inner class:

```
public class ButtonClass {

    public static void main(String [] args) {
        Display display = new Display();
        Shell shell = new Shell(display);
        shell.setSize(200, 200);
        shell.setText("Button Example");

        final Button button = new Button(shell, SWT.PUSH);
        button.setBounds(40, 50, 50, 20);
        button.setText("Click Me");

        final Text text = new Text(shell, SWT.BORDER);
        text.setBounds(100, 50, 70, 20);

        button.addSelectionListener(new SelectionListener()
        {
            public void widgetSelected(SelectionEvent event)
            {
                text.setText("No problem");
            }

            public void widgetDefaultSelected(SelectionEvent event)
            {
                text.setText("No worries!");
```

```
        }
    });
    .
    .
    .
```

 Adapter classes are available for every listener class, and you can extend your listener class from an adapter class instead of implementing the listener's interface. Doing so saves you the trouble of implementing all the listener class's methods. For example, the adapter class for the SelectionListener interface is named SelectionAdapter. For an example showing how this works, see Recipe 9.8.

All you need to complete this example is the code to close the shell when needed (see Example 8-5).

Example 8-5. Using SWT buttons and text widgets

```java
package org.cookbook.ch08;

import org.eclipse.swt.widgets.*;
import org.eclipse.swt.SWT;
import org.eclipse.swt.events.*;

public class ButtonClass {

    public static void main(String [] args) {
        Display display = new Display( );
        Shell shell = new Shell(display);
        shell.setSize(200, 200);
        shell.setText("Button Example");

        final Button button = new Button(shell, SWT.PUSH);
        button.setBounds(40, 50, 50, 20);
        button.setText("Click Me");

        final Text text = new Text(shell, SWT.BORDER);
        text.setBounds(100, 50, 70, 20);

        button.addSelectionListener(new SelectionListener( )
        {

            public void widgetSelected(SelectionEvent event)
            {
                text.setText("No problem");
            }

            public void widgetDefaultSelected(SelectionEvent event)
            {
                text.setText("No worries!");
            }
        });
```

Example 8-5. Using SWT buttons and text widgets (continued)

```
        shell.open();
        while(!shell.isDisposed()) {
           if(!display.readAndDispatch()) display.sleep();
        }
        display.dispose();
    }
}
```

The results appear in Figure 8-6; when you click the button, the text message No problem appears in the text widget.

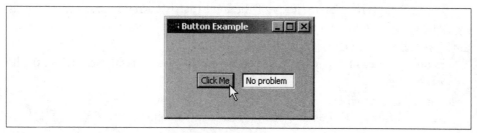

Figure 8-6. Using buttons and text widgets

See Also

Recipe 8.1 on using widgets in SWT; Recipe 8.6 on creating button and text widgets.

8.8   Creating List Widgets

Problem

You need to display multiple items from which the user can select.

Solution

Use a list widget, which can display lists of selectable items. Here's a selection of the most popular list widget methods:

void add(String string)
  Adds the argument to the end of the list widget's list

void add(String string, int index)
  Adds the argument to the list widget's list at the given zero-relative index

void addSelectionListener(SelectionListener listener)
  Adds the listener to the collection of listeners who are notified when the list widget's selection changes

String getItem(int index)
  Returns the item at the given zero-relative index in the list widget

```
int getItemCount( )
    Returns the number of items contained in the list widget
String[] getItems( )
    Returns an array of Strings that are the items in the list widget
String[] getSelection( )
    Returns an array of Strings that are currently selected in the list widget
int getSelectionCount( )
    Returns the number of selected items contained in the list widget
int getSelectionIndex( )
    Returns the zero-relative index of the item that is currently selected in the list
    widget, or -1 if no item is selected
int[] getSelectionIndices( )
    Returns the zero-relative indices of the items that are currently selected in the list
    widget
void setItems(String[] items)
    Sets the list widget's items to be the given array of items
void setSelection(int index)
    Selects the item at the given zero-relative index in the list widget
void setSelection(int[] indices)
    Selects the items at the given zero-relative indices in the list widget
void setSelection(String[] items)
    Sets the list widget's selection to be the given array of items
```

Discussion

As an example, we'll add a multiple-selection list widget to a shell and get the user's
selections with the getSelectionIndices method; this example is named *ListApp* and
can be found at this book's site. Here's how to add a list widget to a shell:

```java
import org.eclipse.swt.*;
import org.eclipse.swt.widgets.*;
import org.eclipse.swt.events.*;

public class ListClass {

    public static void main (String [] args) {
        Display display = new Display ();
        Shell shell = new Shell (display);
        shell.setText("List Example");
        shell.setSize(300, 200);

        final List list = new List (shell, SWT.BORDER | SWT.MULTI | SWT.V_SCROLL);
        list.setBounds(40, 20, 220, 100);
        for (int loopIndex = 0; loopIndex < 9; loopIndex++){
            list.add("Item Number " + loopIndex);
```

```
    }
    .
    .
    .
```

You can add a selection listener to the list widget, as shown in Example 8-6. In this
example, we'll use the list widget's getSelectionIndices method to get an int array
of the selected indices in the list widget. We'll display those selections in a text widget, as you see in the code.

Example 8-6. Using list widgets

```
package org.cookbook.ch08;

import org.eclipse.swt.*;
import org.eclipse.swt.widgets.*;
import org.eclipse.swt.events.*;

public class ListClass {

    public static void main (String [] args) {
        Display display = new Display ();
        Shell shell = new Shell (display);
        shell.setText("List Example");
        shell.setSize(300, 200);

        final List list = new List (shell, SWT.BORDER | SWT.MULTI | SWT.V_SCROLL);
        list.setBounds(40, 20, 220, 100);
        for (int loopIndex = 0; loopIndex < 9; loopIndex++){
            list.add("Item Number " + loopIndex);
        }

        final Text text = new Text(shell, SWT.BORDER);
        text.setBounds(60, 130, 160, 25);

        list.addSelectionListener(new SelectionListener( )
        {
            public void widgetSelected(SelectionEvent event)
            {
                int [] selectedItems = list.getSelectionIndices ();
                String outString = "";
                for (int loopIndex = 0; loopIndex < selectedItems.length;
                        loopIndex++) outString += selectedItems[loopIndex] + " ";
                text.setText("Selected Items: " + outString);
            }

            public void widgetDefaultSelected(SelectionEvent event)
            {
             int [] selectedItems = list.getSelectionIndices ();
             String outString = "";
             for (int loopIndex = 0; loopIndex < selectedItems.length; loopIndex++)
                    outString += selectedItems[loopIndex] + " ";
             System.out.println ("Selected Items: " + outString);
```

Example 8-6. Using list widgets (continued)

```
        }
    });

    shell.open ();
    while (!shell.isDisposed ()) {
        if (!display.readAndDispatch ()) display.sleep ();
    }
    display.dispose ();
  }
}
```

The results appear in Figure 8-7, where the code is displaying the selections the user has made.

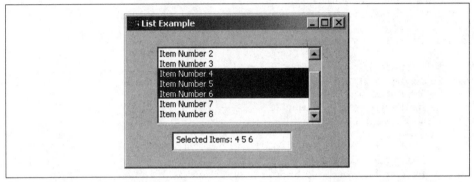

Figure 8-7. Using a list widget

8.9   Creating Composite Widgets

Problem

To create your own custom widget, you need to create a widget that contains other widgets.

Solution

Use a container widget such as a composite widget to create an object from the Composite class. Then add widgets to the composite object as you would to a Shell object.

Discussion

A number of widgets, such as composite widgets, are designed to hold other widgets, which enables you to build composite widgets. Example 8-7 displays a composite widget (*CompositeApp* at this book's site). In this case, we'll display the same labels that we displayed using a grid layout, but in a shell in a composite widget instead. First, we create a composite widget and install a grid layout in it:

```
final Composite composite = new Composite(shell, SWT.NONE);
GridLayout gridLayout = new GridLayout();
gridLayout.numColumns = 4;
composite.setLayout(gridLayout);
```

Now treat the composite widget as a container, just like a shell, and add the label widgets to it, as shown in Example 8-7.

Example 8-7. Using composite widgets

```
package org.cookbook.ch08;

import org.eclipse.swt.*;
import org.eclipse.swt.layout.*;
import org.eclipse.swt.widgets.*;

public class CompositeClass {

    public static void main (String [] args) {
        Display display = new Display ();
        final Shell shell = new Shell (display);
        shell.setSize(300, 300);
        shell.setLayout(new RowLayout());

        shell.setText("Composite Example");

        final Composite composite = new Composite(shell, SWT.NONE);
        GridLayout gridLayout = new GridLayout();
        gridLayout.numColumns = 4;
        composite.setLayout(gridLayout);

        for (int loopIndex = 0; loopIndex < 28; loopIndex++) {
            Label label = new Label(composite, SWT.SHADOW_NONE);
            label.setText("Label " + loopIndex);
        }

        shell.open ();
        while (!shell.isDisposed()) {
            if (!display.readAndDispatch()) display.sleep();
        }
        display.dispose ();
    }
}
```

The composite widget holding the labels appears in the shell, as shown in Figure 8-8.

Besides composite widgets, other widgets that can contain widgets include canvases (designed for drawing) and groups (which can display borders as well).

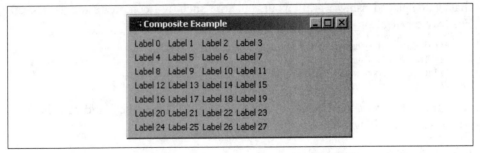

Figure 8-8. Using a composite widget

8.10   Creating Nonrectangular Windows

Problem

You want to wow users with windows of arbitrary shapes, using them to display company logos, game pieces, advertisements, and so on.

Solution

Create a nonrectangular shell using shell regions in Eclipse 3.0. In Eclipse 3.0, SWT shells can now have an irregular shape defined by regions. As an example (*NonRectangularApp* at this book's site), we'll create a blue doughnut-shaped window with an Exit button in it. All you have to do is to create a shell, create a Region object that defines the shape you want to use, and use the shell's setRegion method to configure the shell.

Discussion

In this example, we'll use a method named createCircle to create circular regions. The following example shows how to use that method and those regions to create a doughnut-shaped shell that we'll color blue using the shell's setBackground method. Note that you can add and cut regions from the final shell using the Region class's add and subtract methods:

```
final Display display = new Display();
final Shell shell = new Shell(display, SWT.NO_TRIM);

Region region = new Region();
region.add(createCircle(50, 50, 50));
region.subtract(createCircle(50, 50, 20));
shell.setRegion(region);
shell.setSize(region.getBounds().width, region.getBounds().height);
shell.setBackground(display.getSystemColor(SWT.COLOR_BLUE));
    .
    .
    .
```

To create circles, the createCircle method returns an array of points outlining the circle. Here's how this method does that:

```
static int[] createCircle(int xOffset, int yOffset, int radius) {
    int[] circlePoints = new int[10 * radius];
    for (int loopIndex = 0; loopIndex < 2 * radius + 1; loopIndex++) {
        int xCurrent = loopIndex - radius;
        int yCurrent = (int) Math.sqrt(radius * radius
            - xCurrent * xCurrent);
        int doubleLoopIndex = 2 * loopIndex;

        circlePoints[doubleLoopIndex] = xCurrent + xOffset;
        circlePoints[doubleLoopIndex + 1] = yCurrent + yOffset;
        circlePoints[10 * radius - doubleLoopIndex - 2] = xCurrent + xOffset;
        circlePoints[10 * radius - doubleLoopIndex - 1] = -yCurrent
            + yOffset;
    }

    return circlePoints;
}
```

All that's left is to create an Exit button and add it to the code, which you can see in Example 8-8.

Example 8-8. Creating nonrectangular windows

```
package org.cookbook.ch08;

import org.eclipse.swt.*;
import org.eclipse.swt.graphics.*;
import org.eclipse.swt.widgets.*;

public class NonRectangularClass {

    static int[] createCircle(int xOffset, int yOffset, int radius) {
        int[] circlePoints = new int[10 * radius];
        for (int loopIndex = 0; loopIndex < 2 * radius + 1; loopIndex++) {
            int xCurrent = loopIndex - radius;
            int yCurrent = (int) Math.sqrt(radius * radius - xCurrent
                * xCurrent);
            int doubleLoopIndex = 2 * loopIndex;

            circlePoints[doubleLoopIndex] = xCurrent + xOffset;
            circlePoints[doubleLoopIndex + 1] = yCurrent + yOffset;
            circlePoints[10 * radius - doubleLoopIndex - 2] = xCurrent + xOffset;
            circlePoints[10 * radius - doubleLoopIndex - 1] = -yCurrent
                + yOffset;
        }

        return circlePoints;
    }
```

Example 8-8. Creating nonrectangular windows (continued)

```
public static void main(String[] args) {
    final Display display = new Display();
    final Shell shell = new Shell(display, SWT.NO_TRIM);

    Region region = new Region();
    region.add(createCircle(50, 50, 50));
    region.subtract(createCircle(50, 50, 20));
    shell.setRegion(region);
    shell.setSize(region.getBounds().width, region.getBounds().height);
    shell.setBackground(display.getSystemColor(SWT.COLOR_BLUE));

    Button button = new Button(shell, SWT.PUSH);
    button.setText("Exit");
    button.setBounds(35, 6, 35, 20);
    button.addListener(SWT.Selection, new Listener() {
        public void handleEvent(Event event) {
            shell.close();
        }
    });

    shell.open();
    while (!shell.isDisposed()) {
        if (!display.readAndDispatch())
            display.sleep();
    }
    region.dispose();
    display.dispose();
    }
}
```

That's all you need; you can see the results in Figure 8-9. Very cool.

Figure 8-9. A doughnut-shaped window

8.11 Multithreading SWT Applications

Problem

You're running code in a worker thread, and you need to interact with the user interface in an SWT application.

Solution

Use the `Display.getDefault` method to get access to the main UI thread. Then use the `asyncExec` or `syncExec` methods, passing them a `Runnable` object that will interact with user interface elements.

Discussion

In an SWT application, the main thread, called the *UI thread*, is the thread responsible for handling events and dispatching them to widgets. In other GUI frameworks such as AWT or Swing, you don't have to interact with the UI thread directly, but the SWT architecture is different (SWT uses a message-pump architecture to support plug-ins in Eclipse).

If you've got a lot of intensive work to do, it isn't a good idea to burden the UI thread, and you might want to launch a worker thread. On the other hand, the UI thread is the only thread that can interact with SWT user interface elements without throwing an exception.

So, how do you interact with user interface elements from worker threads? You can use the UI thread's `asyncExec` and `syncExec` methods, passing a `Runnable` object that works with the user interface element you want. Here's an example. In this worker thread code, we want to display some text in a text widget. To do that, you get the current `Display` object using the `Display.getDefault` method and set the text in the text widget like so:

```
Display.getDefault( ).asyncExec(new Runnable( )
{
    public void run( )
    {
        textWidget.setText("Worker thread task has finished.");
    }
});
```

CHAPTER 9

SWT: Dialogs, Toolbars, Menus, and More

9.0 Introduction

This chapter continues our coverage of SWT and demonstrates creating dialog boxes, menus, tables, and toolbars. All of these are powerful controls in SWT, are more complex than the SWT controls you've seen in previous chapters, and merit a closer look. We'll also take a look at the new support in Eclipse 3.0 for embedding Swing and AWT elements in SWT. (Don't find what you want in SWT? Embed it from Swing!)

9.1 Creating Message Boxes

Problem

You need to send a message to the user and/or get a little feedback from the user.

Solution

Use the SWT MessageBox class to create a message box, and check the return value from its open method to determine which button the user clicked.

Discussion

Here are the MessageBox class's methods:

String getMessage( )
  Returns the dialog's message

int open( )
  Makes the dialog visible

void setMessage(String string)
  Sets the dialog's message

You create a message box by passing the current shell to the MessageBox constructor, as well as the style you want to use: MessageBox(Shell parent, int style). Here are some common styles to use:

- SWT.ICON_ERROR
- SWT.ICON_INFORMATION
- SWT.ICON_QUESTION
- SWT.ICON_WARNING
- SWT.ICON_WORKING
- SWT.OK
- SWT.OK | SWT.CANCEL
- SWT.YES | SWT.NO
- SWT.YES | SWT.NO | SWT.CANCEL
- SWT.RETRY | SWT.CANCEL
- SWT.ABORT | SWT.RETRY | SWT.IGNORE.

You use the message box's open method to display it; when the message box is closed, compare this method's int return value to one of the preceding styles such as SWT.YES, SWT.NO, or SWT.CANCEL to determine which button was clicked.

9.2   Creating Dialogs

Problem

You need some input from the user, and a dialog box would be perfect.

Solution

Create a new shell, configure it as a dialog, display it, and recover the data the user entered.

Discussion

SWT has message boxes and a number of prebuilt dialogs that come with it, such as the FileDialog class that creates file dialogs or the FontDialog class that enables users to choose a font. But if you need more than those prebuilt dialogs, you can build your own custom dialog. In this example, we're going to assume you want to confirm the user's decision to delete a file. When the user clicks a button labeled Delete File, the application (*DialogApp* at this book's site) displays a confirming dialog with OK and Cancel buttons. You can then determine which one the user clicked.

The application starts by creating a shell with the Delete File button and a text widget in whch we'll display the response to the user's button click:

```
Display display = new Display( );
Shell shell = new Shell(display);
shell.setText("Dialog Example");
shell.setSize(300, 200);
shell.open( );

final Button button = new Button(shell, SWT.PUSH);
button.setText("Delete File");
button.setBounds(20, 40, 80, 25);

final Text text = new Text(shell, SWT.SHADOW_IN);
text.setBounds(140, 40, 100, 25);
        .
        .
        .
```

To create a dialog, you create a shell and give it the style SWT.APPLICATION_MODAL | SWT.DIALOG_TRIM, making it an application-modal dialog (the user must dismiss it before continuing with the application) and styling the shell as a dialog box. We'll also add to the dialog a "Delete the file?" prompt as well as OK and Cancel buttons:

```
final Shell dialog = new Shell(shell, SWT.APPLICATION_MODAL |
    SWT.DIALOG_TRIM);
dialog.setText("Delete File");
dialog.setSize(250, 150);

final Button buttonOK = new Button(dialog, SWT.PUSH);
buttonOK.setText("OK");
buttonOK.setBounds(20, 55, 80, 25);

Button buttonCancel = new Button(dialog, SWT.PUSH);
buttonCancel.setText("Cancel");
buttonCancel.setBounds(120, 55, 80, 25);

final Label label = new Label(dialog, SWT.NONE);
label.setText("Delete the file?");
label.setBounds(20, 15, 100, 20);
```

That gets you a dialog box, and to display it, all you have to do is to call its open method. So, what about determining which button the user clicked?

To get data from the dialog, we'll use a listener based on an anonymous inner class. To get data from the listener's methods, we'll use a class field. In this example, we'll set a boolean variable, deleteFlag, indicating whether the user clicked the OK button in the button listener's code:

```
package org.cookbook.ch09;

import org.eclipse.swt.*;
import org.eclipse.swt.widgets.*;
```

```
public class DialogClass {
    static boolean deleteFlag = false;
        .
        .
        .
    Listener listener = new Listener() {
        public void handleEvent(Event event) {
            if(event.widget == buttonOK){
                deleteFlag = true;
            }else{
                deleteFlag = false;
            }
            dialog.close();
        }
    };

    buttonOK.addListener(SWT.Selection, listener);
    buttonCancel.addListener(SWT.Selection, listener);
        .
        .
        .
```

All that's left is to display an appropriate message in the text widget depending on the value of deleteFlag, and that's simple enough, as shown in Example 9-1.

Example 9-1. Creating dialogs

```
package org.cookbook.ch09;

import org.eclipse.swt.*;
import org.eclipse.swt.widgets.*;

public class DialogClass {
    static boolean deleteFlag = false;

    public static void main(String [] args) {
        Display display = new Display();
        Shell shell = new Shell(display);
        shell.setText("Dialog Example");
        shell.setSize(300, 200);
        shell.open();

        final Button button = new Button(shell, SWT.PUSH);
        button.setText("Delete File");
        button.setBounds(20, 40, 80, 25);

        final Text text = new Text(shell, SWT.SHADOW_IN);
        text.setBounds(140, 40, 100, 25);

        final Shell dialog = new Shell(shell, SWT.APPLICATION_MODAL |
            SWT.DIALOG_TRIM);
        dialog.setText("Delete File");
        dialog.setSize(250, 150);
```

Example 9-1. Creating dialogs (continued)

```
        final Button buttonOK = new Button(dialog, SWT.PUSH);
        buttonOK.setText("OK");
        buttonOK.setBounds(20, 55, 80, 25);

        Button buttonCancel = new Button(dialog, SWT.PUSH);
        buttonCancel.setText("Cancel");
        buttonCancel.setBounds(120, 55, 80, 25);

        final Label label = new Label(dialog, SWT.NONE);
        label.setText("Delete the file?");
        label.setBounds(20, 15, 100, 20);

        Listener listener = new Listener( ) {
            public void handleEvent(Event event) {
                if(event.widget == buttonOK){
                    deleteFlag = true;
                }else{
                    deleteFlag = false;
                }
                dialog.close( );
            }
        };

        buttonOK.addListener(SWT.Selection, listener);
        buttonCancel.addListener(SWT.Selection, listener);

        Listener buttonListener = new Listener( ) {
            public void handleEvent(Event event) {
                dialog.open( );
            }
        };

        button.addListener(SWT.Selection, buttonListener);

        while(!dialog.isDisposed( )) {
            if(!display.readAndDispatch( )) display.sleep( );
        }

        if(deleteFlag){
            text.setText("File deleted.");
        } else {
            text.setText("File not deleted.");
        }

        while(!shell.isDisposed( )) {
            if(!display.readAndDispatch( )) display.sleep( );
        }
        display.dispose( );
    }
}
```

Run this example now and click the Delete File button that appears in the window, as shown in Figure 9-1.

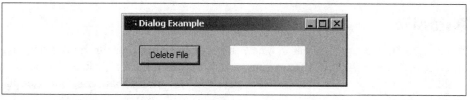

Figure 9-1. The dialog example

Clicking the Delete File button makes the dialog appear, as shown in Figure 9-2.

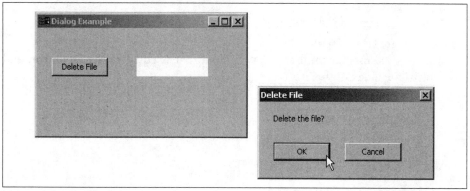

Figure 9-2. The new dialog

Click the OK button now, and a confirming message will appear in the main window's text widget, as shown in Figure 9-3.

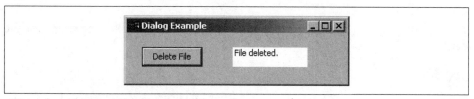

Figure 9-3. Recovering results from a dialog

9.3   Creating Toolbars

Problem

You want to create a toolbar and handle toolbar button clicks.

Solution

Use the SWT `Toolbar` and `ToolItem` classes.

Discussion

We'll create an example toolbar in a new project (*ToolbarApp* at this book's site) and stock it with toolbar buttons, reporting which button the user clicked. To create a toolbar, you use the SWT `Toolbar` class; here's a selection of this class's most popular methods:

`int getItemCount( )`
    Returns the number of items contained in the toolbar

`ToolItem[] getItems( )`
    Returns an array of the items in the toolbar

`int indexOf(ToolItem item)`
    Searches the toolbar until an item is found that is equal to the argument, and returns the index of that item

Here's how you can create a new SWT toolbar:

```
public class ToolbarClass {
    public static void main(String [] args) {
    Display display = new Display( );
    final Shell shell = new Shell(display);
    shell.setSize(300, 200);
    shell.setText("Toolbar Example");

    ToolBar toolbar = new ToolBar(shell, SWT.NONE);
    toolbar.setBounds(0, 0, 200, 70);
        .
        .
        .
```

The next step is to add some buttons to the toolbar; see the following recipe for the details.

See Also

Recipe 9.4 on embedding buttons in toolbars; Recipe 9.5 on handling toolbar events; Recipe 9.6 on embedding combo boxes, text widgets, and menus in toolbars; Chapter 8 in *Eclipse* (O'Reilly).

9.4 Embedding Buttons in Toolbars

Problem

Having created a toolbar, you need to start adding buttons.

Solution

To install buttons in a toolbar you use the ToolItem class, passing the ToolBar object you want to use to the ToolItem constructor.

Discussion

Here's a selection of the ToolItem class's most popular methods:

void addSelectionListener(SelectionListener listener)
> Adds the listener to the collection of listeners that will be notified when the tool item is selected

void setImage(Image image)
> Sets the tool item's image

void setSelection(boolean selected)
> Sets the selection state of the tool item

void setText(String string)
> Sets the tool item's text

void setToolTipText(String string)
> Sets the tool item's tool tip text

void setWidth(int width)
> Sets the width of the tool item

Continuing the example from the previous recipe, we'll create five new toolbar buttons and give them captions. Note that we pass the ToolBar object to the ToolItem constructor:

```
ToolItem toolItem1 = new ToolItem(toolbar, SWT.PUSH);
toolItem1.setText("Save");
ToolItem toolItem2 = new ToolItem(toolbar, SWT.PUSH);
toolItem2.setText("Save As");
ToolItem toolItem3 = new ToolItem(toolbar, SWT.PUSH);
toolItem3.setText("Print");
ToolItem toolItem4 = new ToolItem(toolbar, SWT.PUSH);
toolItem4.setText("Run");
ToolItem toolItem5 = new ToolItem(toolbar, SWT.PUSH);
toolItem5.setText("Help");
    .
    .
    .
```

That installs the toolbar buttons. To handle their click events, see the next recipe.

See Also

Recipe 9.3 on creating toolbars; Recipe 9.5 on handling toolbar events; Recipe 9.6 on embedding combo boxes, text widgets, and menus in toolbars; Chapter 8 in *Eclipse* (O'Reilly).

9.5 Handling Toolbar Events

Problem

You want to catch toolbar click events.

Solution

Add a listener to the toolbar buttons. Just create a new Listener object, and use the toolbar button's addListener method to add that listener.

Discussion

To complete the example discussed in the two previous recipes, create a new listener of the Listener class to handle the buttons, handle click events by displaying the caption of the clicked button (which you can get from the tool item's getText method), and add the new listener to the toolbar buttons. You can see how that works in Example 9-2.

Example 9-2. Creating toolbars

```
package org.cookbook.ch09;

import org.eclipse.swt.*;
import org.eclipse.swt.widgets.*;

public class ToolbarClass {

    public static void main(String [] args) {
        Display display = new Display( );
        final Shell shell = new Shell(display);
        shell.setSize(300, 200);
        shell.setText("Toolbar Example");

        ToolBar toolbar = new ToolBar(shell, SWT.NONE);
        toolbar.setBounds(0, 0, 200, 70);

        ToolItem toolItem1 = new ToolItem(toolbar, SWT.PUSH);
        toolItem1.setText("Save");
        ToolItem toolItem2 = new ToolItem(toolbar, SWT.PUSH);
        toolItem2.setText("Save As");
        ToolItem toolItem3 = new ToolItem(toolbar, SWT.PUSH);
        toolItem3.setText("Print");
        ToolItem toolItem4 = new ToolItem(toolbar, SWT.PUSH);
        toolItem4.setText("Run");
        ToolItem toolItem5 = new ToolItem(toolbar, SWT.PUSH);
        toolItem5.setText("Help");

        final Text text = new Text(shell, SWT.BORDER);
        text.setBounds(55, 80, 200, 25);
```

Example 9-2. Creating toolbars (continued)

```
Listener toolbarListener = new Listener() {
    public void handleEvent(Event event) {
        ToolItem toolItem =(ToolItem)event.widget;
        String caption = toolItem.getText();
        text.setText("You clicked " + caption);
    }
};

toolItem1.addListener(SWT.Selection, toolbarListener);
toolItem2.addListener(SWT.Selection, toolbarListener);
toolItem3.addListener(SWT.Selection, toolbarListener);
toolItem4.addListener(SWT.Selection, toolbarListener);
toolItem5.addListener(SWT.Selection, toolbarListener);

shell.open();

while (!shell.isDisposed()) {
    if (!display.readAndDispatch())
        display.sleep();
}
display.dispose();
    }
}
```

The results appear in Figure 9-4; the toolbar appears at upper left (you can position it where you want using setBounds or using an SWT layout). When the user clicks a button, the code reports his selections, as shown in Figure 9-4.

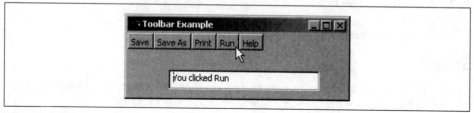

Figure 9-4. Using a toolbar

See Also

Recipe 9.3 on creating toolbars; Recipe 9.4 on embedding buttons in toolbars; Recipe 9.6 on embedding combo boxes, text widgets, and menus in toolbars; Chapter 8 in *Eclipse* (O'Reilly).

9.6 Embedding Combo Boxes, Text Widgets, and Menus in Toolbars

Problem

For many uses, buttons are fine in toolbars. But if you want to impress users, you can add other widgets such as combo boxes or drop-down menus.

Solution

Toolbars can act as widget containers for widgets such as combo boxes. And you can make menus open from inside a toolbar.

Discussion

When you create most widgets, you specify what container you want to use, and you can add widgets to toolbars by making them widget containers. For example, here's how you can add a text widget to a toolbar:

```
Text text = new Text(toolbar, SWT.BORDER);
```

And here's how you can add a combo box widget:

```
Combo combo = new Combo(toolbar, SWT.READ_ONLY);
```

Menus are a little more complex. In SWT, however, you support toolbar menus with context menus, setting their location inside a toolbar and making them visible as needed using code such as this:

```
menu.setLocation(point.x, point.y);
menu.setVisible(true);
```

See Also

Recipe 9.3 on creating toolbars; Recipe 9.4 on embedding buttons in toolbars; Recipe 9.5 on handling toolbar events; Chapter 8 in *Eclipse* (O'Reilly).

9.7 Creating a Menu System

Problem

You want to create and add a menu system to your SWT application.

Solution

Create a menu system with `Menu` and `MenuItem` objects. You create a new `Menu` object for the menu system itself, and new `MenuItem` objects for the individual menus and menu items.

Discussion

You use Menu and MenuItem objects to create menu systems in SWT; to get a handle on this process, we're going to create a menu system here, with File and Edit menus. When the user selects a menu item we'll display the item he has selected in a text widget.

This example is *MenuApp* at this book's site. You start by creating a standard menu system with a Menu object corresponding to the menu bar. Here is a selection of popular Menu methods:

void addMenuListener(MenuListener listener)
  Adds the listener to the collection of listeners who will be notified when menus are hidden or shown

MenuItem getItem(int index)
  Returns the item at the given index

int getItemCount( )
  Returns the number of items contained in the menu

void setVisible(boolean visible)
  Makes the menu visible if the argument is true, invisible otherwise

Here's our menu bar, created with the SWT.BAR style:

```
public class MenuClass
{

    Display display;
    Shell shell;
    Menu menuBar;
    Text text;

    public MenuClass( )
    {
        display = new Display( );
        shell = new Shell(display);
        shell.setText("Menu Example");
        shell.setSize(300, 200);

        text = new Text(shell, SWT.BORDER);
        text.setBounds(80, 50, 150, 25);

        menuBar = new Menu(shell, SWT.BAR);
          .
          .
          .
```

After creating an object corresponding to the menu bar, you create menu items in the menu bar such as the File and Edit menu. However, you don't use the Menu class; you use the MenuItem class. The following is a selection of popular MenuItem methods.

void addSelectionListener(SelectionListener listener)
> Adds the listener to the collection of listeners who will be notified when the item is selected

boolean getSelection( )
> Returns true if the menu item is selected, false otherwise

boolean isEnabled( )
> Returns true if the menu item is enabled, false otherwise

void setAccelerator(int accelerator)
> Sets the item's accelerator

void setEnabled(boolean enabled)
> Enables the menu item if the argument is true, and disables it otherwise

void setImage(Image image)
> Sets the image the menu item will display to the argument

void setMenu(Menu menu)
> Sets the menu item's pull-down menu to the argument

void setText(String string)
> Sets the menu item's text

Here's how to create a File menu header, giving it the caption File and the mnemonic F (which means the menu also can be opened by pressing, for example, Alt-F in Windows or Apple-F in Mac OS X):

```
public class MenuClass
{

    Display display;
    Shell shell;
    Menu menuBar;
    MenuItem fileMenuHeader;
    Text text;

    public MenuClass( )
    {
        display = new Display( );
        shell = new Shell(display);
        shell.setText("Menu Example");
        shell.setSize(300, 200);

        text = new Text(shell, SWT.BORDER);
        text.setBounds(80, 50, 150, 25);

        menuBar = new Menu(shell, SWT.BAR);
        fileMenuHeader = new MenuItem(menuBar, SWT.CASCADE);
        fileMenuHeader.setText("&File");
            .
            .
            .
```

To create the actual drop-down File menu, use the `Menu` class with the `SWT.DROP_DOWN` style, and add that new menu to the File menu header like so:

```
public class MenuClass
{

    Display display;
    Shell shell;
    Menu menuBar, fileMenu;
    MenuItem fileMenuHeader;
    Text text;

    public MenuClass()
    {
        .
        .
        .
        menuBar = new Menu(shell, SWT.BAR);
        fileMenuHeader = new MenuItem(menuBar, SWT.CASCADE);
        fileMenuHeader.setText("&File");

        fileMenu = new Menu(shell, SWT.DROP_DOWN);
        fileMenuHeader.setMenu(fileMenu);
        .
        .
        .
```

This gives you a File menu, as shown in Figure 9-5. How do you add items to this menu? See the next recipe.

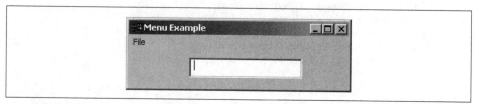

Figure 9-5. A File menu

See Also

Recipe 9.8 on creating text menu items; Recipe 9.9 on creating image menu items; Recipe 9.10 on creating radio menu items; Recipe 9.11 on creating menu item accelerators and mnemonics; Recipe 9.12 on enabling and disabling menu items; Chapter 8 in *Eclipse* (O'Reilly).

9.8 Creating Text Menu Items

Problem

You want to add menu items that display text captions to a menu and handle selection events for those items.

Solution

Use the MenuItem class and the SelectionAdapter class. Create a MenuItem object, use the addSelectionListener method to add a listener to it, and use the setText method to set the text caption in the menu item.

Discussion

To implement a File → Save item to the menu example we started in the previous recipe, create a new MenuItem object with the caption Save, pass the fileMenu object to its constructor, and give this item the style SWT.PUSH:

```
public MenuClass()
    .
    .
    .
    menuBar = new Menu(shell, SWT.BAR);
    fileMenuHeader = new MenuItem(menuBar, SWT.CASCADE);
    fileMenuHeader.setText("&File");

    fileMenu = new Menu(shell, SWT.DROP_DOWN);
    fileMenuHeader.setMenu(fileMenu);

    fileSaveItem = new MenuItem(fileMenu, SWT.PUSH);
    fileSaveItem.setText("&Save");
    .
    .
    .
```

To make this menu item active, connect it to a selection listener class we'll name MenuListener:

```
    fileSaveItem.addSelectionListener(new MenuItemListener());
```

The MenuListener class will extend the SelectionAdapter class. As mentioned in Chapter 8, all SWT listener interfaces have adapter classes with stub implementations of all the interface's methods; if you extend an adapter class, you have to implement only the methods you want to override. In this case, we'll display the text of the selected item by retrieving the menu item widget that caused the event; note that if the selected item was File → Exit, we exit:

```
    class MenuItemListener extends SelectionAdapter
    {
        public void widgetSelected(SelectionEvent event)
        {
```

```
                if(((MenuItem) event.widget).getText().equals("E&xit")){
                    shell.close();
                }
                text.setText("You selected " + ((MenuItem) event.widget).getText());
            }
        }
    }
```

That completes the File → Save menu item; we'll add File → Exit and Edit → Copy items to this example too, as shown in Example 9-3.

Example 9-3. SWT menus

```
package org.cookbook.ch09;

import org.eclipse.swt.widgets.*;
import org.eclipse.swt.SWT;
import org.eclipse.swt.events.*;

public class MenuClass
{
    Display display;
    Shell shell;
    Menu menuBar, fileMenu, editMenu;
    MenuItem fileMenuHeader, editMenuHeader;
    MenuItem fileExitItem, fileSaveItem, editCopyItem;
    Text text;

    public MenuClass()
    {
        display = new Display();
        shell = new Shell(display);
        shell.setText("Menu Example");
        shell.setSize(300, 200);

        text = new Text(shell, SWT.BORDER);
        text.setBounds(80, 50, 150, 25);

        menuBar = new Menu(shell, SWT.BAR);
        fileMenuHeader = new MenuItem(menuBar, SWT.CASCADE);
        fileMenuHeader.setText("&File");

        fileMenu = new Menu(shell, SWT.DROP_DOWN);
        fileMenuHeader.setMenu(fileMenu);

        fileSaveItem = new MenuItem(fileMenu, SWT.PUSH);
        fileSaveItem.setText("&Save");

        fileExitItem = new MenuItem(fileMenu, SWT.PUSH);
        fileExitItem.setText("E&xit");

        editMenuHeader = new MenuItem(menuBar, SWT.CASCADE);
        editMenuHeader.setText("&Edit");
```

Example 9-3. SWT menus (continued)

```
        editMenu = new Menu(shell, SWT.DROP_DOWN);
        editMenuHeader.setMenu(editMenu);

        editCopyItem = new MenuItem(editMenu, SWT.PUSH);
        editCopyItem.setText("&Copy");

        fileExitItem.addSelectionListener(new MenuItemListener());
        fileSaveItem.addSelectionListener(new MenuItemListener());
        editCopyItem.addSelectionListener(new MenuItemListener());

        shell.setMenuBar(menuBar);
        shell.open();
        while (!shell.isDisposed())
        {
            if (!display.readAndDispatch())
                display.sleep();
        }
        display.dispose();
    }

    class MenuItemListener extends SelectionAdapter
    {
        public void widgetSelected(SelectionEvent event)
        {
            if(((MenuItem) event.widget).getText().equals("E&xit")){
                shell.close();
            }
            text.setText("You selected " + ((MenuItem) event.widget).getText());
        }
    }

    public static void main(String[] args)
    {
        MenuClass menuExample = new MenuClass();
    }
}
```

You can see the results in Figure 9-6, where we're selecting File → Save.

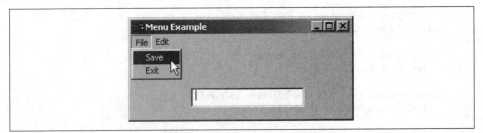

Figure 9-6. Opening the File menu

If you do select File → Save, you'll see the selected item displayed in the application's text widget, as shown in Figure 9-7.

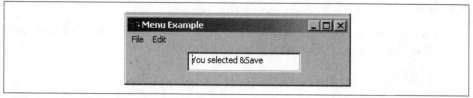

Figure 9-7. Selecting a menu item

See Also

Recipe 9.7 on creating a menu system; Recipe 9.9 on creating image menu items; Recipe 9.10 on creating radio menu items; Recipe 9.11 on creating menu item accelerators and mnemonics; Recipe 9.12 on enabling and disabling menu items; Chapter 8 in *Eclipse* (O'Reilly).

9.9   Creating Image Menu Items

Problem

You want to display images in menu items.

Solution

Use the MenuItem class's setImage method.

Discussion

You can pass an Image object to a MenuItem object's setImage method to add an image to a menu item. Here's an example:

```
Display display = new Display ();
final Image image = new Image (display, "c:\helpitem.jpg");
        .
        .
        .
menuItem.setImage(image);
```

See Also

Recipe 9.7 on creating a menu system; Recipe 9.8 on creating text menu items; Recipe 9.10 on creating radio menu items; Recipe 9.11 on creating menu item accelerators and mnemonics; Recipe 9.12 on enabling and disabling menu items; Chapter 8 in *Eclipse* (O'Reilly).

9.10   Creating Radio Menu Items

Problem

You want to add "selectable" menu items to a menu that, when selected, stay selected until another selectable item is selected instead.

Solution

Use SWT radio menu items, created by setting a `MenuItem` object's style to `SWT.RADIO`.

Discussion

For example, say that you want to add two radio items to the File menu in the menu example developed earlier in this chapter. You want those radio items to set the language used in the application to either German or English. You can create two new `SWT.RADIO` menu items in this way:

```
fileEnglishItem = new MenuItem(fileMenu, SWT.RADIO);
fileEnglishItem.setText("English");

fileGermanItem = new MenuItem(fileMenu, SWT.RADIO);
fileGermanItem.setText("German");
```

To handle their events, we'll create a class named `RadioItemListener`, which extends the `SelectionAdapter` class. Here we're going to catch whichever radio menu item was selected and report which language is in use (if you specifically want to check if a menu item's radio button is selected, call its `getSelection` method):

```
class RadioItemListener extends SelectionAdapter
{
    public void widgetSelected(SelectionEvent event)
    {
        MenuItem item = (MenuItem)event.widget;
        text.setText(item.getText() + " is on.");
    }
}
```

The results appear in Figure 9-8, where you can see the German and English radio menu items. As you select one or the other of these items, SWT toggles their radio buttons on and off.

See Also

Recipe 9.7 on creating a menu system; Recipe 9.8 on creating text menu items; Recipe 9.9 on creating image menu items; Recipe 9.11 on creating menu item accelerators and mnemonics; Recipe 9.12 on enabling and disabling menu items.

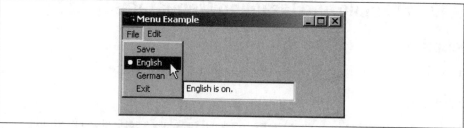

Figure 9-8. Radio menu items

9.11 Creating Menu Item Accelerators and Mnemonics

Problem

You need to add keyboard access to your menu items.

Solution

In SWT, you can support menu item accelerators and mnemonics. To create an accelerator, use the menu item's setAccelerator method; to create a mnemonic, insert an ampersand (&) in the menu item's caption just before the character you want to use as the mnemonic. (Make sure it's a unique mnemonic among those that will be visible at the same time.)

Discussion

Mnemonics are keys you can access as part of a key combination to select a menu item. For example, if a menu item's mnemonic is S, you can access that item by pressing Alt-S in Windows or Apple-S in Mac OS X. You can use a mnemonic when the corresponding menu is already open.

Accelerators, on the other hand, can be used at any time, regardless of whether the corresponding menu is open. As an example, here's how you can give a menu item the mnemonic S and the accelerator Ctrl-S:

```
menuItem.setText("&Spell Check\tCtrl+S");
menuItem.setAccelerator (SWT.CTRL + 'S');
```

See Also

Recipe 9.7 on creating a menu system; Recipe 9.8 on creating text menu items; Recipe 9.9 on creating image menu items; Recipe 9.10 on creating radio menu items; Recipe 9.12 on enabling and disabling menu items; Chapter 8 in *Eclipse* (O'Reilly).

9.12 Enabling and Disabling Menu Items

Problem

You want to disable menu items whose selection is inappropriate.

Solution

To enable and disable menu items, use the MenuItem class's setEnabled method.

Discussion

You can pass a boolean value to the setEnabled method; true enables the item, false disables it.

See Also

Recipe 9.7 on creating a menu system; Recipe 9.8 on creating text menu items; Recipe 9.9 on creating image menu items; Recipe 9.10 on creating radio menu items; Recipe 9.11 on creating menu item accelerators and mnemonics.

9.13 Creating Menu Separators

Problem

You want to separate menu items into groups using horizontal lines.

Solution

Create a new menu item that will act as a separator by setting its style to SWT. SEPARATOR.

Discussion

Here's an example that creates a menu separator and adds it to the File menu:

```
fileMenuSeparator = new MenuItem(fileMenu, SWT.SEPARATOR);
```

See Also

Recipe 9.7 on creating a menu system; Recipe 9.8 on creating text menu items; Recipe 9.9 on creating image menu items; Recipe 9.10 on creating radio menu items; Recipe 9.11 on creating menu item accelerators and mnemonics; Chapter 8 in *Eclipse* (O'Reilly).

9.14 Creating Tables

Problem

You have a lot of data you need to present visually, and you want to arrange that data in columns.

Solution

Use an SWT table based on the `Table` class. SWT tables can display columns of text, images, checkboxes, and more.

Discussion

Here's a selection of the `Table` class's methods:

`void addSelectionListener(SelectionListener listener)`
Adds the listener to the collection of listeners that are notified when the table's selection changes

`void deselect(int index)`
Deselects the item at the given zero-relative index in the table

`TableItem[] getSelection( )`
Returns an array of `TableItem` objects that are selected in the table

`int getSelectionIndex( )`
Returns the zero-relative index of the item which is currently selected in the table (`-1` if no item is selected)

`int[] getSelectionIndices( )`
Returns the zero-relative indices of the items that are currently selected in the table

`boolean isSelected(int index)`
Returns true if the item is selected, false otherwise

`void select(int index)`
Selects the item at the given zero-relative index in the table

As an example (*TableApp* at this book's site), we'll create a simple table displaying text items that catches selection events. We'll create a new table and stock it with items using the `TableItem` class, then report which item has been selected in a text widget. Here are some popular `TableItem` class methods:

`boolean getChecked( )`
Returns true if the table item is checked, false otherwise

`boolean getGrayed( )`
Returns true if the table item is grayed, false otherwise

void setChecked(boolean checked)
> Sets the checked state of the checkbox for this table item

void setGrayed(boolean grayed)
> Sets the grayed state of the checkbox for this table item

void setImage(Image image)
> Sets the table item's image

void setText(String string)
> Sets the table item's text

Here's how to create the table in this example:

```
Table table = new Table(shell, SWT.BORDER | SWT.V_SCROLL | SWT.H_SCROLL);
```

And here's how you can stock it with TableItem objects:

```
for (int loopIndex=0; loopIndex < 24; loopIndex++) {
    TableItem item = new TableItem (table, SWT.NULL);
    item.setText("Item " + loopIndex);
}
```

All that's left is to handle item selection events, which you can do as shown in Example 9-4; you can recover the item selected with the item member of the event object passed to the handleEvent method.

Example 9-4. SWT tables

```
package org.cookbook.ch09;

import org.eclipse.swt.*;
import org.eclipse.swt.widgets.*;

public class TableClass
{
    public static void main(String[] args)
    {
        Display display = new Display();
        Shell shell = new Shell(display);
        shell.setSize(260, 300);
        shell.setText("Table Example");

        final Text text = new Text(shell, SWT.BORDER);
        text.setBounds(25, 240, 200, 25);

        Table table = new Table(shell, SWT.BORDER | SWT.V_SCROLL | SWT.H_SCROLL);

        for (int loopIndex=0; loopIndex < 24; loopIndex++) {
            TableItem item = new TableItem (table, SWT.NULL);
            item.setText("Item " + loopIndex);
        }

        table.setBounds(25, 25, 200, 200);
```

Example 9-4. SWT tables (continued)

```
table.addListener(SWT.Selection, new Listener( )
{
    public void handleEvent(Event event)
    {
        text.setText("You selected " + event.item);
    }
});

shell.open( );
while (!shell.isDisposed( ))
{
    if (!display.readAndDispatch( ))
        display.sleep( );
}
display.dispose( );
    }
}
```

The results appear in Figure 9-9. When you select an item in the table, the application indicates which item was selected.

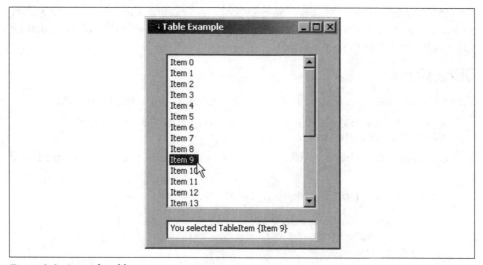

Figure 9-9. A simple table

That's fine up to a point, but this rudimentary example just gets us started with tables (in fact, this simple version looks much like a simple list widget). To add columns, check marks, images, and more, see the following recipes.

 By default, tables allow only single selections. To allow multiple selections, create the table with the SWT.MULTI style instead of the SWT.SINGLE style.

Eclipse 3.0

In Eclipse 3.0, the SWT table widget supports setting the foreground and background colors of individual cells. In addition, the Table widget enables you to set the font for a row or an individual cell.

See Also

Recipe 9.15 on creating table columns; Recipe 9.16 on adding check marks to table items; Recipe 9.17 on enabling and disabling table items; Recipe 9.18 on adding images to table items.

9.15   Creating Table Columns

Problem

You need to add some columns to your SWT table widgets.

Solution

Create TableColumn objects, one for each column, passing the Table object you're working with to the TableColumn constructor. Then create TableItem objects, setting the text for each column individually.

Discussion

To add columns to an SWT table, you start by turning on headers in the table:

```
Table table = new Table(shell, SWT.BORDER | SWT.V_SCROLL | SWT.H_SCROLL);
table.setHeaderVisible (true);
```

You can then create columns using TableColumn objects. In this example, we'll add four columns:

```
String[] titles = {"Col 1", "Col 2", "Col 3", "Col 4"};

for (int loopIndex = 0; loopIndex < titles.length; loopIndex++) {
    TableColumn column = new TableColumn(table, SWT.NULL);
    column.setText(titles[loopIndex]);
}
```

When you stock the table with items, you also set the text for each column, passing the column number as well as the text to use:

```
for (int loopIndex=0; loopIndex < 24; loopIndex++) {
    TableItem item = new TableItem (table, SWT.NULL);
    item.setText(0, "Item " + loopIndex);
    item.setText(1, "Yes");
    item.setText(2, "No");
    item.setText(3, "A table item");
}
```

We'll also pack the columns to adjust them to the width of the text they contain:

```
for (int loopIndex = 0; loopIndex <titles.length; loopIndex++) {
    table.getColumn(loopIndex).pack( );
}
```

And that's it; you can see the results in Figure 9-10. When you select an item, the application indicates which item you selected.

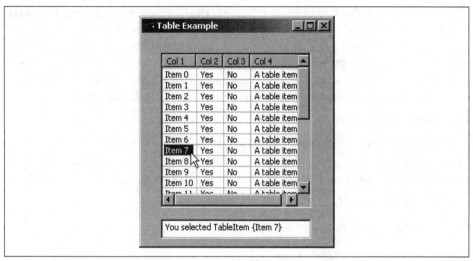

Figure 9-10. A multicolumn table

Eclipse 3.0

In Eclipse 3.0, you can scroll a column into view by calling `Table.showColumn(TableColumn)`.

See Also

Recipe 9.14 on creating tables; Recipe 9.16 on adding check marks to items in a table; Recipe 9.17 on enabling and disabling items in a table; Recipe 9.18 on adding images to table items.

9.16 Adding Check Marks to Table Items

Problem

You want to enable the user to select individual items in your SWT table widgets.

Solution

When you create your table, use the SWT.CHECK style. To determine if an item has been checked, you can use the getChecked method, which returns true if the item is checked.

Discussion

After you've added check marks to a table, you can determine which items have been checked with the table's getSelection method, which returns an array of the selected TableItem objects; with getSelectionIndex, which returns the index of the currently selected item; or with getSelectionIndices, which returns an int array of the indices of the selected items in a multiple-selection table. To see if an individual table item is checked, call its getChecked method or use setChecked to explicitly check it.

For example, here's how to create a table with check boxes:

```
Table table = new Table(shell, SWT.CHECK | SWT.BORDER | SWT.V_SCROLL | SWT.H_SCROLL);
```

You can determine if a newly clicked item has been checked by looking at the detail member of the Event object passed to us in the handleEvent method:

```
table.addListener(SWT.Selection, new Listener()
{
    public void handleEvent(Event event)
    {
        if(event.detail == SWT.CHECK){
            text.setText("You checked " + event.item);
        } else {
            text.setText("You selected " + event.item);
        }
    }
});
```

The results appear in Figure 9-11. As you can see, the application indicates which table item you've checked.

See Also

Recipe 9.14 on creating tables; Recipe 9.15 on creating table columns; Recipe 9.17 on enabling and disabling items in a table; Recipe 9.18 on adding images to table items.

9.17   Enabling and Disabling Table Items

Problem

You want to gray out table items so that they can't be selected.

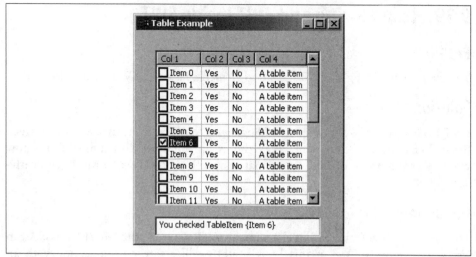

Figure 9-11. A table with check marks

Solution

Use the table item's setGrayed method.

Discussion

To gray out a table item, call that item's setGrayed method with a value of true; to enable the item again, pass the setGrayed method a value of false.

9.18 Adding Images to Table Items

Problem

You want to add images to table items.

Solution

To give a table item an image, call the item's setImage method.

Discussion

Just pass a table item's setImage method an Image object to give the item an image. For more on creating Image objects, take a look at Recipe 9.9 earlier in this chapter.

See Also

Recipe 9.9 on creating image menu items; Recipe 9.14 on creating tables; Recipe 9. 16 on adding check marks to items in a table; Recipe 9.17 on enabling and disabling items in a table.

9.19 Using Swing and AWT Inside SWT

Problem

You want to use Swing or AWT graphical elements *inside* an SWT application.

Solution

SWT (in Eclipse 3.0) supports embedding Swing/AWT widgets inside SWT widgets. Before Version 3.0, such support worked only on Windows. In Eclipse 3.0, it's now working in Windows for JDK 1.4 and later, as well as in GTK and Motif with early-access JDK 1.5.

Discussion

To work with AWT and Swing elements in SWT, you use the SWT_AWT class. As an example (*SwingAWTApp* at this book's site), we'll create an application with an AWT frame and panel, as well as a Swing button and text control. We'll start with a new SWT composite widget:

```
Composite composite = new Composite(shell, SWT.EMBEDDED);
composite.setBounds(20, 20, 300, 200);
composite.setLayout(new RowLayout());
```

Now add an AWT Frame window object to the composite using the SWT_AWT.new_ Frame method, and add an AWT Panel object to the frame:

```
java.awt.Frame frame = SWT_AWT.new_Frame(composite);
java.awt.Panel panel = new java.awt.Panel();
frame.add(panel);
```

We can now work with Swing controls. In this example, we'll add a Swing button and a Swing text control to the AWT panel:

```
final javax.swing.JButton button = new javax.swing.JButton("Click Me");
final javax.swing.JTextField text = new javax.swing.JTextField(20);
panel.add(button);
panel.add(text);
```

All that's left is to connect the button to a listener to display a message when that button is clicked. You can see how that works in Example 9-5.

Example 9-5. Using Swing and AWT in SWT

```
package org.cookbook.ch09;

import java.awt.event.*;

import org.eclipse.swt.*;
import org.eclipse.swt.widgets.*;
import org.eclipse.swt.layout.*;
import org.eclipse.swt.awt.SWT_AWT;
```

Example 9-5. Using Swing and AWT in SWT (continued)

```
public class SwingAWTClass {

    public static void main(String[] args) {
        final Display display = new Display();
        final Shell shell = new Shell(display);
        shell.setText("Using Swing and AWT");
        shell.setSize(350, 280);

        Composite composite = new Composite(shell, SWT.EMBEDDED);
        composite.setBounds(20, 20, 300, 200);
        composite.setLayout(new RowLayout());

        java.awt.Frame frame = SWT_AWT.new_Frame(composite);
        java.awt.Panel panel = new java.awt.Panel();
        frame.add(panel);

        final javax.swing.JButton button = new javax.swing.JButton("Click Me");
        final javax.swing.JTextField text = new javax.swing.JTextField(20);

        panel.add(button);
        panel.add(text);

        button.addActionListener(new ActionListener() {
            public void actionPerformed(ActionEvent event) {
                text.setText("Yep, it works.");
            }
        });

        shell.open();
        while(!shell.isDisposed()) {
            if (!display.readAndDispatch()) display.sleep();
        }
        display.dispose();
    }
}
```

Running this application gives you the results shown in Figure 9-12; a Swing button and text control at work in an AWT frame in an SWT application. Cool.

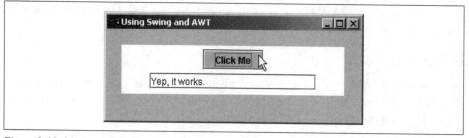

Figure 9-12. Mixing AWT, Swing, and SWT

CHAPTER 10

SWT: Coolbars, Tab Folders, Trees, and Browsers

10.0   Introduction

This final chapter on SWT covers some of the more advanced widgets: coolbars, tab folders, trees, and browsers. All these widgets have their uses, and we're going to put them through their paces here.

The browser widget is a new one in Eclipse 3.0; in earlier versions, browsers were supported only in Windows and had to be started using OLE techniques. In Eclipse 3.0, however, a browser widget is built into SWT, and it's being supported on more and more systems all the time.

10.1   Creating SWT Tab Folders

Problem

Space is at a premium in your application, and you want to divide your widgets into a set of pages.

Solution

Try a tab folder widget, which enables you to stack pages of widgets. Create a new TabFolder object, add TabItem objects to it, and use the TabItem objects as widget containers.

Discussion

Tab folders are not difficult to create and stack with widgets. Just create an object of the TabFolder class, as in the *TabApp* example in the code for the book. Here's a selection of the most popular TabFolder methods:

```
void addSelectionListener(SelectionListener listener)
```
Adds the listener to the collection of listeners who will be notified when the tab folder's selection changes

```
TabItem getItem(int index)
```
Returns the item at the given zero-relative index in the tab folder

```
int getItemCount()
```
Returns the number of items in the tab folder

```
TabItem[] getItems()
```
Returns an array of TabItem objects that are the items in the tab folder

```
void setSelection(int index)
```
Selects the item at the given zero-relative index in the tab folder

Here's how the *TabApp* application creates a tab folder:

```
final TabFolder tabFolder = new TabFolder(shell, SWT.BORDER);
        .
        .
        .
```

After creating a tab folder, add as many TabItem objects as you need to create the pages in the tab folder. Here's a selection of the most useful TabItem methods:

```
TabFolder getParent()
```
Returns the tab item's parent, which must be a TabFolder object

```
void setControl(Control control)
```
Sets the control that is used to fill the client area of the tab item

```
void setImage(Image image)
```
Sets the tab item's image

```
void setText(String string)
```
Sets the tab item's text

```
void setToolTipText(String string)
```
Sets the tab item's tool tip text

In this example, we'll add 10 pages to the tab folder by creating 10 new TabItem objects and connecting them to the tab folder by passing the tabFolder object to the TabItem constructor:

```
final TabFolder tabFolder = new TabFolder(shell, SWT.BORDER);

for (int loopIndex = 0; loopIndex < 10; loopIndex++)
{
    TabItem tabItem = new TabItem(tabFolder, SWT.NULL);
    tabItem.setText("Tab " + loopIndex);
        .
        .
        .
}
```

All that remains is to add widgets—we'll use text widgets in this example—to each tab page using the page's setControl method, and to open the shell, as shown in Example 10-1.

Example 10-1. Using SWT tab folders

```
package org.cookbook.ch10;

import org.eclipse.swt.*;
import org.eclipse.swt.widgets.*;

public class TabClass
{
    public static void main(String[] args)
    {
        Display display = new Display();
        final Shell shell = new Shell(display);
        shell.setText("Tab Folder Example");
        shell.setSize(450, 250);

        final TabFolder tabFolder = new TabFolder(shell, SWT.BORDER);

        for (int loopIndex = 0; loopIndex < 10; loopIndex++)
        {
            TabItem tabItem = new TabItem(tabFolder, SWT.NULL);
            tabItem.setText("Tab " + loopIndex);

            Text text = new Text(tabFolder, SWT.BORDER);
            text.setText("This is page " + loopIndex);
            tabItem.setControl(text);
        }
        tabFolder.setSize(400, 200);

        shell.open();
        while (!shell.isDisposed())
        {
            if (!display.readAndDispatch())
                display.sleep();
        }
        display.dispose();
    }
}
```

You can see this application at work in Figure 10-1. The user can select the tabs to display the various text widgets—a useful control if screen space is at a premium and you want to stack widgets in an easy way.

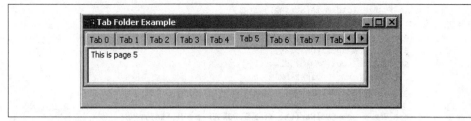

Figure 10-1. A tab folder at work

10.2   Creating SWT Coolbars

Problem

You want to wow users with coolbars, which feature sliding, resizeable toolbars.

Solution

Create a coolbar and add the toolbars you want the user to slide around as cool items in the coolbar. Use the cool items' setControl method to add the toolbars to each cool item.

Discussion

In this example, *CoolBarApp* in the code for this book, we'll put together a coolbar with two sliding toolbars. Here's a selection of the most useful CoolBar methods:

Point computeSize(int wHint, int hHint, boolean changed)
    Returns the preferred size of the coolbar

CoolItem getItem(int index)
    Returns the item that currently is displayed at the given zero-relative index

int getItemCount( )
    Returns the number of items contained in the coolbar

CoolItem[] getItems( )
    Returns an array of CoolItem objects in the order in which they currently are being displayed

Point[] getItemSizes( )
    Returns an array of points whose x and y coordinates describe the widths and heights of the items in the coolbar

Creating the coolbar in this example is easy; just use the CoolBar constructor and set the layout you want to use:

```
public class CoolBarClass
{
    static Display display;
    static Shell shell;
    static CoolBar coolBar;
```

```
public static void main(String[] args)
{
    display = new Display();
    shell = new Shell(display);
    shell.setLayout(new GridLayout());
    shell.setText("CoolBar Example");
    shell.setSize(600, 200);

    coolBar = new CoolBar(shell, SWT.BORDER | SWT.FLAT);
    coolBar.setLayoutData(new GridData(GridData.FILL_BOTH));
      .
      .
      .
```

The next step is to add coolbar items containing toolbars, which we'll cover in the next recipe.

See Also

Recipe 10.3 on adding items to coolbars; Recipe 10.4 on adding drop-down menus to coolbars.

10.3 Adding Items to Coolbars

Problem

You've created a coolbar and you want to add items to it.

Solution

Create CoolItem objects, passing a CoolBar object to their constructors. Use the CoolItem objects' setControl methods to add ToolBar objects to them.

Discussion

To add items such as toolbars to coolbars, you use coolbar items. Here's a selection of the most useful CoolItem methods:

void addSelectionListener(SelectionListener listener)
  Adds the listener to the collection of listeners that will be notified when the item is selected

Point computeSize(int wHint, int hHint)
  Returns the preferred size of the coolbar item

Rectangle getBounds()
  Returns a rectangle giving the coolbar item's size and location

Control getControl()
  Returns the control contained in the coolbar item

Point getMinimumSize( )
    Returns the minimum size to which the coolbar item can be resized

CoolBar getParent( )
    Returns the coolbar item's parent, which must be a CoolBar object

void setControl(Control control)
    Sets the control that is contained in the coolbar item

void setSize(int width, int height)
    Sets the coolbar item's size

Continuing the example begun in the previous recipe (*CoolBarApp* at this book's site), we'll add two toolbars to our coolbar. You begin by creating the toolbars, passing the CoolBar object to their constructors, and creating toolbar buttons:

```
public static void main(String[] args)
{
    display = new Display( );
    shell = new Shell(display);
    shell.setLayout(new GridLayout( ));
    shell.setText("CoolBar Example");
    shell.setSize(600, 200);

    coolBar = new CoolBar(shell, SWT.BORDER | SWT.FLAT);
    coolBar.setLayoutData(new GridData(GridData.FILL_BOTH));

    ToolBar toolBar1 = new ToolBar(coolBar, SWT.FLAT);
    for (int loopIndex = 0; loopIndex < 5; loopIndex++)
    {
        ToolItem toolItem = new ToolItem(toolBar1, SWT.PUSH);
        toolItem.setText("Button " + loopIndex);
    }

    ToolBar toolBar2 = new ToolBar(coolBar, SWT.FLAT | SWT.WRAP);
    for (int loopIndex = 5; loopIndex < 10; loopIndex++)
    {
        ToolItem toolItem = new ToolItem(toolBar2, SWT.PUSH);
        toolItem.setText("Button " + loopIndex);
    }
        .
        .
        .
```

To insert these toolbars into the coolbar, create two new CoolItem objects inside the coolbar and use the items' setControl methods to add the toolbars to them:

```
public static void main(String[] args)
{
        .
        .
        .

    ToolBar toolBar2 = new ToolBar(coolBar, SWT.FLAT | SWT.WRAP);
    for (int loopIndex = 5; loopIndex < 10; loopIndex++)
    {
```

```
        ToolItem toolItem = new ToolItem(toolBar2, SWT.PUSH);
        toolItem.setText("Button " + loopIndex);
    }

    CoolItem coolItem1 = new CoolItem(coolBar, SWT.DROP_DOWN);
    coolItem1.setControl(toolBar1);

    CoolItem coolItem2 = new CoolItem(coolBar, SWT.DROP_DOWN);
    coolItem2.setControl(toolBar2);
        .
        .
        .
```

Finally, size the toolbars to fit the cool items they're embedded within:

```
public static void main(String[] args)
{
        .
        .
        .
    CoolItem coolItem1 = new CoolItem(coolBar, SWT.DROP_DOWN);
    coolItem1.setControl(toolBar1);

    CoolItem coolItem2 = new CoolItem(coolBar, SWT.DROP_DOWN);
    coolItem2.setControl(toolBar2);

    Point toolBar1Size = toolBar1.computeSize(SWT.DEFAULT, SWT.DEFAULT);
    Point coolBar1Size = coolItem1.computeSize(toolBar1Size.x,
            toolBar1Size.y);
    coolItem1.setSize(coolBar1Size);

    Point toolBar2Size = toolBar2.computeSize(SWT.DEFAULT, SWT.DEFAULT);
    Point coolBar2Size = coolItem1.computeSize(toolBar2Size.x,
            toolBar2Size.y);
    coolItem2.setSize(coolBar2Size);
```

And that's all you need; you can see the results in Figure 10-2. Each coolbar item comes with a gripper bar at left; using the mouse, you can resize each toolbar using the gripper bars, as shown in Figure 10-2. You don't have to stop with simple buttons, of course; you also can use all the widgets that can appear in a toolbar—see Chapter 9 for more details.

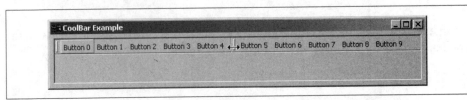

Figure 10-2. Two toolbars in a coolbar

For the complete code for this example, see the code in Recipe 10.4.

See Also

Recipe 9.3 on creating toolbars; Recipe 9.5 on handling toolbar events; Recipe 9.6 on embedding combo boxes, text widgets, and menus in toolbars; Recipe 10.2 on creating SWT coolbars; Recipe 10.4 on adding drop-down menus to coolbars.

10.4 Adding Drop-Down Menus to Coolbars

Problem

You want to add drop-down menus to coolbars.

Solution

Create your own menus, catch the coolbar events you want to handle, and display the menus using the Menu class's setLocation and setVisible methods.

This is the same way context menus are created in SWT.

Discussion

If you give a coolbar item the style SWT.DROP_DOWN, it'll display a *chevron button*, also called an *arrow button*, when the full item can't be displayed. Clicking that button can display a drop-down menu with all the buttons in the coolbar item—if you know what you're doing.

As an example, we'll add a drop-down menu to the coolbar developed in the previous recipe. To make that menu active, we'll catch arrow button clicks (event.detail == SWT.ARROW) in the coolbar with this code in the class CoolBarListener:

```
class CoolBarListener extends SelectionAdapter
{
    public void widgetSelected(SelectionEvent event)
    {
        if (event.detail == SWT.ARROW)
        {
            .
            .
            .
```

```
        }
    }
}
```

The objective here is to display the button captions as menu items, so we start by getting a list of buttons from the toolbar that was clicked:

```
class CoolBarListener extends SelectionAdapter
{
    public void widgetSelected(SelectionEvent event)
    {
        if (event.detail == SWT.ARROW)
        {
            ToolBar toolBar = (ToolBar) ((CoolItem)
                            event.widget).getControl();
            ToolItem[] buttons = toolBar.getItems();
                    .
                    .
                    .
        }
    }
}
```

Next we create a menu with items corresponding to the button captions:

```
class CoolBarListener extends SelectionAdapter
{
    public void widgetSelected(SelectionEvent event)
    {
        if (event.detail == SWT.ARROW)
            {
            ToolBar toolBar = (ToolBar) ((CoolItem)
                            event.widget).getControl();
            ToolItem[] buttons = toolBar.getItems();

            if (menu != null)
            {
                menu.dispose();
            }
            menu = new Menu(coolBar);
            for (int loopIndex = 0; loopIndex < buttons.length;
                        loopIndex++)
            {
                MenuItem menuItem = new MenuItem(menu, SWT.PUSH);
                menuItem.setText(buttons[loopIndex].getText());
            }
                    .
                    .
                    .

        }
    }
}
```

Finally, we determine where the coolbar was clicked using the SelectionEvent class's x and y members and display the menu at that location using the Menu class's setLocation and setVisible methods:

```
class CoolBarListener extends SelectionAdapter
{
    public void widgetSelected(SelectionEvent event)
    {
        if (event.detail == SWT.ARROW)
        {
            ToolBar toolBar = (ToolBar) ((CoolItem)
                        event.widget).getControl( );
            ToolItem[] buttons = toolBar.getItems( );

            if (menu != null)
            {
                menu.dispose( );
            }
            menu = new Menu(coolBar);
            for (int loopIndex = 0; loopIndex < buttons.length;
                        loopIndex++)
            {
                MenuItem menuItem = new MenuItem(menu, SWT.PUSH);
                menuItem.setText(buttons[loopIndex].getText( ));
            }

            Point menuPoint = coolBar.toDisplay(new Point(event.x,
                        event.y));
            menu.setLocation(menuPoint.x, menuPoint.y);
            menu.setVisible(true);
        }
    }
}
```

You can see this new listener class, CoolBarListener, in the final code for *CoolBarApp* in Example 10-2. Note also that we add objects of this class to the two coolbar items as listeners in the code.

Example 10-2. Using SWT coolbars

```
package org.cookbook.ch10;

import org.eclipse.swt.*;
import org.eclipse.swt.events.*;
import org.eclipse.swt.layout.*;
import org.eclipse.swt.widgets.*;
import org.eclipse.swt.graphics.*;

public class CoolBarClass
{
    static Display display;
    static Shell shell;
    static CoolBar coolBar;
    static Menu menu = null;
```

Example 10-2. Using SWT coolbars (continued)

```java
public static void main(String[] args)
{
    display = new Display( );
    shell = new Shell(display);
    shell.setLayout(new GridLayout( ));
    shell.setText("CoolBar Example");
    shell.setSize(600, 200);

    coolBar = new CoolBar(shell, SWT.BORDER | SWT.FLAT);
    coolBar.setLayoutData(new GridData(GridData.FILL_BOTH));

    ToolBar toolBar1 = new ToolBar(coolBar, SWT.FLAT);
    for (int loopIndex = 0; loopIndex < 5; loopIndex++)
    {
        ToolItem toolItem = new ToolItem(toolBar1, SWT.PUSH);
        toolItem.setText("Button " + loopIndex);
    }

    ToolBar toolBar2 = new ToolBar(coolBar, SWT.FLAT | SWT.WRAP);
    for (int loopIndex = 5; loopIndex < 10; loopIndex++)
    {
        ToolItem toolItem = new ToolItem(toolBar2, SWT.PUSH);
        toolItem.setText("Button " + loopIndex);
    }

    CoolItem coolItem1 = new CoolItem(coolBar, SWT.DROP_DOWN);
    coolItem1.setControl(toolBar1);

    CoolItem coolItem2 = new CoolItem(coolBar, SWT.DROP_DOWN);
    coolItem2.setControl(toolBar2);

    Point toolBar1Size = toolBar1.computeSize(SWT.DEFAULT, SWT.DEFAULT);
    Point coolBar1Size = coolItem1.computeSize(toolBar1Size.x,
            toolBar1Size.y);
    coolItem1.setSize(coolBar1Size);

    Point toolBar2Size = toolBar2.computeSize(SWT.DEFAULT, SWT.DEFAULT);
    Point coolBar2Size = coolItem1.computeSize(toolBar2Size.x,
            toolBar2Size.y);
    coolItem2.setSize(coolBar2Size);

    class CoolBarListener extends SelectionAdapter
    {
        public void widgetSelected(SelectionEvent event)
        {
            if (event.detail == SWT.ARROW)
            {
                ToolBar toolBar = (ToolBar) ((CoolItem)
                        event.widget).getControl( );
                ToolItem[] buttons = toolBar.getItems( );

                if (menu != null)
```

Example 10-2. Using SWT coolbars (continued)

```
            {
                menu.dispose( );
            }
            menu = new Menu(coolBar);
            for (int loopIndex = 0; loopIndex < buttons.length;
                    loopIndex++)
            {
                MenuItem menuItem = new MenuItem(menu, SWT.PUSH);
                menuItem.setText(buttons[loopIndex].getText( ));
            }

            Point menuPoint = coolBar.toDisplay(new Point(event.x,
                    event.y));
            menu.setLocation(menuPoint.x, menuPoint.y);
            menu.setVisible(true);
            }
        }
    }

    coolItem1.addSelectionListener(new CoolBarListener( ));
    coolItem2.addSelectionListener(new CoolBarListener( ));

    shell.open( );
    while (!shell.isDisposed( ))
    {
        if (!display.readAndDispatch( ))
            display.sleep( );
    }
    display.dispose( );
    }
}
```

The results appear in Figure 10-3; clicking the chevron button that appears when you resize the coolbar items to partially obscure the first item displays the drop-down menu you see in the figure. Not bad!

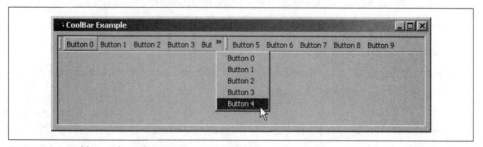

Figure 10-3. Adding a drop-down menu to a coolbar

See Also

Recipe 10.2 on creating SWT coolbars; Recipe 10.3 on adding items to coolbars.

10.5 Creating SWT Trees

Problem

You need to display data items in a hierarchical, collapsible-and-expandable form.

Solution

Use an SWT tree widget, based on the `Tree` and `TreeItem` classes.

Discussion

As an example, we'll create a tree (*TreeApp* at this book's site) that contains several levels of items. Here is a selection of useful `Tree` methods:

`void addSelectionListener(SelectionListener listener)`
> Adds the listener to the collection of listeners who are notified when the tree's selection changes

`void deselectAll( )`
> Deselects all selected items in the tree

`TreeItem[] getItems( )`
> Returns an array of items contained in the tree item

`TreeItem[] getSelection( )`
> Returns an array of `TreeItem` objects that are selected in the tree

`int getSelectionCount( )`
> Returns the number of selected items in the tree

`void selectAll( )`
> Selects all the items in the tree

`void setSelection(TreeItem[] items)`
> Sets the tree's selection to be the given array of items

The code in the *TreeApp* example creates a tree in this way:

```
final Tree tree = new Tree(shell, SWT.BORDER | SWT.V_SCROLL |
    SWT.H_SCROLL);
tree.setSize(290, 260);
```

The items you add to a tree such as this are objects of the `TreeItem` class; here's a selection of `TreeItem` methods:

`boolean getChecked( )`
> Returns true if the tree item is checked, false otherwise

`boolean getGrayed( )`
> Returns true if the tree item is grayed, false otherwise

`int getItemCount( )`
> Returns the number of items contained in the tree item

```
TreeItem[] getItems()
```
Returns an array of TreeItem objects that are children of the tree item

```
void setChecked(boolean checked)
```
Sets the checked state of the tree item

```
void setExpanded(boolean expanded)
```
Sets the expanded state of the tree item

```
void setGrayed(boolean grayed)
```
Sets the grayed state of the tree item

```
void setImage(Image image)
```
Sets the tree item's image

```
void setText(String string)
```
Sets the tree item's text

Adding items to a tree involves passing the parent of the item you're adding to the item's constructor. For example, to add 10 items to the tree widget, you can use code such as this:

```
final Tree tree = new Tree(shell, SWT.BORDER | SWT.V_SCROLL |
        SWT.H_SCROLL);
tree.setSize(290, 260);

for (int loopIndex0 = 0; loopIndex0 < 10; loopIndex0++)
{
    TreeItem treeItem0 = new TreeItem(tree, 0);
    treeItem0.setText("Level 0 Item " + loopIndex0);
        .
        .
        .
}
```

To add subitems to existing tree items, you can pass those existing tree items to the subitems' constructors, down to as many levels as you like. In this example, we'll give each top-level tree item 10 subitems and give each subitem 10 more subitems:

```
final Tree tree = new Tree(shell, SWT.BORDER | SWT.V_SCROLL |
        SWT.H_SCROLL);
tree.setSize(290, 260);

for (int loopIndex0 = 0; loopIndex0 < 10; loopIndex0++)
{
    TreeItem treeItem0 = new TreeItem(tree, 0);
    treeItem0.setText("Level 0 Item " + loopIndex0);
    for (int loopIndex1 = 0; loopIndex1 < 10; loopIndex1++)
    {
        TreeItem treeItem1 = new TreeItem(treeItem0, 0);
        treeItem1.setText("Level 1 Item " + loopIndex1);
        for (int loopIndex2 = 0; loopIndex2 < 10; loopIndex2++)
        {
            TreeItem treeItem2 = new TreeItem(treeItem1, 0);
            treeItem2.setText("Level 2 Item " + loopIndex2);
```

```
            }
        }
    }
```

That creates the tree shown in Figure 10-4.

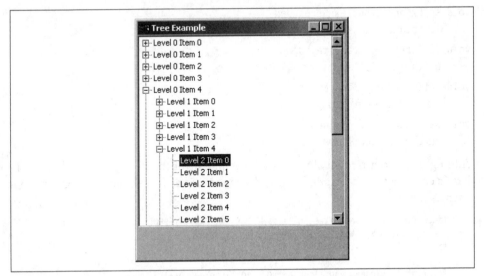

Figure 10-4. An SWT tree

For more on trees, such as handling selection events, see the following recipes.

 For the complete code for this example, see Recipe 10.6.

See Also

Recipe 10.6 on handling tree events; Recipe 10.7 on adding checkboxes to tree items; Recipe 10.8 on adding images to tree items; Chapter 8 in *Eclipse* (O'Reilly).

10.6   Handling Tree Events

Problem

You need to know when the user selects an item in a tree widget.

Solution

Add a new listener to the `Tree` widget, using the `addListener` or `addSelectionListener` methods.

Discussion

As an example, we'll add a listener to the tree developed in the previous recipe. We'll also add a text widget to display the user's selection, as shown in Example 10-3.

Example 10-3. SWT trees

```
package org.cookbook.ch10;

import org.eclipse.swt.*;
import org.eclipse.swt.widgets.*;

public class TreeClass
{
    public static void main(String[] args)
    {
        Display display = new Display();
        Shell shell = new Shell(display);
        shell.setText("Tree Example");

        final Text text = new Text(shell, SWT.BORDER);
        text.setBounds(0, 270, 290, 25);

        final Tree tree = new Tree(shell, SWT.BORDER | SWT.V_SCROLL |
            SWT.H_SCROLL);
        tree.setSize(290, 260);
        shell.setSize(300, 330);

        for (int loopIndex0 = 0; loopIndex0 < 10; loopIndex0++)
        {
            TreeItem treeItem0 = new TreeItem(tree, 0);
            treeItem0.setText("Level 0 Item " + loopIndex0);
            for (int loopIndex1 = 0; loopIndex1 < 10; loopIndex1++)
            {
                TreeItem treeItem1 = new TreeItem(treeItem0, 0);
                treeItem1.setText("Level 1 Item " + loopIndex1);
                for (int loopIndex2 = 0; loopIndex2 < 10; loopIndex2++)
                {
                    TreeItem treeItem2 = new TreeItem(treeItem1, 0);
                    treeItem2.setText("Level 2 Item " + loopIndex2);
                }
            }
        }

        tree.addListener(SWT.Selection, new Listener()
        {
            public void handleEvent(Event event)
            {
                text.setText(event.item + " was selected");
            }
        });
```

Example 10-3. SWT trees (continued)

```
    shell.open( );
    while (!shell.isDisposed( ))
    {
        if (!display.readAndDispatch( ))
            display.sleep( );
    }
    display.dispose( );
  }
}
```

With the new listener and the text widget to display selection events, the *TreeApp* example can display selections the user makes, as shown in Figure 10-5.

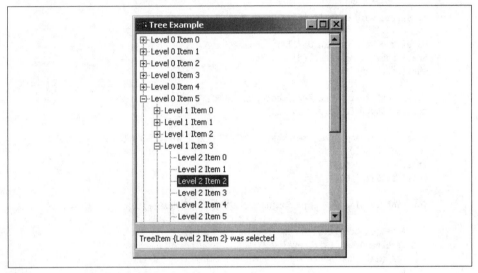

Figure 10-5. Catching tree selection events

See Also

Recipe 10.5 on creating SWT trees; Recipe 10.7 on adding checkboxes to tree items; Recipe 10.8 on adding images to tree items.

10.7 Adding Checkboxes to Tree Items

Problem

You need to enable the user to select items in a tree, and when the items are selected, you want them to stay selected until they're specifically deselected.

Solution

Make your SWT tree support checkboxes by adding the SWT.CHECK style, and make your listener listen for SWT.CHECK events.

Discussion

As an example, we can add checkboxes to the tree (*TreeApp* at this book's site) that we've been developing over the previous two recipes. To add checkboxes, add the SWT.CHECK style to the tree widget when it's created:

```
final Tree tree = new Tree(shell, SWT.CHECK | SWT.BORDER | SWT.V_SCROLL |
        SWT.H_SCROLL);
```

Then listen for SWT.CHECK events in the listener. Here's what that code looks like:

```
tree.addListener(SWT.Selection, new Listener()
{
    public void handleEvent(Event event)
    {
        if (event.detail == SWT.CHECK)
        {
            text.setText(event.item + " was checked.");
        } else
        {
            text.setText(event.item + " was selected");
        }
    }
});
```

You can see the results in Figure 10-6, where each tree item has a checkbox, and checkbox events are detected.

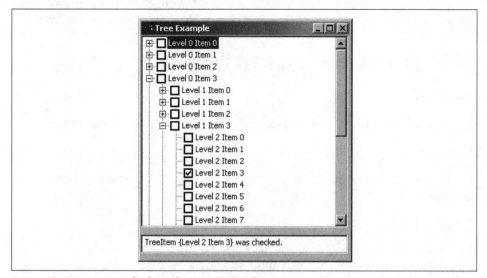

Figure 10-6. Supporting check marks in an SWT tree

You also can handle check marks with the setChecked and getChecked methods.

See Also

Recipe 10.5 on creating SWT trees; Recipe 10.6 on handling tree events; Recipe 10.8 on adding images to tree items.

10.8   Adding Images to Tree Items

Problem

You want to add images to tree items.

Solution

Use the TreeItem class's setImage and getImage methods.

Discussion

To install an image for a tree item, pass the setImage method a new Image object. To see how to create Image objects, take a look at the Recipe 9.9 in Chapter 9. To get the image from a tree item, use the getImage method.

See Also

Recipe 9.9 on creating image menu items; Recipe 10.5 on creating trees in SWT; Recipe 10.6 on handling tree events; Recipe 10.7 on adding checkboxes to tree items.

10.9   Creating SWT Browser Widgets

Problem

You want to give users some online access—for example, to access online help.

Solution

Use an SWT browser widget. Starting in Eclipse 3.0, SWT contains a browser widget built in.

Discussion

In Eclipse 2.x, you do not have much choice for displaying browsers in SWT windows. You really can do so only in Windows, using OLE. Here's how it works. You create an OleFrame object and connect the system's browser to it:

```
import org.eclipse.swt.ole.win32.*;
          .
          .
          .
    OleControlSite oleControlSite;

    OleFrame oleFrame = new OleFrame(shell, SWT.NONE);
    oleControlSite = new OleControlSite(oleFrame, SWT.NONE, "Shell.Explorer");
    oleControlSite.doVerb(OLE.OLEIVERB_INPLACEACTIVATE);
    shell.open();
          .
          .
          .
```

Then you create an OleAutomation object and navigate to the URL you want like so:

```
import org.eclipse.swt.ole.win32.*;
          .
          .
          .
    OleControlSite oleControlSite;

    OleFrame oleFrame = new OleFrame(shell, SWT.NONE);
    oleControlSite = new OleControlSite(oleFrame, SWT.NONE, "Shell.Explorer");
    oleControlSite.doVerb(OLE.OLEIVERB_INPLACEACTIVATE);
    shell.open();

    final OleAutomation browser = new OleAutomation(oleControlSite);

    int[] browserIDs = browser.getIDsOfNames(new String[]{"Navigate", "URL"});
    Variant[] address = new Variant[] {new Variant("http://www.oreilly.com")};
    browser.invoke(browserIDs[0], address, new int[]{browserIDs[1]});
```

Eclipse 3.0

In Eclipse 3.x, life is easier because SWT comes with a built-in browser widget. This widget currently is supported in Windows (using Internet Explorer 5+) and in Linux GTK (using Mozilla 1.4 GTK2). More operating systems will be supported in time. Here are some of the useful navigation methods of this widget:

boolean back( )
> Moves back one page

boolean forward( )
> Moves forward one page

boolean setUrl(String string)
> Navigates to a URL

void stop( )
> Stops the current operation

We'll create an example (*BrowserApp* at this book's site) that shows how to use this widget. This example includes a toolbar with Go, Back, and Stop buttons, and a text widget into which you can enter URLs:

```
public class BrowserClass {
    public static void main(String[] args) {
        Display display = new Display();
        final Shell shell = new Shell(display);
        shell.setText("Browser Example");
        shell.setSize(620, 500);

        ToolBar toolbar = new ToolBar(shell, SWT.NONE);
        toolbar.setBounds(5, 5, 200, 30);

        ToolItem goButton = new ToolItem(toolbar, SWT.PUSH);
        goButton.setText("Go");

        ToolItem backButton = new ToolItem(toolbar, SWT.PUSH);
        backButton.setText("Back");

        ToolItem stopButton = new ToolItem(toolbar, SWT.PUSH);
        stopButton.setText("Stop");

        final Text text = new Text(shell, SWT.BORDER);
        text.setBounds(5, 35, 400, 25);
```

Creating the browser is easy enough in Eclipse 3.x:

```
        final Browser browser = new Browser(shell, SWT.NONE);
        browser.setBounds(5, 75, 600, 400);
```

The listener we'll create will handle the Go, Back, and Stop buttons, calling the appropriate browser methods like so:

```
Listener listener = new Listener() {
    public void handleEvent(Event event) {
        ToolItem item = (ToolItem) event.widget;
        String string = item.getText();
        if (string.equals("Back"))
            browser.back();
        else if (string.equals("Stop"))
            browser.stop();
        else if (string.equals("Go"))
            browser.setUrl(text.getText());
    }
};
```

All that remains is to add a listener for the text widget, which browses to the URL the user typed if she uses the Enter key, and to open the shell that displays the new browser. The code that does this appears in Example 10-4.

Example 10-4. Using an SWT browser widget

```
package org.cookbook.ch10;

import org.eclipse.swt.*;
import org.eclipse.swt.widgets.*;
import org.eclipse.swt.browser.*;

public class BrowserClass {
    public static void main(String[] args) {
        Display display = new Display( );
        final Shell shell = new Shell(display);
        shell.setText("Browser Example");
        shell.setSize(620, 500);

        ToolBar toolbar = new ToolBar(shell, SWT.NONE);
        toolbar.setBounds(5, 5, 200, 30);

        ToolItem goButton = new ToolItem(toolbar, SWT.PUSH);
        goButton.setText("Go");

        ToolItem backButton = new ToolItem(toolbar, SWT.PUSH);
        backButton.setText("Back");

        ToolItem stopButton = new ToolItem(toolbar, SWT.PUSH);
        stopButton.setText("Stop");

        final Text text = new Text(shell, SWT.BORDER);
        text.setBounds(5, 35, 400, 25);

        final Browser browser = new Browser(shell, SWT.NONE);
        browser.setBounds(5, 75, 600, 400);

        Listener listener = new Listener( ) {
            public void handleEvent(Event event) {
                ToolItem item = (ToolItem) event.widget;
                String string = item.getText( );
                if (string.equals("Back"))
                    browser.back( );
                else if (string.equals("Forward"))
                    browser.forward( );
                else if (string.equals("Stop"))
                    browser.stop( );
                else if (string.equals("Go"))
                    browser.setUrl(text.getText( ));
            }
        };

        backButton.addListener(SWT.Selection, listener);
        stopButton.addListener(SWT.Selection, listener);

        text.addListener(SWT.DefaultSelection, new Listener( ) {
            public void handleEvent(Event e) {
                browser.setUrl(text.getText( ));
```

Example 10-4. Using an SWT browser widget (continued)

```
        }
    });

    shell.open();
    browser.setUrl("http://oreilly.com");
    while (!shell.isDisposed()) {
        if (!display.readAndDispatch())
            display.sleep();
    }
    display.dispose();
    }
}
```

The new browser appears in Figure 10-7, where we're browsing to the O'Reilly web site. The user can enter URLs into the address text widget, and the buttons in the toolbar are active. That's the browser widget in Eclipse 3.0—very cool.

Figure 10-7. An SWT browser widget

CHAPTER 11

JSP, Servlets, and Eclipse

11.0 Introduction

This chapter discusses using Eclipse in web development, specifically with JavaServer Pages (JSP) and Java servlets. We're going to use the reference web server for JSP and servlets in this chapter—the Tomcat web server that is available for free from the Apache web site. After installing Tomcat and getting it running, we'll interface Eclipse to that installation, seeing how to edit and install web application files.

 Although we're using Tomcat in this chapter, everything we'll do is applicable to any JSP/servlet container.

11.1 Installing Tomcat

Problem

You need access to a JSP and servlet web container.

Solution

Download and install the Tomcat web server, which is the reference installation for JSP and servlets. You can get Tomcat at *http://jakarta.apache.org/tomcat/* for free. Installation is easy; just download the compressed file for your operating system and uncompress it. Tomcat is a Java application, so no special installation is needed.

Discussion

If you don't have access to a JSP/servlet web server, download Tomcat from *http://jakarta.apache.org/tomcat/*; just select the compressed file for your operating system. One of the good things about Tomcat is that all you have to do to install it is to unzip/untar it. Tomcat is a Java application, so it'll run using your Java installation (see Recipe 11.2 for more information).

We'll use the most recent version of Tomcat as of this writing, Version 5.0.19. Installing it is as easy as downloading it and unzipping or untarring it. Here's the directory structure you get when you do this:

```
jakarta-tomcat-5.0.19
|__bin                        Binary files
|__common                     Classes used by code and web applications
|   |__classes                Common Java classes
|   |__endorsed                Endorsed Java classes
|   |__lib                    Common Java classes in .jar format
|__conf                       Configuration files
|__logs                       The server's log files
|__server                     Internal Tomcat classes
|__shared                     Shared files
|__temp                       Temporary files
|__webapps                    Directory to use for web applications
|__work                       Scratch directory for holding temporary files
```

The *webapps* directory here is the important one; at least in terms of writing web applications; it's where to install your JSPs and servlet applications.

In this chapter, we're going to store examples in a directory named *ch11*, which is a subdirectory of the Tomcat *webapps* directory. Note that this new directory must itself have a subdirectory named *WEB-INF*, which must have two subdirectories, *classes* and *lib*:

```
webapps
|__ch11                       The folder for Chapter 11 examples
     |__WEB-INF                Information about Chapter 11's web applications
          |__classes           Java classes used by Chapter 11's web applications
          |__lib               JAR files used by Chapter 11's web applications
```

Note that although the *WEB-INF*, *classes,* and *lib* directories are empty here, they have to exist, or Tomcat can't serve files to the browser. We'll store the examples in this chapter in the *ch11* directory.

See Also

Recipe 11.2 on starting Tomcat; Chapter 1 in *Tomcat: the Definitive Guide* (O'Reilly); Chapter 4 in *JavaServer Pages (O'Reilly)*; Chapter 9 in *Eclipse* (O'Reilly).

11.2 Starting Tomcat

Problem

You want to get Tomcat running.

Solution

Set the `JAVA_HOME` and `CATALINA_HOME` environment variables, change directories to Tomcat's *bin* directory, and type `startup` in Windows or run `startup.sh` in Unix.

Discussion

Before starting Tomcat from the command line, you must set these two environment variables:

`JAVA_HOME`

> You set this environment variable to the installation directory of Java, the parent directory of the Java *bin* directory; e.g., *C:\jdk1.4* in Windows or */usr/java* in Unix.

`CATALINA_HOME`

> You set this environment variable to the installation directory of Tomcat, the parent directory of the Tomcat *bin* directory; e.g., *C:\tomcat\jakarta-tomcat-5.0.19* in Windows.

You can set these environment variables from the command prompt (in Windows that's the DOS prompt; in Unix it's the shell) as in this example:

```
set JAVA_HOME=C:\jdk1.4
```

How you do this varies by operating system; for example, in the Unix `tcsh` shell, use `setenv` instead. After setting these environment variables, run Tomcat by changing directories to Tomcat's *bin* directory and typing `startup` in Windows, or running `startup.sh` in Unix. Note that in Windows, a new DOS window appears that displays initialization messages. To shut down Tomcat, type `shutdown` in Windows, or run `shutdown.sh` in Unix at the command line.

Now that you've gotten Tomcat running, open a browser, and navigate to *http://localhost:8080*, which should open Tomcat's Welcome page, as shown in Figure 11-1. The localhost part of this URL is what you use for web servers installed on your local machine (corresponding to an IP address of `127.0.0.1`), and 8080 is the port number (web servers usually use port 80, but Tomcat uses 8080 to avoid conflicts with other servers).

> When you store new *.class* files in the Tomcat directories or edit files such as the *web.xml* file you'll see later, you should stop Tomcat and restart it. Doing so makes sure Tomcat copies over your changes from its *webapps* directory to its *work* directory, which is what it actually serves documents from (there are ways to configure Tomcat so that you don't need to restart it this way, but that's beyond the scope of this book.)

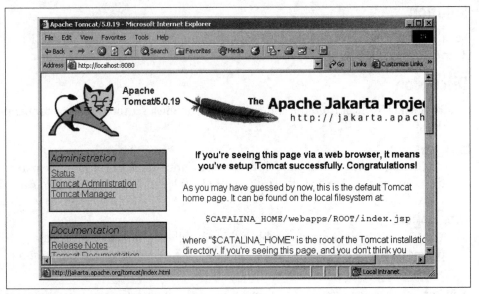

Figure 11-1. The Tomcat 5.0.19 startup page

See Also

Recipe 11.1 on installing Tomcat; Chapter 1 in *Tomcat: the Definitive Guide* (O'Reilly); Chapter 4 in *JavaServer Pages* (O'Reilly); Chapter 9 in *Eclipse* (O'Reilly).

11.3   Creating JSP Files

Problem

You want to write JSP files and view them in a web browser.

Solution

Create and edit JSP files in Eclipse.

Discussion

As with any other project, you can use Eclipse to write and store *.jsp* files that can be used in servlet containers. At its simplest, Eclipse will enable you to create these files, and you can copy them to the correct directory in your web server installation.

JSP files are can hold Java code in scriptlet, declaration, and expression elements. Of these, scriptlets are the most general and can contain general Java code. You enclose a scriptlet between the markup <% and %>, as shown in Example 11-1. In this case, we're using the built-in out object's println method to display text in the JSP page's output in the browser, This JSP is functional..

Example 11-1. A sample JSP

```
<HTML>
    <HEAD>
        <TITLE>JSP Sample</TITLE>
    </HEAD>

    <BODY>
        <H1>JSP Sample</H1>
        <% out.println("This JSP is functional."); %>
    </BODY>
</HTML>
```

An easy way to create this JSP file is to enter it into Eclipse, as shown in Figure 11-2, where we've created a new project, *JSP*, and a new file, *greeting.jsp*, to hold the JSP code. There's no syntax checking going on here; Eclipse is just using its standard, default editor.

 If you do want to check syntax of JSP documents, give the XML editor named XML Buddy a try. It's available for free at *http://www. xmlbuddy.com*.

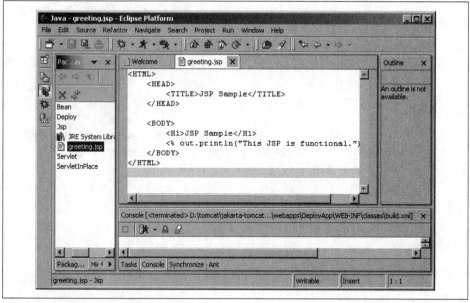

Figure 11-2. Editing JSP code

The next step is to install *greeting.jsp* in your installation of Tomcat; in this case, just copy that file to the directory we're going to use for the examples in this chapter, *webapps\ch11*.

Now restart Tomcat, open a web browser, and navigate to *http://localhost:8080/Ch11/Ch11_01.jsp*. You should see the results that appear in Figure 11-3. Internally, what's happened is that Tomcat has compiled the JSP file into servlet form and has run it, with the results you see in the figure.

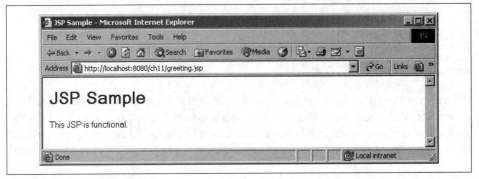

Figure 11-3. A working JSP file

That creates a JSP file. Although Eclipse didn't do much more than act as a text editor here, it can do a lot more; see the following recipes for details.

Eclipse 3.0

Eclipse 3.0 is intended to add more syntax highlighting for JSP files, but as of this writing, that hasn't appeared. Such support for JSP code would be great if it does come to pass.

See Also

Recipe 11.1 on installing Tomcat; Recipe 11.7 on editing *web.xml* in place; Recipe 11.9 on connecting to a JavaBean; Chapter 3 in *JavaServer Pages* (O'Reilly); Chapter 1 in the *Java Servlet and JSP Cookbook* (O'Reilly).

11.4 Creating a Servlet

Problem

You want to use Eclipse to develop servlets.

Solution

Develop the servlet's Java code using Eclipse, and add *servlet.jar* or *servlet-api.jar* (depending on your version of Tomcat) as external *.jar* files. After compiling the servlet, copy it over to your Tomcat installation.

Discussion

JSP files such as that developed in the previous recipe were introduced to make online Java programming easier. JSPs actually are compiled into servlet code, which is pure Java code, with no HTML mixed in. Developing servlets in Eclipse is like developing other Java code: Eclipse can detect problems even before you compile.

You can see the Java code for a servlet in Example 11-2. Servlet code such as this extends the HttpServlet class, and you have to include a *.jar* file in the build path to get that support. In Tomcat 4.x, that *.jar* file is *servlet.jar*; in Tomcat 5.x, it's *servlet-api.jar*.

Example 11-2. A sample servlet

```
package org.cookbook.ch11;

import java.io.*;
import javax.servlet.*;
import javax.servlet.http.*;

public class ServletClass extends HttpServlet
{
    public void doGet(HttpServletRequest request,
        HttpServletResponse response)
        throws IOException, ServletException
    {
        response.setContentType("text/html");
        PrintWriter out = response.getWriter( );

        out.println("<HTML>");
        out.println("<HEAD>");
        out.println("<TITLE>");
        out.println("Servlet Sample");
        out.println("</TITLE>");
        out.println("</HEAD>");
        out.println("<BODY>");
        out.println("<H1>");
        out.println("Servlet Sample");
        out.println("</H1>");
        out.println("This servlet is functional.");
        out.println("</BODY>");
        out.println("</HTML>");
    }
}
```

In this example, the code displays the text:

```
This servlet is functional.
```

To make this happen, create a new project, and call it *Servlet*. Create a new class in this project, ServletClass, in the package org.cookbook.ch11, and add the code from Example 11-2 to it.

To satisfy the imports, include *servlet-api.jar*, which comes with Tomcat 5.x (*servlet.jar* if you're using Tomcat 4.x) in the build path. You can find *servlet-api.jar* at *jakarta-tomcat-5.0.19\common\lib\servlet-api.jar*; right-click the *Ch11_02* project in the Package Explorer, select Properties → Java Build Path → Add External JARs, and add *servlet-api.jar* to the build path.

When you've added *servlet-api.jar* to the build path, you should be able to build the servlet's *.class* file. Select Project → Build Project, creating *ServletClass.class*.

See Also

Recipe 11.5 on installing a servlet in Tomcat; Chapter 2 in *Java Servlet Programming* (O'Reilly); Chapter 2 in *JavaServer Pages* (O'Reilly); Chapter 1 in the *Java Servlet and JSP Cookbook* (O'Reilly).

11.5   Installing a Servlet in Tomcat

Problem

You've created a servlet *.class* file, and you want to run it in Tomcat.

Solution

Place the *.class* file into the correct Tomcat directory (such as *webapps\Ch11\WEB-INF\class\org\cookbook\ch11*). Add servlet data to the *web.xml* file, restart Tomcat, and navigate to your servlet's URL, such as *http://localhost:8080/ch11/org.cookbook.ch11.ServletClass*.

Discussion

To install a *.class* file, you can simply copy it over to the correct directory in the Tomcat directory structure. Because the servlet is in the `org.cookbook.ch11` package, and the directory structure must mirror the package structure, put *ServletClass.class* in *webapps\Ch11\WEB-INF\class\org\cookbook\ch11*:

```
webapps
|__ch11
    |__WEB-INF
        |__classes
        |   |__org
        |   |    |__cookbook
        |   |         |__ch11        Put the servlet's code here
        |__lib
```

To set up this servlet with Tomcat, we'll create the deployment descriptor file, *web.xml*. In this XML file, we'll use two elements, `<servlet>` and `<servlet-mapping>`, to register this servlet with Tomcat. The *web.xml* file we'll use appears in Example 11-3.

Example 11-3. web.xml

```
<?xml version="1.0" encoding="ISO-8859-1"?>
<!DOCTYPE web-app PUBLIC "-//Sun Microsystems, Inc.//DTD Web Application 2.3//EN"
                         "http://java.sun.com/dtd/web-app_2_3.dtd">
<web-app>
  <display-name>Example Applications</display-name>

  <servlet>
    <servlet-name>Servlet</servlet-name>
    <servlet-class>org.cookbook.ch11.ServletClass</servlet-class>
  </servlet>

  <servlet-mapping>
    <servlet-name>Servlet</servlet-name>
    <url-pattern>/org.cookbook.ch11.ServletClass</url-pattern>
  </servlet-mapping>

</web-app>
```

Right-click the Servlet project to create this new XML document and select New →
File. To open *web.xml* in Eclipse, right-click it and select Open With → Text Editor
(unless you have a dedicated XML editor installed in Eclipse, as with a plug-in,
Eclipse opens your XML document in your default XML editor, which is probably a
web browser). Save the file, and copy it to the *ch11* directory's *WEB-INF* directory:

```
webapps
|__ch11
    |__WEB-INF              Store web.xml here
        |__classes
        |__lib
```

Then (re)start Tomcat, giving it a chance to copy everything over to the *work* directory. Now navigate to *http://localhost:8080/ch11/org.cookbook.ch11.ServletClass* in a
browser. You should see the new servlet running, as shown in Figure 11-4.

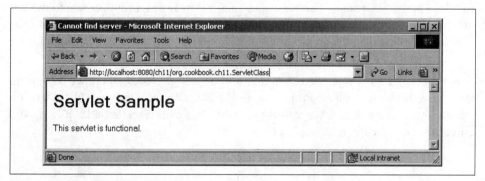

Figure 11-4. A working servlet

We're creating functional compiled servlet code with Eclipse at this point. But
there's no denying it's a pain to have to copy files from the Eclipse directories to the

Tomcat directories. Take a look at the following recipes to see how you can work with files in the Tomcat directories in Eclipse directly.

See Also

Recipe 11.6 on creating a servlet in place; Recipe 11.7 on editing *web.xml* in place; Chapters 2 and 3 in *Java Servlet Programming* (O'Reilly); Chapter 2 in the *Java Servlet and JSP Cookbook* (O'Reilly).

11.6   Creating a Servlet in Place

Problem

You want to develop web applications in place, without having to copy files over from the Eclipse directories.

Solution

Set the project's output folder to the web container's proper target directories.

Discussion

As an example, we'll create a new project here, *ServletInPlace*, and store the needed Tomcat files in Tomcat directories. Create this project by bringing up the New Project folder and entering the name ServletInPlace. To specify that we want the compiled output to go into the Tomcat directories rather than be stored locally, click Next, and click the Browse button next to the Default output folder box to open the Folder Selection dialog.

Next, click the Create new folder button; then click the Advanced button in the New Folder dialog. To connect to the Tomcat directory we want to use, check the "Link to folder in the file system" checkbox and click the Browse button. Browse to the target directory for our compiled code, *jakarta-tomcat-5.0.19\webapps\Ch11\WEB-INF\ classes*, and click OK, bringing up the New Folder dialog again. In that folder, give this new folder the name *output*, as shown in Figure 11-5, and click OK.

When we build this project, all compiled output will be stored where we want it, in the *classes* folder (actually, in this case, in the *classes\org\cookbook\ch11* folder, following the package name we're using). Create the class ServletInPlaceClass, and enter the code you see in Example 11-4.

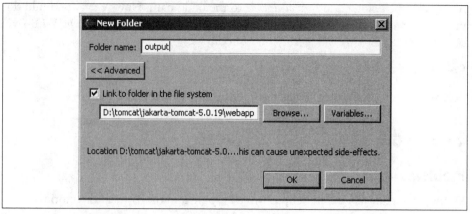

Figure 11-5. Setting up a new output folder

Example 11-4. An in-place servlet

```java
package org.cookbook.ch11;

import java.io.*;
import javax.servlet.*;
import javax.servlet.http.*;

public class ch11_03 extends HttpServlet
{
    public void doGet(HttpServletRequest request,
        HttpServletResponse response)
        throws IOException, ServletException
    {

        response.setContentType("text/html");
        PrintWriter out = response.getWriter();

        out.println("<HTML>");
        out.println("<HEAD>");
        out.println("<TITLE>");
        out.println("A Servlet Example");
        out.println("</TITLE>");
        out.println("</HEAD>");
        out.println("<BODY>");
        out.println("<H1>");
        out.println("Working With Servlets");
        out.println("</H1>");
        out.println("Developing servlets in place");
        out.println("</BODY>");
        out.println("</HTML>");
    }
}
```

As we've done before, add *servlet-api.jar* to the build path. Now when you build this project, *ServletInPlace.class* is stored automatically in the Tomcat *webapps\WEB-INF\classes\org\cookbook\ch11* directory, as it should be.

See Also

Recipe 11.7 on editing *web.xml* in place; Chapter 9 in *Eclipse* (O'Reilly).

11.7   Editing web.xml in Place

Problem

You want to edit *web.xml* in Eclipse while keeping it in the Tomcat directories.

Solution

Link to needed files such as *web.xml* in your project.

Discussion

To get access to *web.xml* in Eclipse, even though it's in the *webapps\ch11\WEB-INF* directory, you can make it a *linked file*. To do that, right-click the *ServletInPlace* project, select New → File, click the Advanced button, check the "Link to file in the file system" checkbox, and click the Browse button. Browse to the *webapps\ch11\WEB-INF* directory, and click Open. Then in the New File dialog that appears, enter the name of the file to link to, *web.xml*, and click OK. This adds *web.xml* to the project, as shown in the Package Explorer at left in Figure 11-6.

You can edit *web.xml* to support the ServletInPlace servlet, as shown in Example 11-5.

Example 11-5. The new version of web.xml

```
<?xml version="1.0" encoding="ISO-8859-1"?>
<!DOCTYPE web-app PUBLIC "-//Sun Microsystems, Inc.
           //DTD Web Application 2.3//EN" "http://java.sun.com/dtd/web-app_2_3.dtd">
<web-app>
  <display-name>Example Applications</display-name>

  <servlet>
    <servlet-name>Servlet</servlet-name>
    <servlet-class>org.cookbook.ch11.ServletClass</servlet-class>
  </servlet>

  <servlet>
    <servlet-name>ServletInPlace</servlet-name>
    <servlet-class>org.cookbook.ch11.ServletInPlaceClass</servlet-class>
  </servlet>

  <servlet-mapping>
```

Example 11-5. The new version of web.xml (continued)

```
    <servlet-name>Servlet</servlet-name>
    <url-pattern>/org.cookbook.ch11.ServletClass</url-pattern>
  </servlet-mapping>

  <servlet-mapping>
    <servlet-name>ServletInPlace</servlet-name>
    <url-pattern>/org.cookbook.ch11.ServletInPlaceClass</url-pattern>
  </servlet-mapping>

</web-app>
```

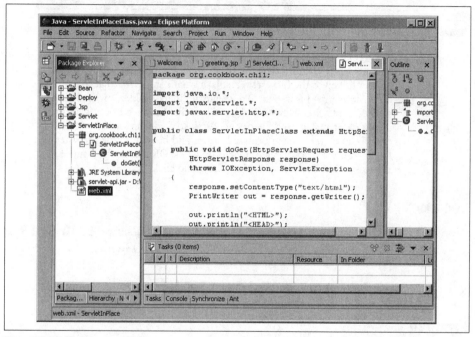

Figure 11-6. Linking to a file

After making these edits to *web.xml*, restart Tomcat. We've already built the servlet's code, so navigate to the new servlet's URL, *http://localhost:8080/ch11/org.*
cookbook.ch11.ServletInPlaceClass, as shown in Figure 11-7.

As you can see, letting Eclipse handle the details of storing compiled files and editing imported files in place makes life much easier than having to change files and
copy them to the web container's directories all the time. This is the way to go if you
are thinking of doing serious web development with JSP/servlets; the whole develop-
ment/testing/revision cycle is made so much easier this way.

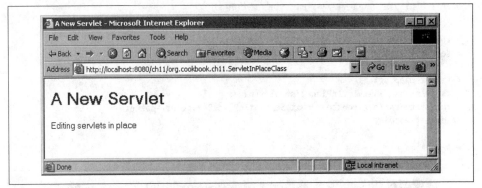

Figure 11-7. Running the servlet developed in place

 You also can create *linked folders* in Eclipse. A folder in an Eclipse project linked to the filesystem displays what's in a particular folder in the computer's filesystem. To create a linked folder, right-click a project, and select New → Folder. Click the Advanced button in the New Folder dialog, and check the "Link to folder in the file system" checkbox; then click the Browse button, and browse to the filesystem folder you want to display in Eclipse. Click OK, enter the name for this new folder in the Folder Name box, and click OK.

See Also

Recipe 11.4 on creating servlets; Recipe 11.5 on installing a servlet in Tomcat; Recipe 11.6 on creating a servlet in place; Chapter 9 in *Eclipse* (O'Reilly).

11.8   Avoiding Output Folder Scrubs

Problem

Now that you're working with the files in a web server's directories, you want to change Eclipse's default behavior of *scrubbing*—that is, deleting—all the files in a build directory because doing so deletes needed files in those directories.

Solution

To stop Eclipse from scrubbing the output directory for a project every time you build the project, select Project → Properties → Java Compiler → Use Project Settings → Build Path, and uncheck the "Scrub output folders on full build" checkbox.

Discussion

When you start working with the files in a web container's directories and not just your local Eclipse workspace, it can become a problem when Eclipse deletes all files in the output directory when you do a build (this is the default behavior). Those files might be other servlets that you need, for example, or configuration files needed by the server. It's not a problem when you're working with a workspace in Eclipse, where one project uses one directory, but when directories are shared by many files, as they are in web containers, it can be a serious problem.

To change this default behavior in Eclipse, select Project → Properties → Java Compiler → Use Project Settings → Build Path, and uncheck the "Scrub output folders on full build" checkbox, as shown in Figure 11-8. That stops Eclipse from scrubbing the output folder by default.

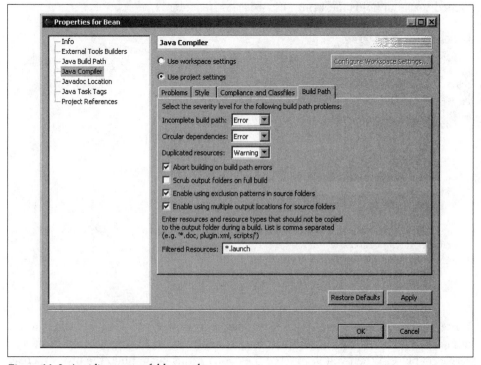

Figure 11-8. Avoiding output folder scrubs

11.9   Interfacing to JavaBeans

Problem

You want to develop JavaBeans and connect them to JSPs in Eclipse.

Solution

Develop the JavaBean code and the JSPs in place. To do that, simply set your project's output folder to the *WEB-INF\classes* directory in which you want the bean code, and create the JSP that uses the bean as a linked file in Eclipse.

Discussion

You can compile Java code into JavaBeans and access that code from JSPs. Now that you know how to use linked files, developing applications with JavaBeans is no problem. As an example, take a look at Example 11-6. This bean sets up a property named text that holds the string This bean is functional..

Example 11-6. A JavaBean

```
package org.cookbook.ch11;

public class BeanClass {
    private String text = "This bean is functional.";

    public BeanClass( )
    {
    }

    public void setText(String message)
    {
        text = message;
    }

    public String getText( )
    {
        return text;
    }
}
```

To set up this example, create a new project named *Bean* and send its output to the *webapps\ch11\WEB-INF\classes* directory, as explained in Recipe 11.6 on creating a servlet in place. When you've entered the code for this bean, build the project, creating and installing *BeanClass.class*.

The JSP file that connects to this bean appears in Example 11-7. Here, we use the JSP <jsp:useBean> element to create a JavaBean object and then the <jsp:getProperty> element to get the value of a bean property.

Example 11-7. Interfacing to a JavaBean

```
<HTML>
    <HEAD>
        <TITLE>Setting a Property Value</TITLE>
    </HEAD>
```

Example 11-7. Interfacing to a JavaBean (continued)

```
    <BODY>
        <H1>Setting a Property Value</H1>

        <jsp:useBean id="bean1" class="org.cookbook.ch11.BeanClass" />

        Got this from the bean: <jsp:getProperty name="bean1" property="text" />
    </BODY>
</HTML>
```

This JSP displays the original message in the msg property and the new value after it's been set. Treating this file as a linked file, store this new JSP file in the *webapps\Ch11* directory, and navigate to *http://localhost:8080/ch11/Bean.jsp*, as shown in Figure 11-9.

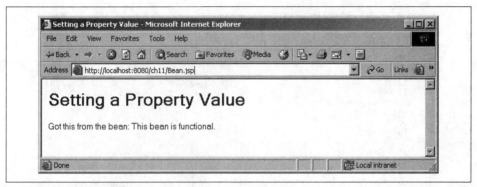

Figure 11-9. Connecting to a JavaBean

As you can see in the figure, the JSP file does indeed connect to the bean. Developing applications using output folders and linked files in this way is no problem.

See Also

Recipe 11.3 on creating JSP files; Chapter 6 in *JavaServer Pages* (O'Reilly); Chapter 7 in the *Java Servlet and JSP Cookbook* (O'Reilly); Chapter 9 in *Eclipse* (O'Reilly).

11.10 Using a Tomcat Plug-in

Problem

You want to automate some of the Tomcat processes, such as starting and stopping Tomcat, as well as debugging Tomcat projects.

Solution

Use a Tomcat plug-in such as the Sysdeo plug-in. Download the plug-in from *http://www.sysdeo.com/eclipse/tomcatPlugin.html*, and expand it in the Tomcat *plugins* directory. It'll add buttons to the Eclipse toolbar for starting and stopping Tomcat.

Discussion

The Sysdeo plug-in enables you to start and stop Tomcat from inside Eclipse, and you can download it for free from *http://www.sysdeo.com/eclipse/tomcatPlugin.html*. You install this plug-in by expanding it in the Tomcat *plugins* directory, then activate it by selecting Window → Customize Perspective, expanding the Other node, and clicking Tomcat, as shown in Figure 11-10.

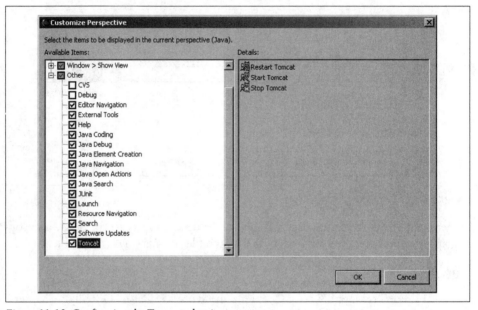

Figure 11-10. Configuring the Tomcat plug-in

 For more on installing, using, and creating plug-ins, see the next two chapters.

As shown in Figure 11-11, this adds a new Tomcat menu to Eclipse and adds three Tomcat buttons to the Eclipse toolbar you can see under the Navigate menu; these buttons start, stop, and restart Tomcat.

You also need to connect the plug-in to your installation of Tomcat. Do that by selecting Window → Preferences, which opens the Tomcat node. Browse to your

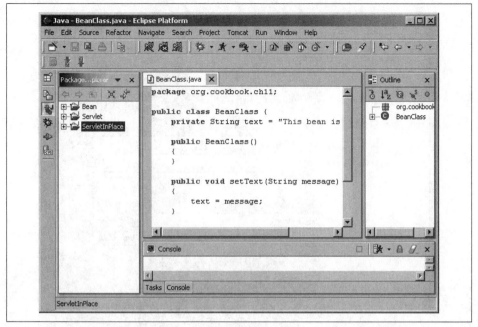

Figure 11-11. Tomcat menu and buttons in the toolbar

installation of Tomcat by clicking the Browse button next to the Tomcat home box, as shown in Figure 11-12.

This plug-in can handle the details of storing your files in the Tomcat installation if you create a Tomcat project. Just select File → New → Project and click Tomcat Project as the type of project, as shown in Figure 11-13.

As shown in Figure 11-14, your project files will be created in the correct Tomcat directories, which will appear in the Package Explorer.

The Sysdeo Tomcat plug-in also enables you to debug Tomcat projects as they're running, using the Eclipse debugger. That's extremely useful for web development because otherwise, all you have to track down errors with are the oblique `Error 500 Server Error` messages Tomcat shows in your browser.

See Also

Chapter 9 in *Eclipse* (O'Reilly).

11.11 Creating WAR Files

Problem

You want to create a deployment file for a web application.

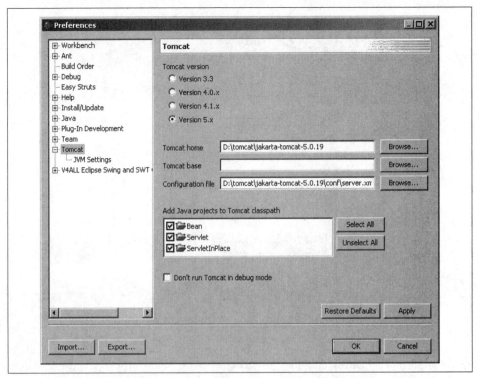

Figure 11-12. Configuring the Sysdeo Tomcat plug-in

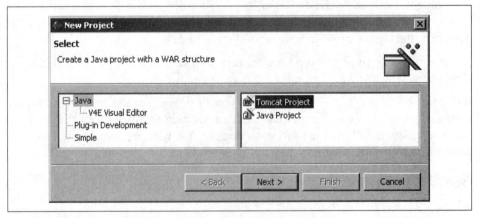

Figure 11-13. Creating a Tomcat project

Solution

Compress the web application into a *.war* file, which is the kind of file you use to deploy web applications. You can create *.war* files from Eclipse using Ant.

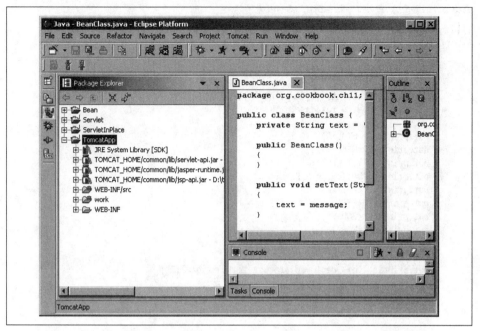

Figure 11-14. A new Tomcat project

Discussion

To get a look at how to deploy web apps using Eclipse, we'll deploy the sample servlet in Example 11-8 for a project named *DeployApp*, which can be found at this book's O'Reilly site. After compressing an application into a *.war* file, you can drop the *.war* file into the Tomcat *webapps* directory. Tomcat then expands and installs it when you restart Tomcat, which deploys the application.

Creating an application to deploy

To make it easier to create the *.war* file, give this project its own folder in the *webapps* directory (i.e., *webapps\DeployApp*). Don't forget to add a *WEB-INF* directory with the subdirectories *classes* and *lib*, and make the *classes* folder the output folder for the project. Then enter the code in Example 11-8 to *DeployClass.java*.

Example 11-8. A servlet to deploy

```
package org.cookbook.ch11;

import javax.servlet.http.HttpServlet;

import java.io.*;
import javax.servlet.*;
import javax.servlet.http.*;
```

Example 11-8. A servlet to deploy (continued)

```
public class DeployClass extends HttpServlet {
    public void doGet(HttpServletRequest request,
        HttpServletResponse response)
        throws IOException, ServletException
    {
        response.setContentType("text/html");
        PrintWriter out = response.getWriter();

        out.println("<HTML>");
        out.println("<HEAD>");
        out.println("<TITLE>");
        out.println("Deploying a Project");
        out.println("</TITLE>");
        out.println("</HEAD>");
        out.println("<BODY>");
        out.println("<H1>");
        out.println("Deploying a Project");
        out.println("</H1>");
        out.println("This deployed project is functional.");
        out.println("</BODY>");
        out.println("</HTML>");
    }
}
```

The *web.xml* file we'll use for this project appears in Example 11-9; place it in the project's *WEB-INF* folder. Then build the project, (re)start Tomcat, and navigate to *http://localhost:8080/DeployApp/org.cookbook.ch11.DeployClass* to confirm that the servlet is working. This is the servlet that we're going to deploy.

Example 11-9. web.xml for the web application to deploy

```
<?xml version="1.0" encoding="ISO-8859-1"?>
<!DOCTYPE web-app PUBLIC "-//Sun Microsystems, Inc.//DTD Web Application 2.3//EN" "http://
java.sun.com/dtd/web-app_2_3.dtd">
<web-app>
  <display-name>Example Applications</display-name>

  <servlet>
    <servlet-name>DeployApp</servlet-name>
    <servlet-class>org.cookbook.ch11.DeployClass</servlet-class>
  </servlet>

  <servlet-mapping>
    <servlet-name>DeployApp</servlet-name>
    <url-pattern>/org.cookbook.ch11.DeployClass</url-pattern>
  </servlet-mapping>

</web-app>
```

Creating a .war file to deploy

We've built the servlet we want to deploy, and the next step is to package it into a deployable *.war* file. The best way to do that in Eclipse is to use Ant, and we'll use the *build.xml* file in Example 11-10. This *build.xml* file takes the output of the *DeployApp* project and compresses it into a *.war* file named *DeployAppWar.war*, storing it in *webapps\DeployApp*.

Example 11-10. build.xml for the servlet to deploy

```xml
<?xml version="1.0" encoding="UTF-8" ?>
<project name="DeployApp" default="Main Build" basedir=".">
  <property name="project" location="d:/tomcat/jakarta-tomcat-5.0.19/webapps/DeployApp" />
  <property name="wardir" location="d:/tomcat/jakarta-tomcat-5.0.19/webapps/DeployApp" />
  <property name="warfile" location="${wardir}/DeployAppWar.war" />

    <target name="Initialize">
        <delete file="${warfile}" />
    </target>
    <target name="War">
        <jar destfile="${warfile}" basedir="${project}" />
    </target>
    <target name="Main Build" depends="Initialize, War">
        <echo message="Building the .war file" />
    </target>
</project>
```

Add *build.xml* to the project. After building the project, right-click *build.xml*, select Run Ant, and click Run to create *DeployAppWar.war*.

Deploying a .war file

After creating *DeployAppWar.war*, you can deploy the application just by placing that file in the Tomcat *webapps* directory on the target machine and (re)starting Tomcat. Tomcat uses the name of the *.war* file, expands that file, and installs the web application in a directory named *DeployAppWar*.

After dropping *DeployAppWar.war* into the *webapps* directory, (re)start Tomcat, and navigate to *http://localhost:8080/DeployAppWar/org.cookbook.ch11.DeployClass* to check this out. You should see the results shown in Figure 11-15. Now you're using Eclipse to create deployment packages for web applications. Not bad.

 You also can use Ant to deploy the *.war* file directly, using such Ant tasks as ftp to send the *.war* file to the web server directory you want on remote machines.

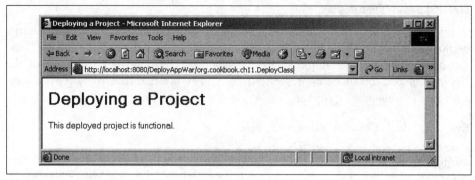

Figure 11-15. A deployed project

See Also

Recipe 7.1 in Chapter 7 on connecting Ant to Eclipse; Chapter 3 in *Tomcat: the Definitive Guide* (O'Reilly); Chapter 2 in the *Java Servlet and JSP Cookbook* (O'Reilly).

CHAPTER 12

Creating Plug-ins: Extension Points, Actions, and Menus

12.0 Introduction

This chapter begins our coverage on creating Eclipse plug-ins. That is, we're going to start extending Eclipse and what it can do. Up to this point, we've been using Eclipse out of the box; now you'll add your own code to augment the development environment.

Being able to create your own plug-ins is one of Eclipse's most powerful features, and although this kind of work isn't for everyone, it's good to know it's possible if you need it. As you'd expect, Eclipse plug-ins are written in Java.

In this chapter, we're going to start with plug-in development and the Plug-in Development Environment (PDE) by creating a plug-in that adds menus and menu items to the Eclipse IDE. When the user selects those custom menu items, our code will respond. By creating a plug-in from scratch, you'll get a good idea of all the details involved.

12.1 Installing a Plug-in

Problem

You want to install an Eclipse plug-in.

Solution

Download the plug-in, and expand it in the Eclipse *plugins* directory.

Discussion

Numerous plug-ins are available already, and many are free for the downloading. To install a plug-in, stop Eclipse if it's running, and download the plug-in to the *eclipse* directory, the directory that contains the *workspace* and *plugins* directories.

You can find more than 450 Eclipse plug-ins at *http://www.eclipse-plugins.2y.net/eclipse/*, and most of them are free. About 7,000 plug-ins are downloaded everyday from this site. Many of them support what Eclipse left out—especially drag-and-drop development for environments such as Swing, Struts, and SWT.

Eclipse plug-ins come zipped or tarred, and you typically uncompress them in the *eclipse* directory. When uncompressed, the files for the plug-ins are stored automatically in the *plugins* and *features* directories.

Each plug-in gets its own folder in the Eclipse *plugins* directory. Typically, you'll find the following files in every plug-in's folder:

*.jar
> The code for the plug-in, stored in a *.jar* file

about.html
> Shown when the user requests information about the plug-in

icons
> Directory for icons (the standard is GIF format)

lib   Holds library *.jar* files

plugin.xml
> The plug-in manifest, which is what describes the plug-in to Eclipse

plugin.properties
> Holds text data used by *plugin.xml*

Although you usually uncompress plug-ins in the *eclipse* directory, some plug-ins are designed to be unzipped in the *plugins* directory. If installation instructions for the plug-in are unavailable, open the plug-in using an unzip or untar tool, and take a look at how it'll expand itself—the file *plugin.xml* always has to go into a subdirectory of the *plugins* directory.

That's all you need to do to install a plug-in. After expanding the plug-in's compressed file, start Eclipse again. You might see a dialog indicating that configuration changes are pending; restart Eclipse again if necessary.

12.2   Creating plugin.xml

Problem

You want to do the minimal work required to create a new plug-in.

Solution

At a minimum, every plug-in needs a *plugin.xml* file that tells Eclipse about it. And if you have a *plugin.xml* file, you have a plug-in—even one that doesn't have any code. Start off *plugin.xml* with a standard XML declaration, add a <plugin> element, and set the id, name, version, and provider-name attributes of this element. Then store *plugin.xml* in a folder in the *plugins* directory to install this rudimentary plug-in.

Discussion

To get a handle on how Eclipse views plug-ins, we'll create a minimal plug-in now, which has only a *plugin.xml* file. This file is called the *plug-in manifest*, and it tells Eclipse all about the plug-in and where to find the Java support code, if any. Because, as far as Eclipse is concerned, all you need to create a plug-in is a plug-in manifest, we'll create one now as an example.

Use any text editor that can save plain text, including Eclipse, to create a plug-in manifest for a plug-in named org.cookbook.simple. Here's what *plugin.xml* looks like when specifying the plug-in's name, ID, version number, and provider name:

```
<?xml version="1.0" encoding="UTF-8"?>
<plugin
    id="org.cookbook.simple"
    name="Simple Plug-in"
    version="1.0.0"
    provider-name="Plug-in Power Corp.">
</plugin>
```

Plug-ins are stored in the *eclipse/plugins* folder, in folders reflecting their name and version number. To indicate that we're creating version 1.0.0 of this simple plug-in, store *plugin.xml* as *eclipse/plugins/org.cookbook.simple_1.0.0/plugin.xml*, then restart Eclipse.

This new plug-in doesn't do anything, but to confirm that Eclipse is treating it as a bona fide plug-in, take a look at the plug-in registry, which you can open by selecting Help → About Eclipse Platform and clicking the Plug-in Details button. You'll see the new, simple plug-in in the plug-in registry, as shown at the bottom of Figure 12-1.

That provides an introduction to working with plug-in manifests. To start creating code for plug-ins, take a look at the next couple of recipes.

See Also

Recipe 12.3 on creating a menu-based plug-in using wizards; Chapters 11 and 12 of *Eclipse* (O'Reilly).

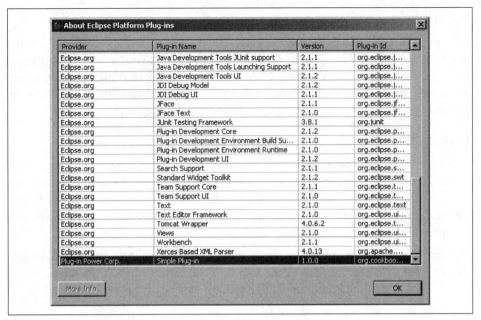

Figure 12-1. The simple plug-in in the plug-in registry

12.3 Creating a Menu-Based Plug-in Using Wizards

Problem

You want to create a plug-in that can add menus and menu items to the Eclipse IDE.

Solution

Use one of the plug-in templates available in the PDE to create a menu-supporting plug-in.

Discussion

With the Eclipse PDE, it's easy to build and modify your own plug-ins. Here are the types of projects the PDE can create for you:

Plug-in projects
    A standard plug-in project

Fragment projects
    A project that acts as an add-on or addition to a plug-in

Feature projects
    Projects that contain one or more plug-ins

Update Site projects
    Web projects that can update features automatically

As an example, we're going to create a new plug-in in a project named *MenuPlugIn* that adds both a menu and a toolbar button to the Eclipse IDE. To create the plug-in project, select File → New → Project. Select Plug-in Development in the left box of the New Project dialog and Plug-in Project in the right box, as shown in Figure 12-2. Then click Next.

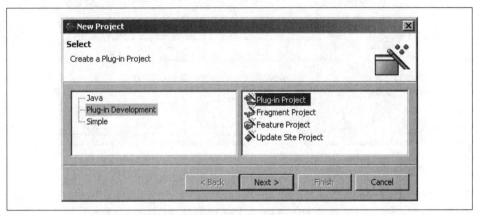

Figure 12-2. Creating a new plug-in project

The following pane of the dialog asks for the plug-in's project name. Call it `org. cookbook.ch12.MenuPlugIn` (this also will be the ID of the plug-in when it comes time to use it in Eclipse), as shown in Figure 12-3. Click Next.

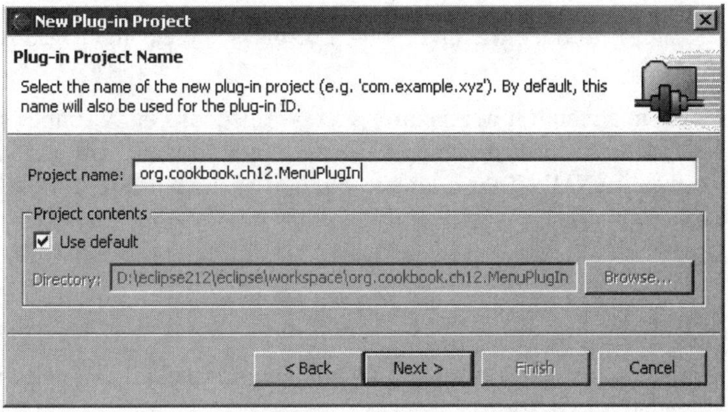

Figure 12-3. Creating a name for the plug-in

In the following pane, accept the defaults shown in Figure 12-4, and click Next, making this a Java-based project.

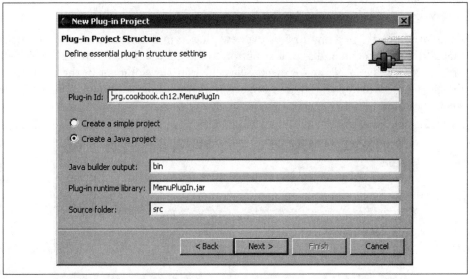

Figure 12-4. Making the project Java-based

In the next pane, you select the wizard to use to create the project. In this case, click Hello, World in the left box, as shown in Figure 12-5, and click Next.

The next pane configures the plug-in. For the provider name we'll enter Eclipse Cookbook; accept the other defaults, as shown in Figure 12-6.

Click Next, and enter the text the plug-in displays when its menu item or toolbar button is selected: This plug-in is functional., as shown in Figure 12-7. Click Finish to generate the code for the plug-in project.

Finally, click Finish to open the PDE, which displays a Welcome page, as shown in Figure 12-8.

Opening a plug-in's manifest in an editor such as this looks fairly simple, but a lot is going on here. This editor is designed to make it easy to work with manifests without going to the raw XML. Take a look at the tabs at the bottom of the editor. They are as follows:

Welcome
> This page describes a plug-in, and you can see an example in Figure 12-8.

Overview
> This displays summary information for the plug-in (including plug-in name, version, provider, and so forth).

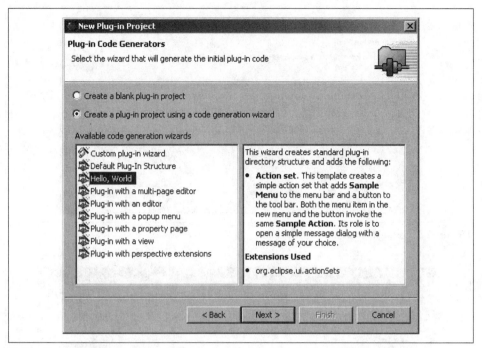

Figure 12-5. Selecting a wizard

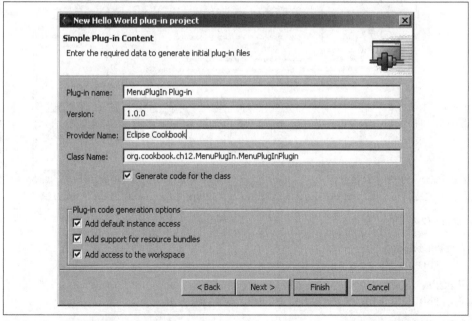

Figure 12-6. Configuring a plug-in

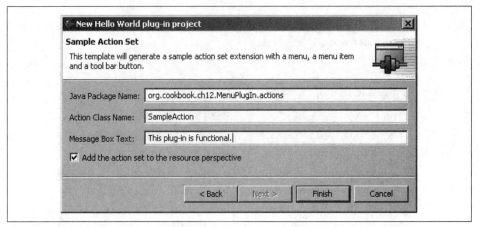

Figure 12-7. Setting the plug-in's display text

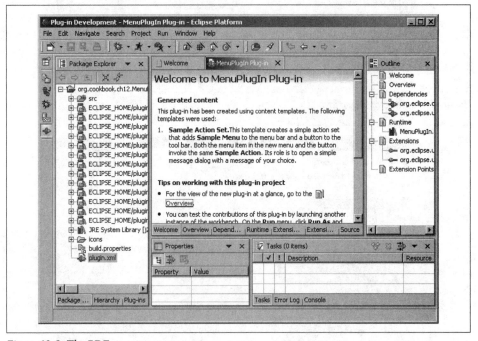

Figure 12-8. The PDE

Dependencies
 This details the plug-ins that are required to run this plug-in.

Runtime
 This details the libraries needed to run this plug-in.

Extensions
 This details the extensions used by the plug-in to build on other plug-ins.

Extension Points
This details the extension points defined by the plug-in.

Source
This is the source for *plugin.xml*, which you can edit directly in an XML editor.

When we start adding our own functionality to plug-ins, we'll come back to the manifest editor.

Eclipse 3.0

As you'd expect, the PDE is being expanded in Eclipse 3.0. For example, the PDE's Plug-in Project creation wizard has an option for creating plug-ins with OSGi bundle manifests (recommended only for plug-ins using the capabilities of the new OSGi-based Platform Runtime). And there's a new build configuration editor in the PDE, which means that if you want to use a *build.properties* file, the PDE gives you a specialized build configuration editor that facilitates the process.

See Also

Recipe 12.2 on creating *plugin.xml*; Recipe 12.4 on testing plug-ins with the Run-time Workbench; Chapter 11 of *Eclipse* (O'Reilly).

12.4 Testing Plug-ins with the Run-time Workbench

Problem

You are developing a plug-in, and you don't want to keep stopping and starting Eclipse each time you want to test the plug-in.

Solution

Launch a runtime workbench, which opens a new workbench with your plug-in already installed for testing purposes.

Discussion

If you want to, you can build the plug-in created in the previous recipe and deploy it to the *plugins* directory (see Recipe 12.5). But for testing purposes, there's an easier way. All you have to do while developing a plug-in is to launch a runtime workbench, which will appear with your plug-in already installed.

To launch a runtime workbench, highlight the plug-in project in the Package Explorer, select Run → Run, click the Run-time Workbench node in the left pane of the Run dialog, and click the New button, creating a new launch configuration, as shown in Figure 12-9. Accept the defaults by clicking Run.

The next time you want to launch the Run-time Workbench, you can simply select Run → Run As → Run-time Workbench.

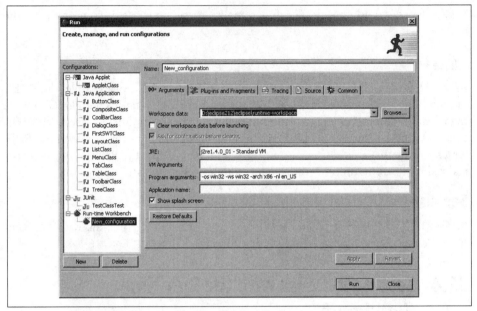

Figure 12-9. Creating a launch configuration

This starts the Run-time Workbench. You can see the menu defined by the plug-in, Sample Menu, and the button (with the Eclipse icon) it adds to the toolbar in Figure 12-10.

If you don't see your plug-in in the Run-time Workbench, select Window → Customize Perspective → Other, check the "Sample Action Set" checkbox defined by the plug-in we created, and click OK.

To verify things are working as they should, select Sample Menu → Sample Action or click the New button. The plug-in displays a message box with the message This plug-in is functional., as shown in Figure 12-11.

Cool—you've now created and run an Eclipse plug-in. To quit, close the Run-time Workbench.

You can debug plug-in code as you'd expect; just select Run → Debug As → Run-time Workbench.

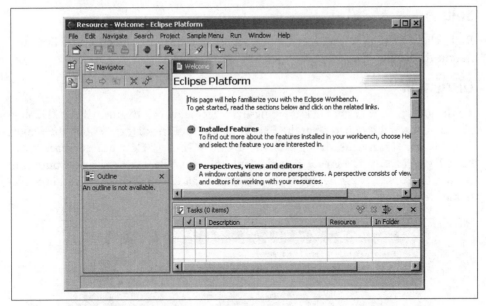

Figure 12-10. A runtime workbench

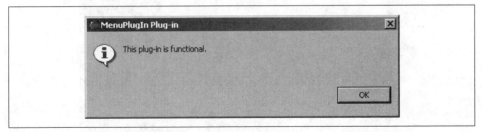

Figure 12-11. The plug-in's message

Eclipse 3.0

Eclipse 3.0 offers a new option on the Plug-ins tab of the Run-time Workbench launch configuration dialog that enables you to select a set of plug-ins to include while testing your plug-in. And as far as testing goes, the Eclipse 3.0 PDE has a new launcher for JUnit-based unit test suites for plug-ins. In fact, that's one of the big changes in Eclipse 3.0: you can use JUnit to test plug-ins.

12.5   Deploying a Plug-in

Problem

You want to deploy a plug-in you've created.

Solution

Right-click the plug-in project, click Export, and follow the directions. Eclipse will handle the details.

Discussion

To deploy a plug-in, right-click the plug-in project and click Export. Check "Deployable plug-ins and fragments" in the Export dialog, and click Next to open the Export Plug-ins and Fragments dialog shown in Figure 12-12. Select `org.cookbook.ch12.` `MenuPlugIn (1.0.0)`. To create a single deployable *.zip* file, use the Browse button to browse to *eclipse/workspace/org.cookbook.ch12/MenuPlugIn*; Eclipse will add the filename *MenuPlugIn_1_0_0.zip*. Then click Finish.

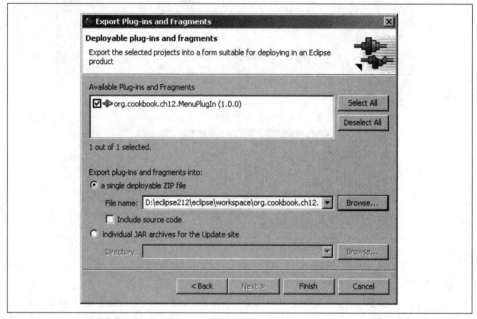

Figure 12-12. Exporting a plug-in

Clicking Finish creates *MenuPlugIn_1_0_0.zip*, ready for deployment. This file contains two files: *MenuPlugIn.jar* and *plugin.xml*. This *.zip* file, *MenuPlugIn_1_0_0.zip*, is what you deploy to users—all they've got to do is to unzip it.

> You can specify the name of the *.jar* file the project will create when you create the project initially in the third pane of the New Plug-in Project dialog.

12.6   Writing a Plug-in from a Skeleton

Problem

You want to develop the code for a plug-in yourself, from scratch.

Solution

You can create a skeletal plug-in project in the Plug-in Code Generators pane by selecting Default Plug-In Structure. We'll do that here and develop the rest of the plug-in from that starting point.

Discussion

As an example, we'll create the plug-in created earlier in this chapter that displayed menus, but this time, we'll do the work ourselves instead of relying entirely on a wizard. We will use a wizard to get started, however, so select File → New → Project. In the New Project dialog, select Plug-in Development in the left box and Plug-in Project in the right box, and click Next. In the next pane, enter the new project's name, org.cookbook.ch12.MenuPlugInFromScratch, and click Next to open the Plug-in Project Structure pane. Click Next again to accept the defaults.

In the Plug-in Code Generators pane, select Default Plug-In Structure, as shown in Figure 12-13, and click Next.

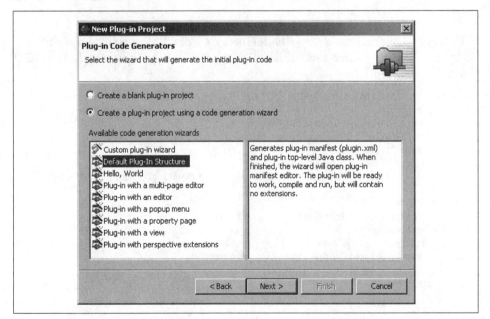

Figure 12-13. Selecting a plug-in wizard

The next dialog enables you to set the provider name, which we'll set to Eclipse Cookbook. Because we'll be writing our own code here, uncheck the items in the "Plug-in code generation options" box, as shown in Figure 12-14, and click Finish.

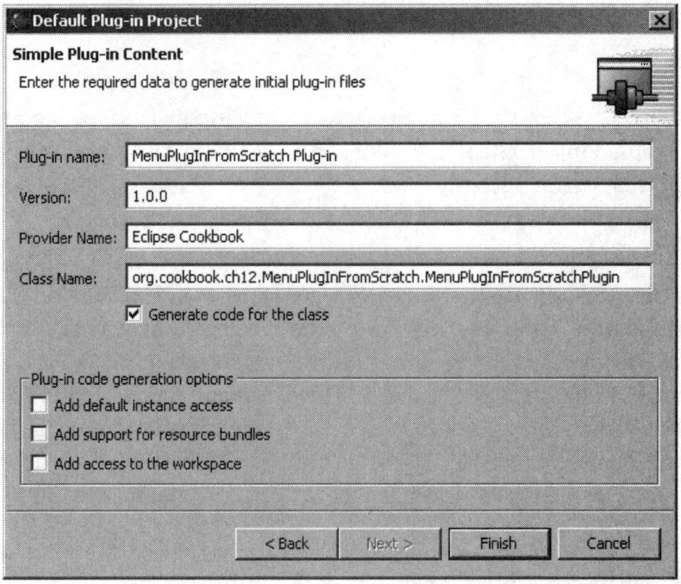

Figure 12-14. Setting the provider name

Clicking Finish creates the MenuPlugInFromSratch plug-in, opening its manifest in Eclipse. Click the Source tab, which displays the XML in *plugin.xml*. That XML should look like this:

```xml
<?xml version="1.0" encoding="UTF-8"?>
<plugin
    id="org.cookbook.ch12.MenuPlugInFromScratch"
    name="MenuPlugInFromScratch Plug-in"
    version="1.0.0"
    provider-name="Eclipse Cookbook"
    class="org.cookbook.ch12.MenuPlugInFromScratch.MenuPlugInFromScratchPlugin">

    <runtime>
        <library name="MenuPlugInFromScratch.jar"/>
    </runtime>
    <requires>
        <import plugin="org.eclipse.core.resources"/>
        <import plugin="org.eclipse.ui"/>
    </requires>

</plugin>
```

That's our new plug-in's manifest. Our goal in this plug-in is to add a new menu item and a button in the toolbar. To make things happen in a plug-in, you define *actions* and *action sets*. See the following recipe for further details.

See Also

Recipe 12.2 on creating *plugin.xml*; Recipe 12.9 on creating an action set; Recipe 12.10 on coding an Eclipse action; Chapters 11 and 12 in *Eclipse* (O'Reilly).

12.7 Responding to User Actions in a Plug-in

Problem

You want to let your plug-in respond to user actions in the Eclipse IDE.

Solution

Create an action set, and support it in your plug-in's code. You can do this with the New Extension wizard.

Discussion

An *action* represents an action the user can perform; for example, you can connect actions to elements such as menus and toolbars. To specify what happens when an action is activated, you extend the Action class. After you've created an action, you can use it in a variety of places, such as menu item selections or toolbar button clicks; the same action object will make the same thing happen in either case. An *action set* is, as the name implies, a set of actions. You connect actions to items such as menus and toolbars using an action set.

To develop action sets, you use *extension points*. An extension point lets one plug-in build on what another plug-in exports. Action sets such as those that enable you to implement menu and toolbar actions are extensions of the org.eclipse.ui. actionSets extension point.

 Plug-ins can use only those classes that are exported by other plug-ins, which makes extension points especially important. Much support for custom plug-ins is already built into several standard plug-ins that come with Eclipse. To let a plug-in use your Java code, you can put that code in a *.jar* file; then you can wrap the *.jar* file inside a plug-in so that other plug-ins can access your code.

To create an action set which ties a menu and toolbar button to an action, click the Extension tab in the *MenuPlugInFromScratch* project's plug-in manifest editor, and click Add to open the New Extension wizard shown in Figure 12-15. Select Generic

Wizards in the left box, select Schema-based Extension in the right box, and click Next.

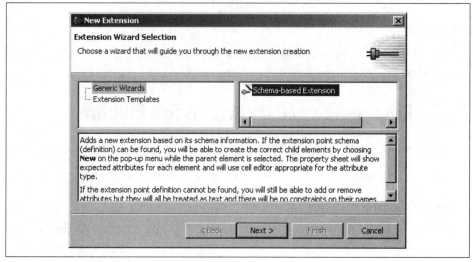

Figure 12-15. Using the New Extension wizard

The next dialog enables you to select the extension point on which you want to build, as shown in Figure 12-16. Because we want to create an action set to support toolbar buttons and menu items, we'll use the `org.eclipse.ui.actionSets` extension point. Select it, as shown in the figure, and click Finish.

When you click Finish, an entry for the `org.eclipse.ui.actionSets` extension point is added to the Extensions pane in the Eclipse manifest editor, as shown in Figure 12-17. To create a new action set, right-click `org.eclipse.ui.actionSets` in the All Extensions box and select New → actionSet, creating a new action set, as shown in the figure.

To set the properties of this new action set, select it and, in the Properties view at the bottom of the Eclipse window, set the `label` property to `Action Set 1` and the `visible` property to `true`, as shown in Figure 12-18.

That creates the new action set.

12.8 Creating a Plug-in Menu from Scratch

Problem

You have a plug-in action set, and you want to create a new menu using it.

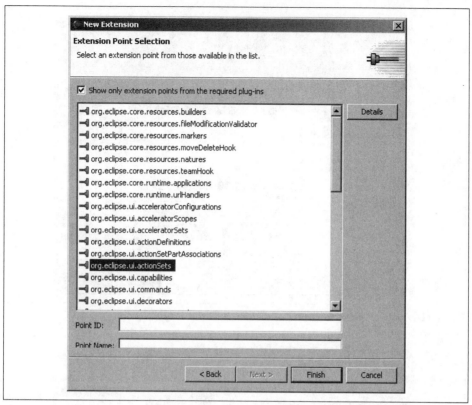

Figure 12-16. Selecting an extension point

Solution

To create a new menu, right-click an action set in the Extensions tab, and select New → Menu.

Discussion

We'll continue the example developed in the previous recipe by adding a new menu to the action set created in that recipe. Right-click Action Set 1 in the Extensions tab, and select New → Menu. In the Properties view, set the id property of the new menu to Menu1 and the label property to Menu 1, as shown in Figure 12-19, where the new menu appears under Action Set 1.

We're going to add a menu separator to this menu as a placeholder that will enable us to add other items to the menu later, grouping menu items together. To create a menu separator, right-click the menu, Menu 1, and select New → Separator. Set the separator's name property to Group1, in the Properties view, as shown in Figure 12-20.

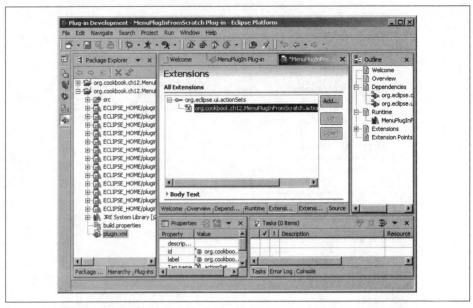

Figure 12-17. A new action set

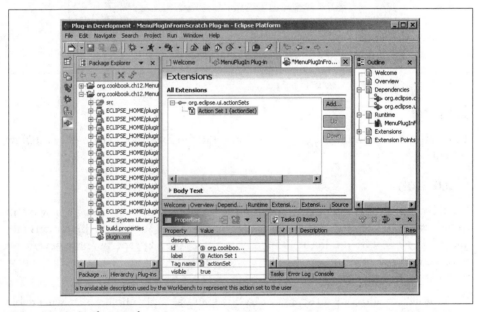

Figure 12-18. Configuring the action set

This creates a new menu and adds it to the action set. Now you've got to create some menu items and connect an action to them to make something happen. See the next recipe for details.

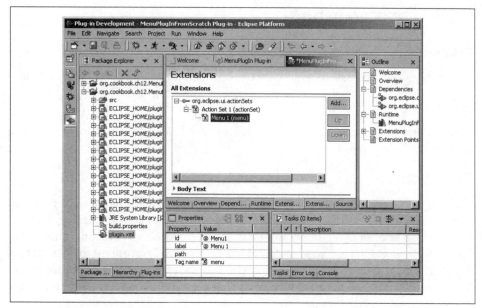

Figure 12-19. A new menu

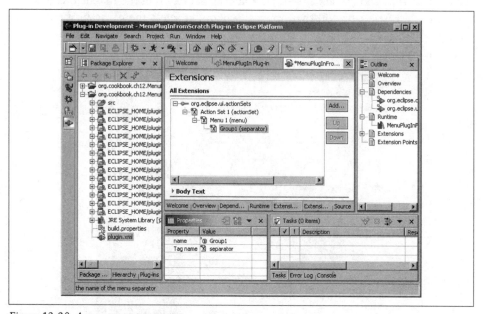

Figure 12-20. A new menu separator

See Also

Recipe 12.9 on creating actions; Recipe 12.10 on coding plug-in actions; Chapters 11 and 12 of *Eclipse* (O'Reilly).

12.9 Creating Actions

Problem

You want to create menu items and toolbar buttons and connect Java code to them.

Solution

Create a new action, add menu items and toolbar buttons, and implement what you want to have happen in Java.

Discussion

Building upon the example developed in the previous two recipes, we'll now add menu items and a toolbar button to the plug-in. Right-click Action Set 1 in the Extensions box of the plug-in manifest editor and select New → Action. In the Properties view, set the label property to Action 1, the toolTip property to This action is functional., and the id property to Action1. Next, set the menubarPath property to Menu1/Group1 and the toolbarPath property to Group1. That connects the action to the menu item and toolbar button.

To connect the action to code, select the action, Action 1, in the Extensions box, and click the ellipsis (...) button that appears when you select the class property in the Properties view. This opens the Java Attribute Editor shown in Figure 12-21.

Figure 12-21. Creating an action class

Select the "Generate a new Java class" radio button, enter `org.cookbook.ch12.`
`MenuPlugInFromScratch` in the "Package name" box (or click the Browse button and
select that package), and name the class `Action1`, as shown in the figure. Then click
Finish. This creates the new action and adds its Java support file, *Action1.java*, to the
project.

See Also

Recipe 12.7 on responding to user actions in a plug-in; Recipe 12.10 on coding a
plug-in action; Chapter 11 of *Eclipse* (O'Reilly).

12.10 Coding a Plug-in Action

Problem

You have an action, and you need to make it actually do something.

Solution

Edit its *.java* file, and implement the support you need.

Discussion

Continuing the example developed over the previous three recipes, open *Action1.
java* now if it's not already open. This file contains plenty of TODOs, such as adding
code to the action's constructor to customize it, which we'll ignore in this example.
Here, we'll display a message box when the user selects our menu item or clicks our
toolbar button, as the plug-in developed earlier in this chapter did.

To do that, we'll need an object that implements the Workbench window interface,
IWorkbenchWindow. The object we need is passed to the init method in *Action1.java*,
so we'll begin by creating a private class variable, window, to hold it:

```
public class Action1 implements IWorkbenchWindowActionDelegate {
    private IWorkbenchWindow window;
        .
        .
        .
```

Then we'll store the Workbench window passed to us in the init method in this
variable like so:

```
public void init(IWorkbenchWindow window) {
    this.window = window;
}
```

We can use this variable and the openInformation method of the MessageDialog class
to display a message box with the message This plug-in is functional. in the

action's run method. To use the `MessageDialog` class, we first import it and then call it in the run method:

```
import org.eclipse.jface.dialogs.MessageDialog;
    .
    .
    .
public void run(IAction action)  {
    MessageDialog.openInformation(
    window.getShell( ),
    "New Plug-in",
    "This plug-in is functional.");
}
```

That finishes the plug-in. Now save all files, and rebuild the project. To test this new plug-in, launch the Run-time Workbench.

Note that there's one more step to load the plug-in, which wasn't necessary with the plug-in developed using a wizard in the earlier part of this chapter. We have to explicitly add the new plug-in to the current perspective to see it, so select Window → Customize Perspective in the Run-time Workbench, select the box next to Action Set 1, as shown in Figure 12-22, and click OK.

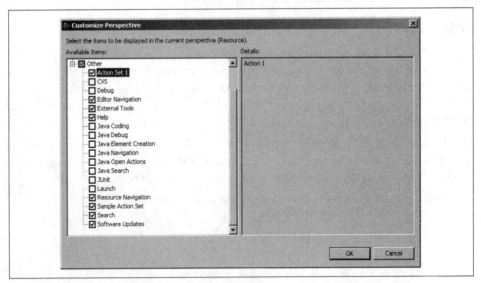

Figure 12-22. Customizing the perspective

You should now see the default square button icon that Eclipse uses for toolbar buttons and the new menu, Menu 1, as shown in Figure 12-23.

Select New Menu → Action 1, or click the New button. You should see the New Plug-in message box, as shown in Figure 12-24. Congratulations, you're an Eclipse plug-in developer.

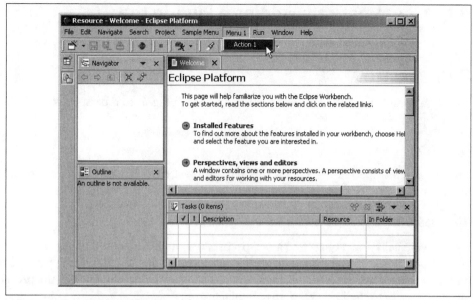

Figure 12-23. A new plug-in at work

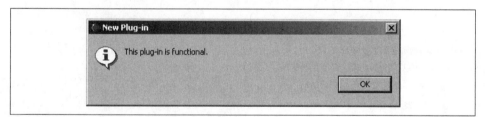

Figure 12-24. The message from the new plug-in

Having to customize the perspective every time you launch a new plug-in using Window → Customize Perspective is a little cumbersome. Take a look at the next recipe to see how to get around it.

See Also

Recipe 12.7 on responding to a user's action; Recipe 12.9 on creating Action sets; Recipe 12.11 on adding a plug-in to a perspective.

12.11 Automatically Adding a Plug-in to a Perspective

Problem

You don't want users to have to explicitly add your plug-in to a perspective by customizing it.

Solution

Use the extension point org.eclipse.ui.perspectiveExtensions in *plugin.xml* to add the plug-in to the perspective automatically.

Discussion

To automatically add a plug-in to a perspective, use the extension point org.eclipse. ui.perspectiveExtensions in *plugin.xml*. You can make this just by editing the XML in *plugin.xml*. Here's how to automatically add the plug-in developed over the previous few recipes to the Java perspective in *plugin.xml*:

```xml
<?xml version="1.0" encoding="UTF-8"?>
<plugin
    id="org.cookbook.ch12.MenuPlugInFromScratch"
    name="MenuPlugInFromScratch Plug-in"
    version="1.0.0"
    provider-name="Eclipse Cookbook"
    class="org.cookbook.ch12.MenuPlugInFromScratch.MenuPlugInFromScratchPlugin">

    <runtime>
        <library name="MenuPlugInFromScratch.jar"/>
    </runtime>
    <requires>
        <import plugin="org.eclipse.core.resources"/>
        <import plugin="org.eclipse.ui"/>
    </requires>

    <extension
            point="org.eclipse.ui.actionSets">
        <actionSet
            label="Action Set 1"
            visible="true"
            id="org.cookbook.ch12.MenuPlugInFromScratch.actionSet1">
            <menu
                label="Menu 1"
                id="Menu1">
                <separator
                    name="Group1">
                </separator>
            </menu>
            <action
                label="Action 1"
```

```
              class="org.cookbook.ch12.MenuPlugInFromScratch.Action1"
              tooltip="This action is functional."
              menubarPath="Menu1/Group1"
              toolbarPath="Group1"
              id="Action1">
      </action>
    </actionSet>
  </extension>
  <extension
     point = "org.eclipse.ui.perspectiveExtensions">
     <perspectiveExtension
        targetID="org.eclipse.ui.javaPerspective">
        <actionSet
           id="org.cookbook.ch12.MenuPlugInFromScratch.actionSet1">
        </actionSet>
     </perspectiveExtension>
  </extension>
</plugin>
```

Save *plugin.xml* after editing it, and restart the Run-time Workbench. When you do, the new plug-in should appear on startup.

 Other perspectives can be reached using similar nomenclature. For example, to add a plug-in to the Resource perspective, use org.eclipse.ui.resourcePerspective.

CHAPTER 13

Creating Plug-ins: Wizards, Editors, and Views

13.0 Introduction

In this chapter, we're going to expand our plug-in power by creating plug-ins that display wizards, editors, and views. It's not as hard as you might think, especially because you can rely on templates that the PDE can create for you and modify them as needed. We'll see how that works in this chapter.

13.1 Creating a Plug-in That Supports Wizards and Editors

Problem

You want to create a plug-in that uses a wizard to create files and an editor to edit them.

Solution

Use a PDE Wizard template. Create a new plug-in project, select the "Plug-in with a multi-page editor" template, and follow the onscreen directions to create a skeletal template, ready to be customized.

Discussion

In this example, we're going to create a plug-in that Eclipse will associate with the file extension *.new*. The plug-in's wizard will enable the user to create files with this extension, and when the user double-clicks those files, they'll appear in the plug-in's editor.

The PDE can help us out here by creating a template for our plug-in. Select New → Project. In the New Project dialog, select Plug-in Development in the left box and

Plug-in Project in the right box, and click Next. Specify the name of the project as org.cookbook.ch13.EditorPlugIn in the following dialog, as shown in Figure 13-1.

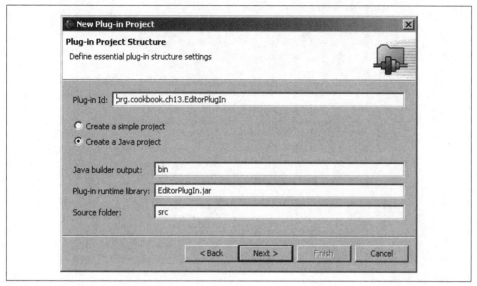

Figure 13-1. Naming the plug-in

Click Next once again to bring up the Plug-in Code Generators dialog shown in Figure 13-2. Select the "Plug-in with a multi-page editor" template, as shown in the figure, and click Next.

In the next dialog, give the provider name as Eclipse Cookbook, as shown in Figure 13-3, and click Next.

The following dialog enables you to give the extension you want to use for the files created by this plug-in; enter new here, as shown in Figure 13-4. Then click Next.

In the last dialog, shown in Figure 13-5, set the file extension to new, and enter document.new as the initial filename.

Finally, click Finish to create the code template for the plug-in. The following files are created by the PDE and added to the *org.cookbook.ch13.EditorPlugIn* project.

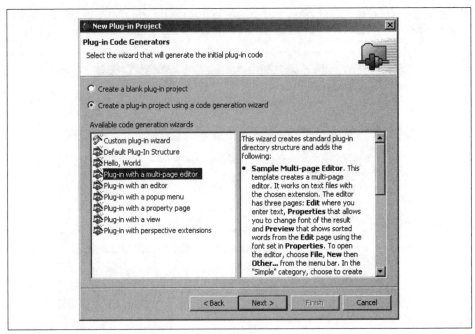

Figure 13-2. Creating a plug-in with a multipage editor

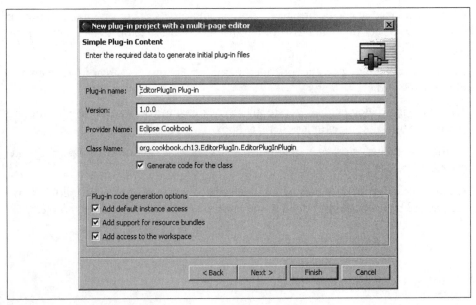

Figure 13-3. Giving the provider name

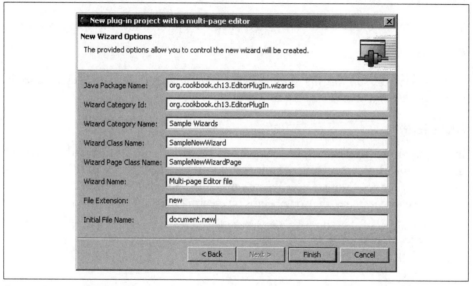

Figure 13-4. Configuring the plug-in's editor

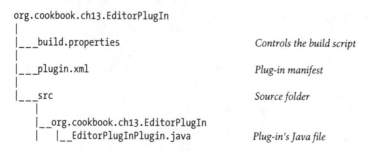

Figure 13-5. Configuring the wizard

```
org.cookbook.ch13.EditorPlugIn
    |
    |___build.properties                    Controls the build script
    |
    |___plugin.xml                          Plug-in manifest
    |
    |___src                                 Source folder
        |
        |__org.cookbook.ch13.EditorPlugIn
        |    |__EditorPlugInPlugin.java     Plug-in's Java file
```

```
        |
        |__org.cookbook.ch13.EditorPlugIn.editors
        |  |__MultiPageEditor.java              Editor's code
        |  |__MultiPageEditorContributor.java   Editor actions
        |
        |__org.cookbook.ch13.EditorPlugIn.wizards
           |__SampleNewWizard.java              Wizard's code
           |__SampleNewWizardPage.java          Wizard's page
```

See Also

Recipe 13.2 on customizing a wizard; Recipe 13.3 on customizing editors; Chapter 12 of *Eclipse* (O'Reilly).

13.2   Customizing a Wizard

Problem

You want to customize a template you created for a plug-in that includes a wizard.

Solution

Edit the wizard's support file (*SampleNewWizard.java* in the example created in the previous recipe) to customize the code.

Discussion

In the plug-in created in the previous recipe, the wizard creates files with the default name *document.new*, inserting default text into those files. This wizard is supported by the two files *SampleNewWizard.java* and *SampleNewWizardPage.java*. In *SampleNewWizard.java*, the code begins by creating the page the wizard will show:

```java
public class SampleNewWizard extends Wizard implements INewWizard {
    private SampleNewWizardPage page;
    private ISelection selection;

    /**
     * Constructor for SampleNewWizard.
     */
    public SampleNewWizard() {
        super();
        setNeedsProgressMonitor(true);
    }

    /**
     * Adding the page to the wizard.
     */

    public void addPages() {
        page = new SampleNewWizardPage(selection);
```

```
        addPage(page);
    }
        .
        .
        .
```

In the createControl method of *SampleNewWizardPage.java*, the wizard's appearance is created. As you can see here, the SWT controls—labels, text controls, and so on—are added and positioned:

```java
public void createControl(Composite parent) {
    Composite container = new Composite(parent, SWT.NULL);
    GridLayout layout = new GridLayout( );
    container.setLayout(layout);
    layout.numColumns = 3;
    layout.verticalSpacing = 9;
    Label label = new Label(container, SWT.NULL);
    label.setText("&Container:");

    containerText = new Text(container, SWT.BORDER | SWT.SINGLE);
    GridData gd = new GridData(GridData.FILL_HORIZONTAL);
    containerText.setLayoutData(gd);
    containerText.addModifyListener(new ModifyListener( ) {
        public void modifyText(ModifyEvent e) {
            dialogChanged( );
        }
    });

    Button button = new Button(container, SWT.PUSH);
    button.setText("Browse...");
    button.addSelectionListener(new SelectionAdapter( ) {
        public void widgetSelected(SelectionEvent e) {
            handleBrowse( );
        }
    });
    label = new Label(container, SWT.NULL);
    label.setText("&File name:");

    fileText = new Text(container, SWT.BORDER | SWT.SINGLE);
    gd = new GridData(GridData.FILL_HORIZONTAL);
    fileText.setLayoutData(gd);
    fileText.addModifyListener(new ModifyListener( ) {
        public void modifyText(ModifyEvent e) {
            dialogChanged( );
        }
    });
    initialize( );
    dialogChanged( );
    setControl(container);
}
```

If you want to customize the wizard's page, do it here. This is where that page is created; if you want a different appearance and different controls, this is the place to configure things as you want them.

The actual work that the wizard does for your plug-in begins when the Finish button is clicked in the wizard's page, calling the doFinish method in *SampleNewWizard. java*. We'll customize this code to insert our own text into the newly created document. That method runs in a worker thread, and it begins by finding the path of the file to create and creates that file this way; if you want to create files in another location, this is the spot to customize:

```
private void doFinish(
    String containerName,
    String fileName,
    IProgressMonitor monitor)
    throws CoreException {
    // create a sample file
    monitor.beginTask("Creating " + fileName, 2);
    IWorkspaceRoot root = ResourcesPlugin.getWorkspace( ).getRoot( );
    IResource resource = root.findMember(new Path(containerName));
    if (!resource.exists( ) || !(resource instanceof IContainer)) {
        throwCoreException("Container \"" + containerName +
        "\" does not exist.");
    }
    IContainer container = (IContainer) resource;
    final IFile file = container.getFile(new Path(fileName));
            .
            .
            .
```

To set the contents of the new file, the code next calls a method named openContentStream and uses that method to fill the file:

```
try {
    InputStream stream = openContentStream( );
    if (file.exists( )) {
        file.setContents(stream, true, true, monitor);
    } else {
        file.create(stream, true, monitor);
    }
    stream.close( );
            .
            .
            .
```

We'll customize the openContentStream method to change the default text put into the *document.new* file created by the wizard. Here's what that method looks like now:

```
private InputStream openContentStream( ) {
    String contents =
        "This is the initial file contents for *.new file that should
                be word-sorted in the Preview page of the multi-page editor";
    return new ByteArrayInputStream(contents.getBytes( ));
}
```

Change that to this, where we're installing our own custom text:

```
private InputStream openContentStream( ) {
    String contents =
```

```
        "Welcome to document.new";
    return new ByteArrayInputStream(contents.getBytes( ));
}
```

Making this change customizes the wizard for our purposes. In Recipe 13.3, we will customize the editor this plug-in displays.

See Also

Recipe 13.1 on creating plug-ins that support wizards and editors; Recipe 13.3 on customizing an editor.

13.3   Customizing an Editor

Problem

You've created a new plug-in using a PDE wizard, and you want to customize the editor.

Solution

Customize the editor's *.java* file.

Discussion

If you followed the discussion over the previous two recipes, you already have in hand a good template for a plug-in with an editor, and customizing that template is easy. The editor is supported by two files, *MultiPageEditor.java* and *MultiPage-EditorContributor.java*. The toolbar and menu support is in *MultiPageEditor-Contributor.java*, and the actual Java support for the editor is in *MultiPageEditor.java*.

In this example, we'll take a look at the code for *MultiPageEditor.java* and modify it. As it stands, this code displays three pages: the text in the document created by the plug-in's wizard, a page that enables you to select the display font, and a page that displays the words in the document in sorted order. We don't need all that in our example; we'll just make use of the first page, which displays the text in the document in a text editor.

To display the text in the first page of the editor, the code uses an `org.eclipse.editors.ui.text.TextEditor` object named editor. After creating that object, you can use the `MultiPageEditorPart` class's `addPage` method to add the new page to the editor. Here's how it works; the code starts by creating a new `TextEditor` object (the `MultiPageEditor` class extends `MultiPageEditorPart`, which uses an SWT tab control to display multiple editor pages).

```
public class MultiPageEditor extends MultiPageEditorPart {

    private TextEditor editor;
        .
        .
        .

    void createPage0() {
        try {
          editor = new TextEditor();
              .
              .
              .

        }
    }
```

To install this editor in the page, you just use the addPage method, passing it the editor object and using the getEditorInput method to get the text in the editor. To set the text in the page's tab, you use the setPageText method:

```
public class MultiPageEditor extends MultiPageEditorPart {

    private TextEditor editor;
        .
        .
        .

    void createPage0() {
        try {
          editor = new TextEditor();
          int index = addPage(editor, getEditorInput());
          setPageText(index, editor.getTitle());
        } catch (PartInitException e) {
          ErrorDialog.openError(
                  getSite().getShell(),
                  "Error creating nested text editor",
                  null,
                  e.getStatus());
        }
    }
```

That's all it takes to install an editor object in a page in this plug-in. To add your own controls to a plug-in page, you can create an SWT Composite control, set the layout in the composite, add the controls and listeners you want to the composite, and pass the composite to addPage.

The method that calls the various page-creating methods is called createPages. We're going to need only the first editor page in this example, created by the createPage0 method, so comment out the other two pages created by the PDE wizard:

```
protected void createPages() {
    createPage0();
//    createPage1();
//    createPage2();
```

To run this new plug-in, start the Run-time Workbench, and create a new Java project, *TestProject*. Right-click TestProject, and select New → Other to open the New dialog shown in Figure 13-6. Select Sample Wizards in the left box and Multi-page Editor file in the right box, and click Next to open the new wizard.

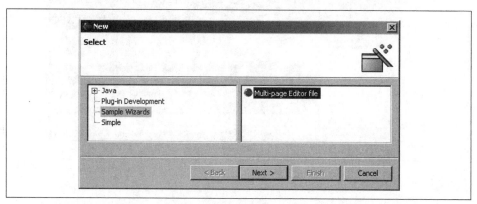

Figure 13-6. Using a new wizard

The new wizard indicates that it'll name the new file *document.new* by default, as shown in Figure 13-7, although you can change that name here. You have to associate a project with the new file, so click the Browse button, and navigate to TestProject.

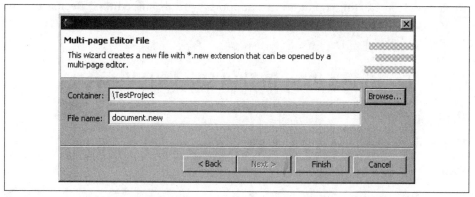

Figure 13-7. Creating a new document

Click Finish to create the new document, *document.new*, which is added to the project you specified, *TestProject*, and opened in the plug-in's editor, as shown in Figure 13-8. You can see the name of the document in the editor's tab, and the default text we placed in the file. Very cool.

If you double-click a file with the extension *.new* in views such as the Package Explorer or Navigator, that file is opened in the editor automatically. And you can

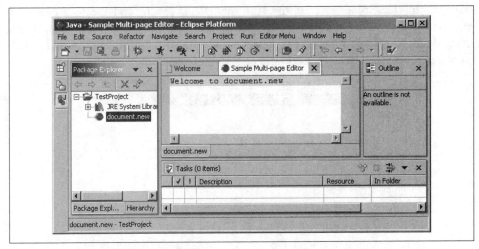

Figure 13-8. The new file

edit the file and use Eclipse's File → Save or File → Save As menu items or the matching toolbar buttons. For that matter, note that adding other pages to the editor is not difficult; just use the addPage method and set the text in the new page's tab with setPageText.

See Also

Recipe 13.1 on creating a plug-in that supports wizards and editors; Recipe 13.2 on customizing wizards; Recipe 10.1 on creating tabbed folders in SWT; Chapter 12 of *Eclipse* (O'Reilly).

13.4 Creating a Plug-in That Supports Views

Problem

You need your plug-in to support a view.

Solution

Use the PDE template "Plug-in with a view."

Discussion

This next example will build a plug-in that supports a view—in this case, a clickable tree of items. To follow along, create a new plug-in project named *org.cookbook. ch13.ViewPlugin*. In the Plug-in Code Generators dialog, shown in Figure 13-9, select "Plug-in with a view" and click Next.

In the next dialog, set the provider name to Eclipse Cookbook, as shown in Figure 13-10.

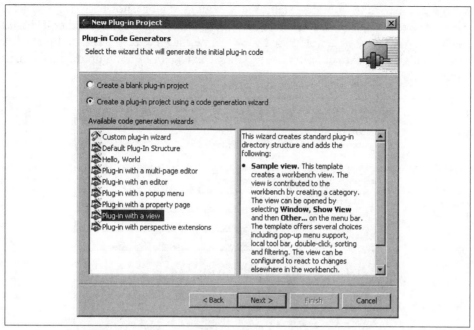

Figure 13-9. Configuring a plug-in with a view

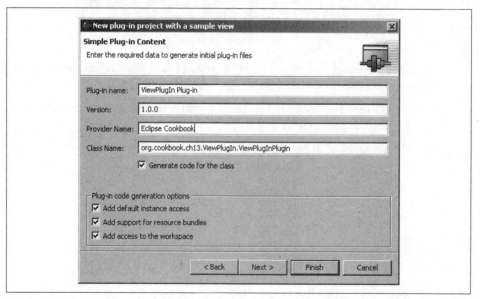

Figure 13-10. Setting the provider name

Clicking Next brings up the Main View Settings dialog shown in Figure 13-11. Here's where you customize the view, setting its name, as well as a whether it should be a tree-based view or a table-based view. Name the view Item View, and make it a tree-based view, as shown in the figure. Click Next again to bring up the final dialog of this wizard.

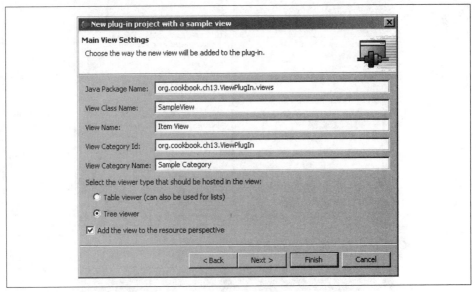

Figure 13-11. Setting view options

In the last dialog, you configure the view's actions. Leave the defaults selected, and click Finish to create the template for this plug-in (see Figure 13-12).

After you click Finish, the template for this plug-in is created, and these files are created and added to the project's *src* folder:

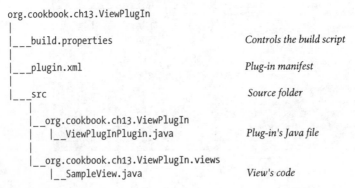

```
org.cookbook.ch13.ViewPlugIn
 |
 |___build.properties                       Controls the build script
 |
 |___plugin.xml                             Plug-in manifest
 |
 |___src                                    Source folder
 |    |
 |__org.cookbook.ch13.ViewPlugIn
 |    |__ViewPlugInPlugin.java              Plug-in's Java file
 |    |
 |__org.cookbook.ch13.ViewPlugIn.views
      |__SampleView.java                    View's code
```

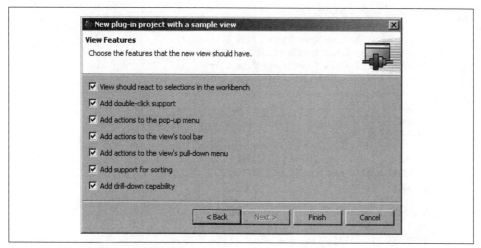

Figure 13-12. Configuring the view's actions

To customize this new plug-in by adding items to the view and making them do something, see the next two recipes.

See Also

Recipe 13.5 on adding items to a view; Recipe 13.6 on configuring the actions in a view; Chapter 12 of *Eclipse* (O'Reilly).

13.5 Adding Items to a View

Problem

You've created a plug-in that supports a view, and you want to add items to that view.

Solution

If you've created the plug-in with a PDE template, just customize the initialize method.

Discussion

How you customize the items in a view depends on whether you've based that view on an SWT table or an SWT tree. In the example developed in the previous recipe, *ViewPlugIn*, our view was based on a tree. You create the tree structure under a TreeParent object named invisibleRoot in the initialize method of *SampleView. java*. The following code creates a tree of nodes in the view (note that in a real application, you'd build this tree to reflect your data model).

```
private void initialize() {
    TreeObject to1 = new TreeObject("Item 1");
    TreeObject to2 = new TreeObject("Item 2");
    TreeObject to3 = new TreeObject("Item 3");
    TreeObject to4 = new TreeObject("Item 4");
    TreeParent p1 = new TreeParent("Parent 1");
    p1.addChild(to1);
    p1.addChild(to2);
    p1.addChild(to3);
    p1.addChild(to4);

    TreeObject to5 = new TreeObject("Item 5");
    TreeParent p2 = new TreeParent("Parent 2");
    p2.addChild(to4);

    TreeParent root = new TreeParent("Root");
    root.addChild(p1);
    root.addChild(p2);

    invisibleRoot = new TreeParent("");
    invisibleRoot.addChild(root);
    }
}
```

This configures the tree object that will appear in the view. To make these items actually do something when clicked (with either mouse button) or double-clicked, see the following recipe.

See Also

Recipe 13.4 on creating a plug-in that supports views; Recipe 13.6 on configuring the actions for a view; Chapters 11 and 12 of *Eclipse* (O'Reilly).

13.6   Configuring a View's Actions

Problem

You need to make the items in a view do something when clicked, right-clicked, or double-clicked.

Solution

Configure the view's actions. If you've used a PDE template to create your plug-in, edit the makeActions method.

Discussion

In the previous two recipes, we created a plug-in that supports a view based on an SWT tree control. To make the items created in the previous recipe do something when the user interacts with them, edit the code in the makeActions method in *SampleView.java*. In the code, you can get access to the item that was clicked, right-clicked, or double-clicked using the following line:

```
Object obj = ((IStructuredSelection)selection).getFirstElement()
```

Here's how to modify the code in makeActions to create actions that will handle menu selections when you right-click or double-click the items in the view:

```java
private void makeActions() {
    action1 = new Action() {
        public void run() {
            showMessage("You selected Action 1");
        }
    };
    action1.setText("Action 1");
    action1.setToolTipText("Action 1 tooltip");
    action1.setImageDescriptor(PlatformUI.getWorkbench().getSharedImages().
        getImageDescriptor(ISharedImages.IMG_OBJS_INFO_TSK));

    action2 = new Action() {
        public void run() {
            showMessage("You selected Action 2");
        }
    };
    action2.setTex("Action 2");
    action2.setToolTipText("Action 2 tooltip");
    action2.setImageDescriptor(PlatformUI.getWorkbench().getSharedImages().
        getImageDescriptor(ISharedImages.IMG_OBJS_TASK_TSK));
    doubleClickAction = new Action() {
        public void run() {
            ISelection selection = viewer.getSelection();
            Object obj =
                ((IStructuredSelection)selection).getFirstElement();
            showMessage("You double-clicked " + obj.toString());
        }
    };
}
```

To work with Item View, start the Run-time Workbench, and select Window → Show View → Other. Select Item View in the Sample Category folder, as shown in Figure 13-13, and click OK to display the new view.

Our new view appears at the bottom of Figure 13-14. That's a new, functional view that we've added to the Eclipse IDE. Not bad.

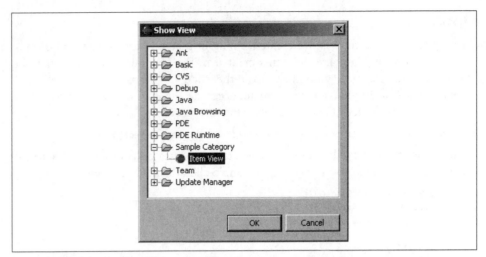

Figure 13-13. Selecting Item View

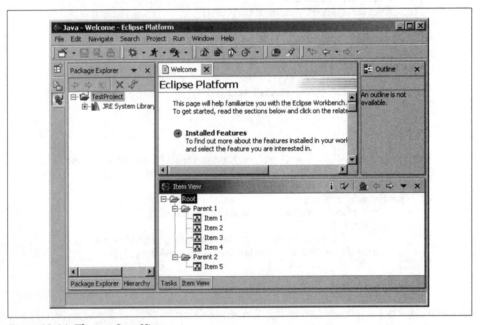

Figure 13-14. The new Item View

Double-clicking an item in the view activates the action for double-clicks, as shown in Figure 13-15.

For that matter, you also can right-click an item, and select Action 1 or Action 2 from the context menu which appears. A message box indicates which action you selected, as shown in Figure 13-16.

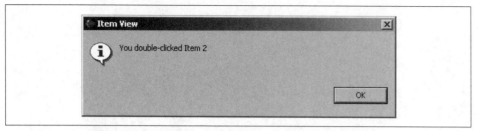

Figure 13-15. Double-clicking an item

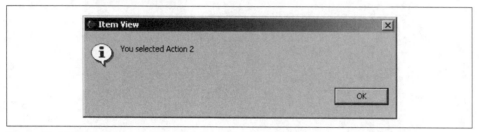

Figure 13-16. Selecting a context menu item

That gets our view plug-in working. You can see that adding a view to Eclipse isn't so hard after all. You can create a template using PDE tools and modify the template's code. You aren't restricted to basing your view on tables or trees, although those are traditional, and you can use an SWT composite control to host your own collection of controls in the view.

See Also

Recipe 13.4 on creating plug-ins that support views; Recipe 13.5 on adding items to a view; Chapters 11 and 12 of *Eclipse (O'Reilly)*.

Index

We'd like to hear your suggestions for improving our indexes. Send email to *index@oreilly.com*.

D

Debug perspective, 13
  Breakpoints view, 119
  Expressions view, 119
  Navigator view, 32
Debug view, 118
debugging
  breakpoints, 119
    conditions, 130
    exception breakpoints, 134
    method breakpoints, 132
    setting, 120
  expressions, 128
    evaluating, 135
  on the fly, 138
  starting, 117
  stepping through, 122
    breakpoints and, 125
  stopping execution at specific point, 127
  variables and, 128
    value assignment, 137
  watchpoints, 132
delegate methods, 67
deleting
  files, restoring, 49
  projects, Package Explorer view, 28
deploying plug-ins, 301
dialogs (SWT), creating, 215
directories
  plugins, 291
  workspace, 7
displaying data, views, 12
do/for/if/while constructs, enclosing
        code, 67
downloading
  Eclipse, 1
    versions, 2
  plug-ins, 291
dragging editors, 33
drop-down menus, coolbars (SWT), 251

E

Eclipse
  building applications with Ant, 171
  connect to CVS repository, 143
  connecting to Ant, 165–171
  downloading, 1
    versions, 2
  installation, 3
    multiple installation, 9

  reinstallation, 29
  running, 3
Eclipse Search dialog, 90
edit location, returning to, 39
editing, views and, 12
editors
  accessing, 38
  Ant, appearance, 181
  code, 12
  customizing, plug-ins and, 323
  definition, 12
  dragging, 33
  edit location, returning to, 39
  GUIs and, 13
  Java code editor, 12
  JDT, increase speed, 54
  maximizing, 37
  multiple, 13
  navigation history, 38
  perspectives, 12, 13
    built-in, 14
  plug-ins and, 316
  positioning, 36
  previous, 38
  restoring to position, 36
  tabs, reordering, 40
  tiling, 36
  views
    linking, 39
    switching between, 41
  Word window, 12
  XML editor, 12
elements, moving, 86
embedding
  buttons in toolbars, 220
  combo boxes in toolbars, 224
  menus in toolbars, 224
  text widgets in toolbars, 224
enabling/disabling
  menu items, 234
  table items, 240
errors
  Quick Fix, 24
  syntax, fixing automatically, 24–27
event handling
  SWT widgets, 202
  toolbars (SWT), 222
  trees (SWT), 258
exception breakpoints, debugging and, 134
expressions, debugging and, 128
  evaluating during, 135
Expressions view, 119

extensibility, plug-ins and, 8
extension points, action sets, 305
external tools, Ant as, 184

F

factory methods, converting constructors
    to, 72
fast views, creating, 47
field breakpoints, 132
fields
    delegate methods, creating, 67
    renaming, 85
File Search tab, Search dialog, 90
file sharing (see CVS)
files
    accessing, 35
    comparing, 93
    comparing, local history and, 94
    deleting, restoring, 49
    JSP, creating, 270
    labeling, version control, 149
    restoring from local history, 96
    scrubbing, 280
    .war files, 285
filters, code-stepping and, 122
final classes, 18
FirstApp.java code, 10
FirstSWTApp project, 192
folders
    linked, 279
    tab folders, creating, 244

G

getter/setter methods, creating, 66
Go to Last Edit Location option, 39
GUIs (graphical user interfaces)
    editors and, 13
    Java and, 186

H

head, CVS, 141
help component, 8
Help, customizing, 48
Help search tab, Search dialog, 90
hiding views, 32
Hierarchy view, Java perspective, 15

I

icons
    label decorations, 42
    resource information, 41
images
    menu items, creating, 231
    tables, adding, 241
    tree items (SWT), 262
installation
    CVS server, 141
    Eclipse, 3
        multiple installations, 9
        reinstallation, 29
    Java servlets in Tomcat, 274
    JUnit, 109
    plug-ins, 291
    Tomcat, 267
Integration builds, downloading, 2
interfaces
    extracting from classes, 88
    implementing, 89

J

.jar files, 101
JAR files, SWT classes, 194
Java
    classes
        creating, 16–19, 60
        private, 18
        protected, 18
        public, 18
    code, running, 22
    Eclipse startup, 4
    methods
        creating, 61
        overriding, 63
    packages, creating, 58
    projects
        class creation, 16–19
        creating, 9, 56
    runtime, selecting, 98
Java code editor, 12
Java perspective, 11, 14–16
    Console view, 16
    Hierarchy view, 15
    Outline view, 16
    Package Explorer view, 15
    Task view, 16
Java Search tab, Search dialog, 90

Java servlets, 267
  creating, 272
    in place, 276
  installation in Tomcat, 274
JavaBeans, JSP interface, 281
JAVA_HOME environment variable
  Tomcat installation and, 269
JDT editor
  breakpoints, setting, 120
  renaming elements, 83
JDT (Java Development Toolkit), 5
  editor, speed increase, 54
JNI (Java Native Interface), code
    support, 196
JSPs (Java Server Pages), 267
  file creation, 270
  JavaBeans interface, 281
JUnit, 108
  installation, 109
  naming conventions, 112
  testing applications, 111
  tests, 108
JUnit Wizard, 112

K

kernel, platform kernel (see platform kernel)
key bindings, creating, 41
keyboard shortcuts, 41
keywords, implements, 89

L

label decorations, icons, 42
launch, configuration, 105
launching applications, SWT, 196
Libraries tab, 57
linked folders, 279
links, views and editors, 39
list widgets (SWT), 205
listeners (SWT)
  button events, 200
  widget events, 202
local history
  file comparison and, 94
  restoring files from, 96
locking files, CVS, 141
logical modules, CVS, 141

M

main method, 19
maximizing
  editors, 37
  views, 37
menu-based plug-ins, wizards and, 294–299
menus
  accelerators, 233
  drop-down, coolbars (SWT), 251
  enabling/disabling items, 234
  image items, creating, 231
  item creation, 310
  mnemonics, 233
  radio items, 232
  Run menu, 99
  separators, 234
  SWT applications, 224
  SWT, embedding in toolbars, 224
  text items, creating, 228
message boxes (SWT), 214
MessageBox class (SWT), 214
method breakpoints, 132
methods
  creating, code assist and, 62
  delegate, creating, 67
  factory, converting constructors to, 72
  getter/setter, creating, 66
  Java
    creating, 61
    overriding, 63
  main, 19
  open, 192
  parameters
    hints, 64
    inserting names in code, 65
  refactoring name, 85
  renaming, 83
  testing, JUnit, 113
mnemonics, menu items, 233
modules, CVS, 140
moving
  elements, 86
  toolbars, 33
  views, 33
multiple windows, 8
  multiple workspaces, 8
multithreading, applications (SWT), 212

N

naming conventions, JUnit, 112
navigation, Go to Last Edit Location
    option, 39
Navigator view, Debug perspective, 32
New Project dialog, 10
Nightly builds, downloading, 3
nondefault workspaces, 43
nonrectangular windows, 210

O

on the fly debugging, 138
open method, 192
optimistic locking, CVS, 141
Order and Export tab, 57
outline synchronization, JDT
    turn off, 55
Outline view, Java perspective, 16
overriding methods, Java, 63
overview bar, 20
overview ruler, JDT, 55

P

Package Explorer view, 13
    Java perspective, 15
    projects, deleting, 28
Package Explorer, working sets, 74
package statement, 19
packages
    Java, creating, 58
    renaming, 85
parameters
    inserting names in code, 65
    methods, hints, 64
    renaming, 85
path, SWT classes, 194
PDE (Plug-in Development Environment),
    5, 291
perspectives
    closing, 13
    creating, 52
    customizing, 50
    CVS Repository Exploring, 144, 150
    Debug, 13
    definition, 12
    editors, 13
        built-in, 14
    hidden files, 35
    Java, 11

Java perspective, 14–16
    Console view, 16
    Hierarchy view, 15
    Outline view, 16
    Task view, 16
    opening, 13
    plug-ins, adding automatically, 314
    Resource, 3
    restoring, 51
    shortcut bar, 14
    views, built-in, 14
pessimistic locking, CVS, 141
physical modules, CVS, 141
platform kernel, 6
Plug-in Code Generators, 317
Plug-in Development Environment (PDE),
    5, 291
plug-in manifest, 293
Plug-in Search tab, Search dialog, 90
plug-ins, 5
    action sets, menu creation, 306
    actions, coding, 311
    creating, 292
        writing from skeleton, 303
    deploying, 301
    downloading, 291
    editor support, 316
    editors, custom, 323
    extensibility and, 8
    installation, 291
    menu-based, wizards and, 294–299
    perspectives, 314
    testing, run-time workbench, 299
    Tomcat, 283
    uncompressing files, 292
    user actions, responses, 305
    view support, 326
        actions, custom, 330
        adding items, 329
    wizard support, 316
    wizards, customizing, 320
    (see also PDE)
plugins directory, 291
plugin.xml, creating, 292
private classes, 18
problem indicators, JDT, 55
projects
    Applet, 186
    checking out of repository, 152
    creating
        Java, 56
        Java project, 9

FirstSWTApp, 192
Java, class creation, 16–19
overview, 10
Package Explorer view, deleting from, 28
renaming, 85
storing, CVS repository, 146
workspaces, 7
  nondefault, 43
Projects tab, 57
properties, Ant, 180
protected classes, 18
public classes, 18

Q

Quick Fix, 24

R

radio items, menus, 232
recovery, reinstallation, 29
refactoring
  introduction, 82
  method names, 85
reinstallation, 29
Release builds, downloading, 2
Rename Method dialog, 85
renaming
  methods, 83
  variables, 83
reordering
  editor tabs, 40
  view tabs, 40
Resource perspective, 3
resources
  information, displaying with icons, 41
  renaming, 85
responses to user actions, plug-ins, 305
Restore from Local History option, 50
restores
  files
    deleted, 49
    from local history, 96
  perspectives, 51
Run menu, 99
  debugging, starting, 117
running code, 99
running Eclipse, 3
runtime, selecting, 98
run-time workbench
  launching, 9
  plug-ins, testing, 299

S

Save Perspective As dialog, 52
saving to repository (CVS), 148
scrapbook pages, 23
scrubbing files, 280
searches, 90
  curly braces, 68
segments, toolbars, 33
servers, CVS installation, 141
ServletInPlace project, 276
servlets (see Java servlets)
Share Project with CVS Repository
        dialog, 146
sharing (see CVS)
shortcut bar, perspectives, 14
shortcuts, key binding creation, 41
showing views, 32
snippets, running, 23
source control, CVS, 140
source folders, renaming, 85
Sources tab, 57
Stable builds, downloading, 2
startup, increasing speed, 5
stepping through code
  breakpoints and, 125
  debugging, 122
Swing, 188
SWT (Standard Widget Toolkit), 186
  applications
    creating, 191
    launching, 196
    menu system creation, 224
    multithreading, 212
  AWT elements inside, 242
  browser widget creation, 262
  classes, path, 194
  combo boxes, embedding in
        toolbars, 224
  coolbars
    adding items, 248
    creating, 247
    drop-down menus, 251
  dialogs, creating, 215
  listeners
    button events and, 200
    widget events, 202
  menus
    accelerators, 233
    embedding in toolbars, 224
    enabling/disabling items, 234
    image items, creating, 231
    mnemonics, 233

trees (SWT)
  checkboxes in items, 260
  creating, 256
  event handling, 258
  images in items, 262
try/catch blocks, enclosing code, 67
type hierarchies, Hierarchy view, 16
types, Ant, 180

U

UI thread, 213
updating code from CVS repository, 152
updating files, CVS, 140
user action responses, plug-ins, 305

V

variables
  debugging and, 128
  renaming, 83
  value assignment, debugging and, 137
version control
  code patches and, 156
  labeling files, 149
  naming versions, 159
  synchronizing versions, 155
  (see also CVS)
versions of Eclipse, downloading, 2
views
  actions, customizing, 330
  Ant, 183
  Console view, Java perspective, 16
  Debug, 118
  definition, 12
  displaying data and, 12
  dragging, 33
  editing and, 12
  editors
    linking, 39
    reordering, 40
    switching between, 41
  fast views, creating, 47
  hiding, 32
  Hierarchy, Java perspective, 15
  items, adding, 329
  maximizing, 37
  moving, 33
  Outline view, Java perspective, 16
  Package Explorer, 13
    Java perspective, 15

perspectives, 12
  built-in, 14
  plug-ins and, 326
  reopening, 12
  showing, 32
  tabs, reordering, 40
  Task view, Java perspective, 16
virtual modules, CVS, 141

W

.war files, creating, 285
watchpoints, 132
web.xml file, editing in place, 278
widgets (SWT)
  availability, 189
  browser widgets, 262
  button, 200
  composite, 208
  custom, 208
  event handling, 202
  list widgets, 205
  listing reference, 189
  position in shell, 198
  text, creating, 200
windows
  multiple, 8
  multiple in multiple workspaces, 8
  multiple in same workspace, 8
  shapes, SWT, 210
  SWT, Opening, 193
  views, 12
wizards, plug-ins and, 316
  custom, 320
  menu-based, 294–299
Word, editors and, 12
workbench, 6
  runtime workbench, launching, 9
  SWT and, 7
workbench editor, navigation history, 38
working sets, creating, 74
workspace, 5, 7
  directory, 7
  multiple, multiple windows, 8
  nondefault, 43
  projects, 7
  windows, multiple, 8
wrapping text, strings, 69
writing plug-ins from skeleton, 303

X

XML editor, 12

About the Author

Steve Holzner is an award-winning author who has been writing about Java topics since Java first appeared. He's a former *PC Magazine* contributing editor whose many books have been translated into 18 languages around the world. His books have sold more than 1.5 million copies, and many of his bestsellers have been about Java. Steve has also written *Eclipse* for O'Reilly.

Steve graduated from MIT and got his Ph.D. from Cornell; he's been a very popular member of the faculty at both MIT and Cornell, teaching thousands of students over the years and earning an average student evaluation of over 4.9 out of 5.0. He also runs his own software company and teaches week-long classes on Java to corporate programmers around the country.

Colophon

Our look is the result of reader comments, our own experimentation, and feedback from distribution channels. Distinctive covers complement our distinctive approach to technical topics, breathing personality and life into potentially dry subjects.

The animals on the cover of *Eclipse Cookbook* are pole shrimp (*Macrobrachium rosenbergii*). These crustaceans can be found in freshwater streams and waterholes as well as in the brackish water and estuaries of the Indo-Pacific region.

Shrimp are similar to crayfish, but their arms are long with fine claws. As with most arthropods, a pole shrimp has an exoskeleton; instead of muscles connected over a bony internal skeleton, its muscles attach underneath, on the rigid, calcium-impregnated carapace. Six long feelers covered with chemoreceptor cells allow the shrimp to detect the smell of food in the water. The pole shrimp continually uses these feelers to scrub itself, removing pieces of dirt that may affect its function.

Like all crustaceans, pole shrimp grow through molting. Before molting, they grow a new shell beneath their old one; this new carapace is soft and somewhat folded, something like an empty balloon. The new carapace inflates with water, splitting the old one at the weakened points. The old carapace splits in half, and the entire head section slides out of the old shell. A sharp flick of the tail leaves the old exoskeleton lying at the bottom of the sea.

Mary Anne Weeks Mayo was the production editor and proofreader, and Audrey Doyle was the copyeditor for *Eclipse Cookbook*. Phil Dangler and Emily Quill provided quality control. Jamie Peppard and Mary Agner provided production assistance. Tom Dinse wrote the index.

Emma Colby designed the cover of this book, based on a series design by Edie Freedman. The cover image is a 19th-century engraving from *Cuvier's Animals*. Emma produced the cover layout with QuarkXPress 4.1 using Adobe's ITC Garamond font.

Melanie Wang designed the interior layout, based on a series design by David Futato. This book was converted by Julie Hawks to FrameMaker 5.5.6 with a format conversion tool created by Erik Ray, Jason McIntosh, Neil Walls, and Mike Sierra that uses Perl and XML technologies. The text font is Linotype Birka; the heading font is Adobe Myriad Condensed; and the code font is LucasFont's TheSans Mono Condensed. The illustrations that appear in the book were produced by Robert Romano and Jessamyn Read using Macromedia FreeHand 9 and Adobe Photoshop 6. The tip and warning icons were drawn by Christopher Bing. This colophon was compiled by Mary Anne Weeks Mayo.

Related Titles Available from O'Reilly

Java

Ant: The Definitive Guide
Eclipse: A Java Developer's Guide
Enterprise JavaBeans, *3rd Edition*
Hardcore Java
Head First Java
Head First Servlets & JSP
Head First EJB
J2EE Design Patterns
Java and SOAP
Java & XML Data Binding
Java & XML
Java Cookbook
Java Data Objects
Java Database Best Practices
Java Enterprise Best Practices
Java Enterprise in a Nutshell, *2nd Edition*
Java Examples in a Nutshell, *3rd Edition*
Java Extreme Programming Cookbook
Java in a Nutshell, *4th Edition*
Java Management Extensions
Java Message Service
Java Network Programming, *2nd Edition*
Java NIO
Java Performance Tuning, *2nd Edition*
Java RMI
Java Security, *2nd Edition*
Java ServerPages, *2nd Edition*
Java Serlet & JSP Cookbook
Java Servlet Programming, *2nd Edition*
Java Swing, *2nd Edition*
Java Web Services in a Nutshell
Learning Java, *2nd Edition*
Mac OS X for Java Geeks
NetBeans: The Definitive Guide
Programming Jakarta Struts
Tomcat: The Definitive Guide
WebLogic: The Definitive Guide

O'REILLY®

Our books are available at most retail and online bookstores.
To order direct: 1-800-998-9938 • *order@oreilly.com* • *www.oreilly.com*
Online editions of most O'Reilly titles are available by subscription at *safari.oreilly.com*

Keep in touch with O'Reilly

1. Download examples from our books

To find example files for a book, go to:

www.oreilly.com/catalog

select the book, and follow the "Examples" link.

2. Register your O'Reilly books

Register your book at *register.oreilly.com*

Why register your books?
Once you've registered your O'Reilly books you can:

- Win O'Reilly books, T-shirts or discount coupons in our monthly drawing.
- Get special offers available only to registered O'Reilly customers.
- Get catalogs announcing new books (US and UK only).
- Get email notification of new editions of the O'Reilly books you own.

3. Join our email lists

Sign up to get topic-specific email announcements of new books and conferences, special offers, and O'Reilly Network technology newsletters at:

elists.oreilly.com

It's easy to customize your free elists subscription so you'll get exactly the O'Reilly news you want.

4. Get the latest news, tips, and tools

www.oreilly.com

- "Top 100 Sites on the Web"—PC Magazine
- CIO Magazine's Web Business 50 Awards

Our web site contains a library of comprehensive product information (including book excerpts and tables of contents), downloadable software, background articles, interviews with technology leaders, links to relevant sites, book cover art, and more.

5. Work for O'Reilly

Check out our web site for current employment opportunities:

jobs.oreilly.com

6. Contact us

O'Reilly & Associates
1005 Gravenstein Hwy North
Sebastopol, CA 95472 USA

TEL: 707-827-7000 or 800-998-9938
      (6am to 5pm PST)

FAX: 707-829-0104

order@oreilly.com
For answers to problems regarding your order or our products. To place a book order online, visit:

www.oreilly.com/order_new

catalog@oreilly.com
To request a copy of our latest catalog.

booktech@oreilly.com
For book content technical questions or corrections.

corporate@oreilly.com
For educational, library, government, and corporate sales.

proposals@oreilly.com
To submit new book proposals to our editors and product managers.

international@oreilly.com
For information about our international distributors or translation queries. For a list of our distributors outside of North America check out:

international.oreilly.com/distributors.html

adoption@oreilly.com
For information about academic use of O'Reilly books, visit:

academic.oreilly.com

O'REILLY®

Our books are available at most retail and online bookstores.
To order direct: 1-800-998-9938 • *order@oreilly.com* • *www.oreilly.com*
Online editions of most O'Reilly titles are available by subscription at *safari.oreilly.com*